INJECTING CHANGE

A Mother's Journey through Vaccine Injury

Bridget Long

ISBN: 1532804970
ISBN 13: 9781532804977
Library of Congress Control Number: 2016906486
CreateSpace Independent Publishing Platform
North Charleston, South Carolina

DEDICATION

To my wonderful children, I love you.
Thank you for waiting patiently while I wrote.
One day, you will understand the value.

To the parents who know vaccine injury,
I hope my words travel from my heart to yours.
We are not alone. Please forgive yourself.

I am a mom. This is my personal story.
My words are not medical advice, but an expression of thoughts, feelings,
and experiences in a life forever changed by vaccine injury.

TABLE OF CONTENTS

CHAPTER 1

I FELL IN LOVE

I am a mom. As I sit and hold my newborn baby in the narrow hospital bed, I am in an unfamiliar world I never expected to join. This new life became real as soon as I heard those first cries. The journey starts here, at this magical moment, but I must go backwards before I move forward, or the story wouldn't begin at all.

My little girl was born two days before my eleventh wedding anniversary. We planned for the big day and committed to the lifetime to follow, but I didn't grow up with "Mom" on my list of goals. I didn't envision my life's path leading to motherhood. At nineteen, when I said, "I do," thoughts of parenting were far from my mind.

I thought choosing a life of teaching would lead me away from motherhood, as I threw my whole life into my work. Mothering is not the kind of job that fits nicely into a summer vacation, and I wasn't sure I had the time or the skills to perform two very challenging roles to my very high standards. Besides, I have always felt that the world might be too harsh for the innocence of children,

1

so I chose to include kids in my life by making a positive difference for the ones who were already here.

As a teacher, I never imagined the day would come when "Mrs. Long" would be called "Mommy." Sometimes students would call me "Mom," but it was just an accidental mix-up of familiarity from spending quality time together, and it always ended with a shy embarrassed smile. A child's endearing mistake was most often a compliment, but it didn't entail any of the responsibilities of parenting.

As I skip backwards in time, through the stepping stones of my life, it was my own school experiences that led me to teaching, a formidable foundation which held the roots of my being, my own student years stuck firmly in place, cemented through long nights of studying, an unwavering focus on grades, and the constant need for the approval of teachers.

I was a good pupil, but school filled me with disappointment. Overworked and exhausted, I resented the homework that ate through my precious time. As hours dissolved into the past, the years of my youth had disappeared. I hadn't meant to trade childhood play for classroom burnout, prioritizing school work above all else. In exchange, I had a bunch of report cards and some award trinkets. I learned real skills through repetitive practice and hard work. But something was missing. I lost my interest in learning.

With the completion of high school, punch clocks replaced school bells. Eight hour obligations seemed relatively leisurely in comparison to the seemingly endless nights of homework after a full day of classes. I didn't think the point of school was to make the world of work seem easy, but maybe it was...

Without homework, the work day actually ended, and I found myself with free time! Open time in idle hands added some excitement to life. With the space and freedom to enjoy learning experiences, I found pleasure in the process of discovery and the accrual of information. Without forced assignments or pressure to write about everything I read, learning became fun again.

Through observation and osmosis, my school years taught me how to teach. As an attentive student, I was paying close attention to not only the subject matter, but also the ways schools and educators conducted business. My own school experiences had been far from satisfying, and I couldn't turn off my brain from the abundance of thoughts flowing in with ideas for betterment. Students deserve wonderfully enriching and enjoyable school opportunities, and I wanted to put forth my best efforts to give it to them.

Visions of teaching filled my brain. Flipping pages of books or magazines sparked ideas for lesson plans. Saturday morning environmental shows and educational programming triggered an emotional response, a yearning that reminded me how much I wanted to make a difference by working with children. I couldn't wait to get back into the classroom as the lead role.

The lack of a degree slowed down the arrival at my destination, a fortuitous lack that invited invaluable learning opportunities. College completion took longer because it came second to the full time job needed to pay the bills. As I strolled along employment paths beneficial to my future career, I was grateful for the experiences that taught me what life was like outside of a school. I was thankful for the occasions outside of the classroom that would help me immensely when I earned my way back in. Work experience was a way for me to incorporate real world applications into the lesson plans and curriculum.

The touch of grace landed me into the field of human resources, where the grass was pretty green as I sat surrounded by some nice people, tasks that I enjoyed, and daily growth in my abilities. I had on-the-job practice with my interviewing and presentation skills and a boss who taught me the mannerisms of business. Time in human resources was a priceless opportunity where I absorbed relevant skills transferrable to any teaching situation. It was an excellent situation to get lost in for a while, making the virtue of patience seem far less challenging. I might have stayed, but the company relocated, and I was free to finish college full time.

Master's degree in hand, I was hired immediately upon graduation by a lovely school in a nearby town. That piece of paper was my ticket to the real reward, a wonderful group of fifth graders, and my very own space to share with them. Beaming with enthusiasm and energy, I proudly entered my classroom to greet each day. As students poured through the door, I welcomed them as a family of learners. Dressed in business attire, I flashed my most important accessory, the giant smile worn across my face.

I started the year with greetings and handshakes at the door, respectful habits I picked up from my days spent in the office. My grin widened as I watched young faces momentarily age with delight from feeling all grown up. I loved that these kids were still kids but I could talk to them like adults, without needing to alter my voice into the high pitched baby tone that appeals to the younger children. Fifth grade is a big year for many children, when they cross the bridge into abstract thinking. As they crossed the threshold into our classroom, they were about to start their journey. We were a family for the year, a team, and we would accomplish some serious growing together.

Tree-lined streets dotted my commute to work. Located in an idyllic rural setting, my new school was an older brick building filled to the brim with children from kindergarten through sixth grade. As I pulled into the drive each day, feelings of serenity grounded me from the surreal thoughts that I had the unbelievable privilege of working there. Spending my days with a classroom of pleasant coworkers, I had arrived, and had no plans to go anywhere else.

With my charmingly cozy school and a job that I loved, I was grateful for everything. I appreciated that I worked in an older building with windows that could be open to let in the fresh air. I appreciated that we still had real chalkboards that hadn't been replaced by whiteboards and smelly markers. I appreciated that we had a sink with a water fountain in the classroom for convenient hand washing and sips to drink. I appreciated card stock, the binding machine, and the laminator that helped us create beautiful books. I appreciated that we still valued human connection and hadn't gone completely high tech. But most of all, I appreciated every single minute I got to spend with my special students. I worked in the upper elementary school of an older building, and I fit perfectly.

It took a lot of hours behind the scenes to step onto the class-room stage prepared, dedicating time long beyond what is required for the paycheck. Unlike my high school homework, I enjoyed this work. Passion poured through my efforts, and the time spent felt meaningful rather than wasteful. Being a teacher is a very satisfying way to spend a life, rewarded daily with the smiles of my students.

Teaching brought out the best in me. Blessed with a wonderful group of young scholars, I received far more rewards than a salary. I helped highlight my students' strengths, and they introduced me to mine. Each day, I was learning something new from a room full of my young teachers. My students taught me that I didn't always need to be serious to be respected. They taught me to be fully present in the moment, an essential skill to keeping a classroom of 25 "managed." They taught me to have hope for the future, because their existence was good for the world, and good for me.

Those kids… their light lit that fire in my belly that ignited sparks of enthusiasm. I couldn't contain my joy. My face burst into a smile so big it ached my jaw muscles whenever I talked about my students and all the wonderful experiences we were having together. Success achieved, my dream had come true! I was deeply fulfilled and so happy. These kids were amazing, and as big of an impact I was hop-ing to make in their lives, they were positively impacting mine. My heart had been touched by their souls, and I fell in love.

CHAPTER 2
THE PATH TO MOTHERHOOD

My bliss was interrupted when the winds of change flowed right out of the principal's mouth. Staff meeting news announced budget cuts that could end the employment of all non-tenured staff. I didn't think my calling was a wrong number, but maybe it was just a job. To the business of a school district, teachers were just employees, some numbers on a budget. I expected the quality of work to count in the evaluations of our worth, but tenure trumps all, and our performances couldn't override a lack of money. As a teacher, this was my first real lesson in decisions where values and money don't always meet.

As word of a layoff spread through the air, my body froze in disbelief. Suddenly, I was knocked into real reality, and not the ideal one I was creating in my classroom. Surprise probably shouldn't have been my first reaction. This wasn't the first layoff notice of my lifetime, but I was living my dream, being forced to wake up too quickly, like the alarm clock that abruptly ends the perfect fantasy. I was too optimistic to think about such possibilities and having too much fun to ever want it to end.

On a mission to collect my things, I walked down the empty corridor to my classroom. It had been a long day, ending harshly at the staff meeting, and it was time to go home. Normally, I felt at home here, in this old brick school building, but now that they were considering evictions, I just wanted to go to my real home, where I could process the information from the comforts of my couch with my little dogs snuggled up at my sides. Believing I was alone, I released my eyes from their duty of restraint and let the tears flow.

With my guard down and my focus cloudy, I was surprised by the soft touch of a hand upon my back. My principal offered a small gesture of humanity and kindness, both of us hoping that my name wasn't going to be on one of those pink slips. I didn't want to leave, and she didn't want to see me go. My teaching position was so much more than a job. It had become my life.

Teaching was a natural passion. I had love for the children and was good at creating a community of cooperative learners based on kindness and respect. I presented lessons with energy and enthusiasm. I had a strong work ethic, the classroom management skills, and students who were improving their math and writing scores. I had lots of skills that make great teachers. But in school, it was all about tenure, and I didn't have that.

I was at home, fully myself, fully present, bringing everything that was me to the job. I thought I had earned my keep through my hard work and dedication, but axes were expected to fall, cutting the cord to my second home and family. My heart and my spirit were on display each day, shining inner light through my pores. Maybe I had given too much of myself for it not to feel personal. My soul was exposed, leaving me completely vulnerable.

The district was taking this merger one year at a time, while I looked straight through to the grave, committing to a lifelong union when there were no such promises or guarantees in return. The work that I cherished dangled precariously from an unraveling string. Its loss would be devastating. With the ability to end it all too soon, cuts happen in an instant, in sharp contrast to the lengths it took to get here, with years of preparation in time, money, education, and work. Long hours of commitment can be lost in a snap.

As the district went looking for money, I searched deeply inside myself, going within for reflection, forcing myself to reconsider the sacrifice, to reevaluate life and my choices. As I contemplated life, I reflected upon kids and motherhood, parenting and family, careers and work, decisions and regrets, tradeoffs and commitments. Facing the realization of a layoff stirred something within me, leading to the conception of a new idea; maybe we could have kids of our own.

After collecting my thoughts, I went outward, toward my husband, and we discussed future possibilities in deep conversations, as we tried to imagine what life would look like with children of our own. We wondered if regret would one day fester in our lives if we passed through our window of opportunity alone, without any young ones by our side, when we settled into an age too old to change our minds.

Parenting and teaching are both difficult jobs when done well, so I thought I had to choose just one. I leaned towards career, knowing I needed to earn a living, and I chose a role in teaching because I thought it might be the best job in the world. With all that schooling, it just seemed that I was being trained for something besides motherhood, because there certainly wasn't any taking care of baby classes in all that learning. I felt I needed to put all those grades and studying to good use or maybe it would have been a waste of time.

Maybe it was too much of a sacrifice to be giving up a family of my own for a family of students with a revolving door that flipped faces and personalities every academic year. Our obligations to each other get fulfilled, while their real families enjoy them for a lifetime. Teachers get a beautiful glimpse into the development of a child, but the time is fleeting. There is no future commitment to witness the emergence and blossoming of a full life. We nurture the seedlings, but the flowers fully unfold in front of someone else's eyes.

Saying goodbye each day, watching students go home to their families, I wondered about family life. I imagined the joy that children bring to a home, just like the laughter they bring to a classroom. I wanted into this private world filled with morning hugs and bedtime routines, sharing life with the love of my own child. I wanted time as a family, to witness the beauty of metamorphosis, watching tiny babies grow into a rewarding friendship of an adult child. The long term rewards of parenthood were the kind of commitment worthy of a life, an experience I decided I didn't want to live without.

I didn't have an opinion on childhood vaccines or care to know the shot status of my students. My business was the education of children, focused on mental and emotional health, more concerned with building a high self-esteem than a strong immune system.

I was conscious of germs and encouraged hand washing several times each day, but I never let the kids feel like they had cooties or kept my distance in fear. The only bacteria that concerned me was tuberculosis, because a positive TB test meant I wouldn't be allowed to teach. But I never once worried that I was going to catch this from one of my students.

To keep us healthy, I did my part to make sure our classroom was free of chemicals and negativity. We filled our sinks with regular soap and water, while filling our days with creativity, learning, discussion, and laughter. I focused on making the kids feel good about themselves and good about learning. By creating a positive environment where happy kids wanted to come to school, I offered my own version of a boost to immunity.

What did concern me was the world the children lived in, the world my potential child would join. I was afraid of a hostile environment full of dangers and potential threats. I wasn't sure earth was a healthy place to live, with Mother Nature crumbling, and all the chemicals and pollution that were destroying life.

As a teacher, I was not boggled down with the uneasiness that consume a parent's thoughts. Real parents have all the fear and worries that this naturally anxious teacher was trying to avoid. Even after overcoming each hurdle, there would still be a lifetime full of frets about accidents and heartaches, disappointments and loss. I knew my heart was big enough for the love, but would it be strong enough to withstand a lifetime of worries? Children of my own would invite lots of fears into my own personal universe, because I was afraid of everything that could go wrong.

But, to see what was right in this world, all I had to do was look at my students. My students were good children who drew me in with their light. Bursting with unique qualities and special talents, they showed me the potential of the younger generation. Their fresh young perspectives brought promise, and the beauty of their hearts gave me hope for the future. Their infectious love of life made me believe that there was lots of goodness in this world, being fostered in the hearts and minds of our young people.

Mothering instincts started to flow as I spent my days with children in the nurturing environment I created. My classroom offered up a gentleness to soften some of the harshness of the world. I was used to making kids feel at home, but as a mother, it would be my own home, where "parents are a child's first teacher."

Class time often involved meaningful heart to heart discussions about writing, books, current events, illustrations, and art, all the same things I might discuss with my own children through bedtime stories and teachable moments. I valued those qualities that teachers cannot grade, and as a parent, those are the qualities I could help polish and shine, revealing hidden talents and uniqueness. My heart was full of love to share, and as I reflected on the love for my students, I knew I had an overflow to transfer to my own child.

"When one door closes another one opens." Fortunately, the layoff never materialized for me that year, leaving my classroom door wide open. My arms were filled, once again, with textbooks and a briefcase full of paperwork, leaving no free hands for holding and no free arms for hugging. I was happy to still be employed, but we had already decided to open that second door to a family, and this time, we weren't going to close it for a job. I needed to drop some of the load to balance my life, making room for a family, not yet fully realizing that the weight of a baby sets everything off balance.

Spurred by the love for my students and the threat of a layoff, this is how I, who never planned on becoming a mother, willfully and happily made the decision to become a mom on purpose. It took a role in teaching to lead me down the path to motherhood, where I held hands with my husband and led the way.

CHAPTER 3
THE NEWS

With a firm decision to start a family, we welcomed the possibilities. I was going to try my best at having it all, because I didn't want to give up the career that I loved, even if it was just a job. The planner in me arranged for child care before I even conceived, because I was still a teacher at heart, with all intentions of returning to work.

Days spent avoiding pregnancy turned into days filled with excited anticipation. A pregnancy that we once feared now brought nervous jitters of hope. I thought pregnancy would have blossomed instantly if it were unplanned, but as months came and went, we were surprised that this process might require patience. In six months, I had conceived, but I felt certain that an accident would have happened quicker.

Our morning news came to us from our bathroom, delivering joy at the first sign of new life growing inside. I had never viewed urine with such enthusiasm, but that little pregnancy stick brought excitement to an otherwise ordinary Sunday. We placed our keepsake into a plastic baggy for preservation, where it made its new home in a bin above the toilet next to the washcloths and toiletries. Should this tangible memory be the first addition to our baby's scrapbook? Not quite, but it was our proof that this was real. We were going to have a baby!

What is early pregnancy supposed to feel like? Will I notice the difference right away? I didn't know, so I called the doctor's office to ask. I established myself as a patient when I visited prior to conception and walked out with a prescription for prenatal vitamins.

Only two weeks into the pregnancy, and I was experiencing some belly pain. Maybe I just had a bad lunch, but I was not sure, because I had never been pregnant before. Instead of a quick phone conversation with a nurse, to answer what I thought was a simple question, I was told to come in for an appointment, that day. I didn't stop to think and ask myself if that was what I wanted. I was trained to obey, and I followed the instructions. Pregnancy had already filled my brain.

When I arrived at the obstetrician's office, I had no idea what to expect. I completely trusted that this recommended doctor would know best, as I was introduced to the internal ultrasound wand that searched my insides for an ectopic pregnancy. I could see the value in an ultrasound if ectopic pregnancies could be life threatening, but I left with no clear answers, only instructions to return the following week. I wished I had just kept the questions to myself. My appointment seemed as futile as my phone call, but I was so excited to be pregnant, that I still walked out smiling.

I returned the following week with my husband by my side. As I lay flat on the exam table, I looked down the length of my body towards the little fuzzy black and white screen above my feet. In this moment, it was too early to see anything that even remotely resembled a baby. Completely optimistic, I was not concerned at all. I didn't really know why I was there, but I didn't seem to mind, because I was discovering, for the first time, the mysteries behind the walls at an actual obstetrician's office.

The ultrasound concluded quickly, and the technician silently walked out the door. She returned with the doctor, but they were keeping quiet, not saying anything. An elephant filled the room with coldness. Shivers tingled up my spine. My husband and I exchanged glances and tightened the grasp of our hands, our silent communication that we are a team, through thick and thin. In dead silence, our ears sensed there was something wrong. This seemed to be some private understanding between the doctor and the technician, but clearly it involved me.

The quiet was maddening. Tension thickened. Friendly faces morphed into hardened stones, cold, silent, and heavy. Finally, the doctor's words broke the air, "You can get dressed. Then, come meet me in my office."

We entered the office together, my husband and I, hand in hand. Two chairs waited for us, directly across from the doctor, who was now sitting behind his desk. We hesitatingly sat down, my husband to my left, our hands still embraced. Then, we stared down the doctor as he delivered some bad news.

The doctor proceeded to tell us that I had no baby growing inside, just an empty sac where a baby should be, but isn't. He told me that I needed to prepare myself for an impending miscarriage to occur at any time, any day. He assured us that he "is not wrong about these things," with words that were confidently clear. He was "over 95% sure" we were losing our baby, but he would allow us another ultrasound in a week, before he scheduled a D&C.

A D&C. I knew this is a procedural term that someone wanting to keep her pregnancy does not want to hear. Questions sprang forth from my lips, flying out of my mouth in fast succession, explaining information that he needed to make an accurate assessment. I knew my body better than his machine's reading. He was missing the fact that sometimes I had extra-long menstrual cycles and often ovulated on days when textbook women might be getting their periods.

I reiterated several times that I thought I was only three weeks pregnant. He believed that I was five weeks pregnant and didn't see what he had expected to see for the gestation period. "But, I am only three weeks pregnant," I heard myself saying, like a broken record that had become mere background noise.

I was the patient who was being ignored. He was the doctor who wasn't listening. Maybe he was too arrogant to hear me. I wanted to scream, "It's my baby! It's my body! Why won't you listen to me?" But I was far too reserved for that. But I knew that I was correct about this too. Three weeks never miraculously changes into five weeks, without two more weeks passing. That is impossible math.

When I finally felt like he may have heard me, he said that he had the same conclusion regardless. He was trying to shut me up. He advised that my next step was to schedule a D&C if the miscarriage didn't happen as expected, because he was very confident that he was correct. He was supposed to be the expert, and I guess I trusted him more than I trusted myself. My balloon of happiness was deflated, and I left with silent tears slowly dripping from my eyes.

CHAPTER 4
WHAT?

I walked into school with tears flowing down my face, because they hadn't stopped from the day before. The floodgates were open, and my usual smile was absent. The empty hallway to my classroom seemed longer, and the concrete walls felt so cold.

This was the first time I cried at school, and the first time I emanated sadness instead of enthusiasm. My students could see that I was upset, but thankfully didn't ask any questions. Instead, they showed their caring concern through their actions. My class supported me with their kindness and flawless behavior, collectively making the day run as smoothly and easily as possible. My students were my blessing and my inspiration, and on this difficult day, I felt their love.

I didn't know what to do. The doctor told me to expect a miscarriage at any moment, and I was waiting for the moment to arrive. The doctor had me convinced that I had already lost my baby, that this fate was inevitable. His words echoed clearly, "I am not wrong about these things."

What would happen to my students if the bleeding loss starts right here at school? I probably should have turned to my principal for support. I should have known that she was the person to go to, that she would understand. But I was trained in student teaching to solve problems myself, and principals were not to be bothered. I turned to my fifth grade teaching team instead. We worked well together and knew how to support each other.

I had hoped to be sharing happy news when I reached the three month pregnancy mark, but now, I was disseminating my sadness. I gathered my teaching team into an empty classroom and revealed my personal disappointment. Between us, I was sure we could figure out coverage. Who could watch my class if I needed to leave in an emergency? We could pull together for a group movie, or the classroom aide from across the hall could fill in if needed. We only had another day and a half to get through before a week off for our winter vacation.

Oops. I forgot to mention that I would like this personal information kept private. While I spent the day holed up with my students, my news was quickly spreading outside my classroom. Words fly fast, even when they are heavy, even when they are meant to be secret. My impending misfortune became the gossip of the day. Maybe I would have had more privacy if I had simply gone to the principal...

I wasn't really upset over the words traveling outside my door. I was only upset for the loss I felt inside. Maybe I should have just taken two personal days and cried at home, but to wallow in misery by myself seemed like an awful choice compared to days with my students. The tears dripped on and off sporadically, but it was good to be with my class. I needed to be with them, for me.

Vacation brought a continued sadness. How was I to enjoy a vacation with the dark cloud looming overhead? The pain was worse now, because I was alone waiting for the miscarriage with an impending feeling of doom. I missed the love of my students and the pleasant distraction days at school could provide, because I didn't like wallowing in this pain by myself. My one visitor seemed oblivious to my emotions, didn't seem to notice that I was crying, and couldn't stop talking about babies. I reconsidered. Maybe, sometimes, it is better to be alone.

I grieved the loss of life growing inside. I wept for the lost dreams. I counted the days of waiting before we would be able to try again. I worried about the surgical procedure I wanted to avoid, praying nature takes the right course. Confusion filled my insides, where I had once imagined my baby. The doctor seemed so sure of himself that I allowed myself to believe him.

The week passed slowly until the day our follow up ultrasound arrived. I was still crying, even though a part of me felt numb. The doctor's words replaced my hope. My movements felt a bit mechanized as I removed my clothing and climbed onto the table. Last week, I was glowing in my visions of becoming a new mom. This week, I felt like a test subject, a bit lifeless at the anticipation of impending death. I was not interested in looking at the screen. I was not interested in being here. I let my mind wander to avoid the feelings.

I was expecting confirmation of the bad news, when I heard, "There's the heartbeat," in a calm, casual voice.

"Excuse me?" I asked, suddenly with full attention.

"There's the heartbeat," the technician repeated.

"What?" This wasn't really a question. This was shock. I sprung to life upon hearing these words. I was immediately flooded with emotions, elation, relief, confusion, shock, but most of all, an ecstatic surprise. I started laughing and smiling with my husband in a complete childlike giddiness. My baby was alive, my growing miracle, there all along. The baby we expected to lose was ours again.

The doctor's confidence had me so convinced of miscarriage that I forgot to remember the other possibility, that my baby was fine. His tragic words had me give up hope. Today, the doctor congratulated us, never apologizing, never mentioning the conversation from the week before. He was expecting a thank you before he sent us on our way.

I was too happy to yell at him in this moment, but I won't forget the unnecessary pain the obstetrician caused. If the heart starts beating at week four of gestational development, then there is a huge transformational difference between three weeks pregnant and five weeks pregnant. Her heart needed time to grow. As the clock ticked on for another week, her heart developed the ability to tick on its own. As the expert, he should have known that.

I briefly touched on the understanding of miscarriage. My short-lived grief gave me a taste of the pain without having to live the actuality of the loss. My mind may have listened to his prognosis with disbelief and confusion, while still accepting his words as truth and expecting his fate. Thankfully, my body didn't hear any of it and kept on growing my baby, exactly as nature intended, right on its own time. As my outside was gloomy, my inside was working away in beautiful precision, growing the life of my little girl.

That night, I couldn't relax. The day's wildly changing emotions unsettled me. When darkness set in and the day became quiet, I started to process my feelings. The nighttime came and awakened my anger. I wanted to feel only happiness and gratitude, yet there was an underlying fury surging in my belly.

I was terribly upset with the doctor. How could he be so irresponsible in his diagnosis and so cocky in his tone? How could he not understand that it might be traumatic to suffer a mistaken miscarriage when there was no need for alarm? Instead of adding my input to his evaluation, he added extra stress to my pregnancy. Why didn't he listen to me? Why didn't he believe me? How dare he act like the hero today, flying in with good news and rescuing me from my sadness. If only he had listened to me, none of this needed to happen in the first place.

Late in the evening, when quiet filled the house, I couldn't sleep with thoughts and emotions swirling in my brain. Grabbing my notebook, I got out of bed and made my way into the living room to do what I always did when I had anger to release, write. Getting cozy on the couch, I turned on the television for company and started drafting a letter of angry disappointment to the doctor. All was still, except my hand, writing in a flurry.

Something else was happening that same night, at the exact same time, in a nightclub not too far away. The day I found out that my baby was going to live, was the same day that many people lost their lives in a Rhode Island nightclub fire. As I vented my frustration through my writing, the heartbreaking news came on in the background.

As that tragedy unfolded, my anger fell away, and my thoughts went out to the victims. On a night that I was feeling such anger at the doctor for putting us through needless turmoil, I quickly realized my good fortune. Any one of those lives lost could have been my husband or his friends, a bunch of guys who enjoyed watching the '80s hairbands of our youth. That fire could have consumed my husband, but he was asleep in our bed, while I sat on our couch, still pregnant with our child.

The smoke brought clarity to my visions. We were lucky. I was blessed to have a future as a new mom and grateful to have my husband still by my side to experience it with me. In that moment, I was able to let go of my anger and appreciate all the gifts I had in my life.

My angry fire was contained to my belly, while their very real inferno exploded dreams into a lifetime of suffering. My bad news was a short lived mistake, while theirs was an actual reality full of pain. As the anger left my heart that night, it made a special space for the night club victims to fill.

CHAPTER 5
PREGNANCY

My words remained tucked inside my notebook, while the recommended obstetrician went about his days with patients. Maybe the others were impressed with the sound of his voice when he uttered big words in his regal accent. Maybe they liked that he offered a delivery of fresh flowers as a congratulatory gesture after the delivery of the baby. Maybe they liked being treated like a helpless maiden in distress, the role he had just cast me in with the label of "high risk," earned through my tendency towards long menstrual cycles and his inability to listen.

Instead of my writing, the obstetrician's office received a phone call, requesting my medical records, while informing them that I would be leaving the practice. The doctor would not release my medical records until I spoke with him personally, because with the "good news" he had just given me, he was actually surprised by my decision.

Medical records revealed that the doctor performed those ultrasounds to check for "viability of embryo." Discovering that I had undergone unnecessary tests to result in a needless diagnosis infuriated me. If an embryo is not viable, there is nothing the doctor can do to save it. Time would expose the fate.

Three irrelevant ultrasounds created tears of grief for a hurtful conclusion that wasn't even true. My ovum wasn't blighted. It was filled with a growing life. I think awful thoughts when I wonder how many women, who really wanted to become moms, may have unknowingly been subjected to unwanted abortions through procedures of misdiagnosis. I imagine they would rather not know anything other than what they already believe.

I reminded myself that I walked into motherhood with a positive attitude, expecting a positive outcome, and I trusted the innate wisdom of my body. I hadn't stepped into pregnancy in fear, but the first doctor scared me off track with his inaccurate assessment. I let go of the negative thoughts to start fresh for the remaining days on the countdown to baby. In contrast to the miscarriage scare, I wanted to relish the rest of my baby's gestation in peace, settling myself into a happy anticipation and appreciation.

My pregnancy evolved without complications. The first movements surprised me at four months gestation. I felt those first kicks with amazement and wonder, connecting with my baby, tangibly feeling her presence at a level far beyond the morning sickness that only reminded me she was there.

I often gazed at the growing size of my belly, pulling my shirt taut into a form fitting display of unmistakable bulge. With a nudge or a tap-tap on my protruding skin, I would get a responsive kick or punch in return. With each of my baby's rolls, my belly took on new alien shapes as body parts distorted, pushing here and there, creating rolls and bumps, constantly pulsing with life. The baby's movements brought humor and laughs as we watched the shifting routines of our growing acrobat.

I was busy teaching into June, but then I had several months of free time to prepare for my baby's arrival. As I pulled my car into the parking lot of the baby megastore, I saw empty spots right up front, with a sign declaring, "Reserved for expectant mothers." Pregnancy had not hindered my ability to walk, but I took advantage of this tiny perk. In only a few short months, I will fully transition into the role of new mother. But right then, I was savoring pregnancy and enjoying the label of expectant mom.

This store was huge, an entire building devoted to babies. I felt special here relishing in my new identity, engulfed in these new surroundings. I wasted lots of time here over my summer vacation, while my husband and friends spent their days at work. Savoring moments of peace among all this colorful stuff, I walked aisles and aisles of things I never expected would become part of my life.

Rows of plastic goodies, bright colors, and tacky designs looked strangely appealing. I took the time to stroll each aisle, meticulously examining each potential purchase. I believed most of my purchases were the necessities, however, my concept of necessities was a bit skewed as I bought into the consumer driven belief that my baby needs everything. I couldn't wait to bring all that stuff home and start playing house with my little girl.

Normally, I would enjoy spending summer mornings at the ocean, but with a growing baby inside, I purposely avoided going anywhere near the radioactive nuclear power plant that sits right on my favorite beach. Mutations scared me, so I did my best to avoid radiation, the same way I tried to avoid pollution, chemicals, and electromagnetic waves. So, this summer, I found other things to fill my time as I anticipated the arrival of my child. I spent my summer days in the company of my two dogs. We took walks in the neighborhood, and we rested together on the couch as I watched reruns of my favorite afternoon show, *Dharma and Greg*. I read, I prepared the house for baby, and I spent lots of time visiting my new favorite store.

I was preparing for my baby's arrival by making sure the house was in order and having all the important supplies on hand. Feeling prepared brought feelings of peace during this nesting process. Clothing from birth to twelve months sat washed and folded in drawers. Diapers were stacked neatly next to the changing area, and the diaper pail was lined and waiting for its first deposit.

In the living room, we had a pop up hamper filled with toys and teddies, and a bin filled with board books. Then there was the bassinet, car seat, stroller, play pen, bathtub, baby swing... As my developing baby grew bigger, our living space seemed to grow smaller. At just over 1000 feet, my tiny abode was filling up fast. Our house had become a home ready to welcome its newest resident.

As I was showered with gifts, we had a good time. I didn't hear one person mention anything about healthcare, choosing a pediatrician, or vaccines. And everyone seemed to keep hush about their own deliveries. I had plenty of time to do my homework before the birth, but I didn't realize there was more beyond what I had already done.

I had already prepared by performing what I thought were the serious duties. We interviewed pediatricians and attended classes in childbirth and infant CPR. The house was baby proofed and all potential poisons were far out of reach. I read product comparisons online, read safety reports on car seats, and kept up to date on recalled items. I thought this was the kind of stuff that mattered, making sure I didn't expose my baby to any items that might be considered dangerous.

As my due date approached, I started to see the mismatch of ideals with my second obstetrician, as he began to ignore what I wanted to push what he wanted. The doctor asked to induce me so the timing of my baby's birth would coincide with his duty at the hospital. I desired birth to come naturally, so I declined his offer. It didn't feel right for me to pick my daughter's birthday. I was leaving that one up to God.

Apparently, the doctor had other plans, rushing me along to fit his own agenda. As I was leaving my last prenatal appointment with aching insides, I knew that the doctor had done something more than the routine dilation check. Needing to understand what had just happened to me, I asked the nurse. She didn't seem to like that I would question the doctor, but she told me that he had stretched my cervix. As I reiterated over and over that I wanted my daughter to come when she was ready, he knew I wouldn't have given consent to this unnatural tactic to hurry nature along.

Another recommended doctor, this obstetrician was probably no better than the last. He had the same problem with listening. He also had trouble honoring wishes and respecting women's bodies. Unfortunately, his flaws didn't reveal themselves until the very end, near the day my baby was due, and I was too far along to switch providers. It was the end of my pregnancy, and I was hospital ready.

CHAPTER 6

HOSPITAL BIRTH

I thought birthing might come as naturally as breathing, with the instinctual intelligence living in our genes. Of course our bodies would know how to have babies or our species would never have survived. The idea of researching to have a baby seemed a bit counterintuitive as I never researched my other bodily functions. But curiosity swirled, so I read books and took childbirth classes that left me with the illusion that I could have a natural birth in a hospital.

I was not unprepared for birth. My body had been preparing for weeks, practicing contractions and making a steady progress towards a full dilation. But nothing I had learned prepared me for the alternate universe where technology and interventions override a mother's innate wisdom and human capabilities. As the doors flapped open, I entered another dimension, where everything I had learned became irrelevant because it wasn't allowed entry into the delivery room.

Hospital protocols tossed aside my ideas and began hooking me up to machines. Not because there was anything wrong, but because it was standard procedure. I asked not to be confined, but was told that they had no wireless monitors and I needed that belt wrapped around my belly hooked up to the noisy machine at my bedside. They told me I needed the IV drip in my arm to pulse antibiotics through my veins to avoid a strep infection. I had learned about the importance of movement during labor, expecting large birthing balls and walks down the hallway, but they hooked me up instead, tethering me to the hospital bed.

As I lay unguarded, the doctor informed me that he was going to do a dilation check, but his true intent was instantly evident when liquid gushed upon the mattress and excruciating pain filled my body. Breaking my waters burst all remaining hopes I had for that natural birth.

Apparently, women should expect to be impaled as part of their natural deliveries at hospitals. The obstetrician inserted a long needle to break my baby's soft cushion of wetness, performing an entirely different procedure without my knowledge or consent. Lying to me again, just like the day when he snuck in the stretch, he made sure to violate me when I was exposed and vulnerable, while my husband was on a coffee break, outside of the room and unable to protect me.

I am told the instrument looks like a long crochet hook, but I wouldn't know, because I didn't see it coming. I would have said, "No," had I been aware I was going to be assaulted in this manner, so the doctor took it upon himself not to ask. Yet, it would be helpful to warn someone even if only for the sake they keep still, so there aren't any poking accidents, where sharp tools and delicate tissue meet.

The pain immediately intensified to a level I couldn't understand, immensely greater than the waves of contractions that rolled through my belly. I freaked out in horror, as this insanely unnecessary procedure inflicted intolerable cruelty. In my instinctual attempts to control it, I got off the bed to literally shake it off in hysteria. My body was in shock. As my unknowing husband entered the room, I fell into his arms. I don't know if I had a moment of unconscious, but my eyes were completely open and all I saw was blackness.

That prick unnecessary morphed an uncomfortable experience into an unnaturally painful one, as the trauma ripped through my core, stealing my eyesight and my strength. I was suddenly scared, but I had to wait for the shock to subside so I could return my body to stillness in preparation for another big needle. This time it was in my back as I agreed to an epidural in panic. Momentary blindness can do that to a person, cause them to freak out, losing a sense.

That one unauthorized procedure alone changed the course of my delivery. With his hasty behaviors to rush delivery, the doctor inadvertently created a cascade of consequences that slowed down the progression of my labor.

The intrusions on my body made me feel less safe, less confident, and unsure of my basic rights. Falling into my husband's arms, I wanted him to save me from all this. I wanted to go home, but it was too late. I knew I didn't want any of this, but what could I do now that I was here? Sometimes the only way out is through, and I wasn't leaving without a baby in my arms.

Why did an inner process as intimate as birth have to be ruined by the bombardment of so much outside intervention? Birth is an inner journey, a gentle dance between mother and baby, an innate knowing. I expected childbirth to take time, I expected it to hurt, and I expected my body would know what to do. None of the interventions or machines could duplicate the efforts of a mom.

My silent meditations were interrupted by noise machines and intrusive prods. The constant distractions, interruptions, and body violations cut connection to myself. I was trying to figure out how to be in tune with my body and my baby, while someone kept turning the stations. A chaotic external environment created chaos within that impeded silent communication to urge baby's arrival.

When the doctor threatened me with a C-section for the third time, something inside me snapped. My aversion towards this man had been growing every minute. My anger peaked at his final warning, and I yelled at him to leave the room. My own doctor had me uncomfortable and on edge with the energy of his presence, hindering my ability to perform such an intimate task in his company.

He thought I was taking too long, while I thought I could take as long as I needed. There were no emergencies or distress, and I hadn't even been in the hospital twelve hours. He grew increasingly impatient as the clock ticked closer to midnight. If he was that tired, I certainly didn't want him slicing me open. With my doctor's threat, I suddenly understood the seriousness of this situation before he would be allowed to start violating me some more.

The doctor's impatience had already altered the course of my delivery, but now his threat could change the course of my whole life. I knew deep down that if I had a C-section, my daughter would be my only child. I didn't want my future options cut by an impatient obstetrician. My whole life could change simply because my doctor wants to go home.

This was my life, not his, and I believed in myself in a way that my male doctor could not understand. I would have to live with the consequences of the day's events, while he would move on to forget me and the day altogether.

My goal was crystal clear. I was certain I did not want a C-section, so I asked the nurses for help. I wanted to be rescued from the situation, and not "rescued" by the doctor with a C-section. When I snapped at the third surgical threat, my survival instincts kicked in to rescue myself from a fate I didn't want.

I was so grateful to a nurse who wasn't even assigned to me, but stepped in at the most critical time. She brought her loud cheering voice and years of experience. With a burst of Pitocin, added to my shear conviction, I was able to summon that inner strength, fueled by my anger and that boiling blood, with the wonderful nurse by my side. With her encouragement and my determination, we succeeded, together.

Tremendous gratitude inflated my chest. I couldn't have done it without her. The special nurse was my angel sent to help me achieve what I believed, because even though I trusted that birthing was innate, I still believed that most of us could use some help with the process.

A few final pushes was all my baby needed, fully crowned and ready to emerge into the world. Nurses must not be allowed this final responsibility because the doctor was called in last minute to pull my baby out. But just before, he made sure to cut me, even though I had said, "No," many times before, and in writing, getting that one last nick at me before this was all through. Maybe it was a form of retaliation or maybe he just cut himself a bigger paycheck, but it was not necessary. A few more minutes of patience was all that was needed for natural stretching, minutes the machines were telling me I had.

My baby emerged seemingly healthy, with nearly perfect Apgar scores to prove it. I wondered if the extra interventions will affect her in some way, but she was not showing any outward signs of harm. Me, on the other hand, I was wounded, both physically and emotionally, from unwanted procedures and complete disregard from my doctor. My delivery had ended, and it looked nothing like the beautiful picture I had imagined. The after effects of the delivery had me shaking so uncontrollably, I couldn't even hold my baby.

I was subjected to bodily violations I would surely have believed criminal had I not been in an environment where I was supposed to be safe. In one day, I had been sliced and impaled. It certainly wasn't consensual. If this wasn't a hospital and he weren't a doctor, I certainly would have believed he was going to jail.

My human rights seemed to have gotten tossed right alongside with my birth plan. My doctor had his own stubborn ideas about birth-things and he didn't leave much space for variation. Even though I told him my wishes, typed them out too, and gave him more than one copy, on more than one occasion, it didn't matter. His vision conflicted with my own and he had his way with me.

One medical intervention led to the next, racking up charges, as I paid the price, suffering consequences of all the manipulations and interventions — broken waters led to an epidural, which led to delayed progress, which led to Pitocin, and then the doctor threw in an episiotomy, just for the heck of it.

There was nothing out of the ordinary to my birth, just standard procedures and the usual body violations, the normal experience for many women. Many might actually say I was one of the "lucky" ones, fortunate to have made it out alive with a healthy baby. I was in a lot of physical pain, but a deep level of pain hit me on an emotional level. Mixed feelings stirred from a wide spectrum of positive and negative, right alongside the love and appreciation for my healthy baby. She is worth it, but I innately knew that birth is supposed to be different, better, and my one chance with my first baby was over.

CHAPTER 7
MY NEW BABY

I never thought I would get here, but here I am, a mom holding my newborn. Propped up on the narrow hospital bed, I hold my beautiful baby Bella, swaddled in the thin flannel, standard issue blanket that comes adorning all newborns. I admire her loveliness, gazing at this little person we created from within ourselves. Cradled in my arms, my little girl fills my air with love and euphoria. I feel complete peace in her presence, even surrounded by an environment I find unsettling.

Our spirits intermingle in an instantaneous mother child bond. Inhaling her energy, I take her in, absorbing her being with my senses: smelling the top of her head, caressing her delicate fingers, watching her soft scalp pulse with the beating of her heart, listening for tiny breaths, and just staring in amazement at my incredible gift. I can't believe that she is mine.

The door to our hospital room opens and closes a lot with the comings and goings of workers. It is nighttime when our moment of peaceful bliss is disturbed by a nurse entering the room to perform routine checks of my baby. When the thermometer reading indicates that my little girl has a fever, the mood shifts quickly from serene to panic.

As my baby is pulled from my arms, I am told that I overheated her with my smothering love. Her blanket is hastily stripped before she is placed to rest uncovered in the hospital crib. Then, the nurse swiftly leaves the room, while I am left confused and crying, separate from my baby, waiting for her to cool down.

I can see my baby through the clear plastic sides of the crib. She is still sharing the same room, but I am not allowed to hold her. My little darling and I were so comfortable together; I didn't want to let her go. Certainly a mother's arms provide the nurture that a cold crib lacks.

All seemed perfect. My baby seemed fine. She was in my embrace, sharing a most beautiful moment in time. I don't see how our abrupt separation is going to make her better. But I believe she will be okay, because she was okay only moments ago when she lay in my arms. I don't think I have anything to worry about or I might feel differently.

Bella's temperature returns to normal and she is clear for release. I dress my little angel in a soft pink fleece coverall, perfect baby attire for a crisp fall day. Heading home with our new baby is both exciting and a little scary, full responsibility in our hands. When we walk out the doors, we will no longer be under hospital control. Thankful to make it out of this place alive, we are going home. The three of us are going home, to the place where we become a family.

But, no one is letting us leave until we produce visible proof of a car seat. That is my husband's job, because I can't lift the heavy thing right now.

As we are walking out the door, a nurse hands me a small blue booklet. "What's this?" I ask.

"It's your baby's vaccination booklet," she replies as she opens it up to show me the first entry.

"You gave her a vaccine?" Completely blindsided, I think I am in shock again, from another needle. I didn't know that hospitals vaccinated babies at birth, but my ignorance wouldn't have mattered if I were asked permission. I should have known, but they should have asked. What is Hepatitis B anyway? It certainly isn't something I fear.

This shouldn't have happened. I asked lots of questions at admission, and read the forms that I signed. I was told that as long as I was conscious, I could make the decisions to consent or decline treatments. But they hadn't even let me make decisions for myself, why should I have expected anything different for my daughter? Maybe it was all some giant misunderstanding, but I had been given reassurances of misinformation that didn't ring true.

Why the sense of urgency? Did staff declare the lack of a Hepatitis B vaccine to be a medical emergency, a life or death situation, that they felt it necessary to perform the intrusion while I was sleeping? They woke me up for everything else, but not this? I didn't even think that sleeping and unconscious had the same meaning. Maybe they jabbed her while I was awake, but didn't think to ask. Either way, it never occurred to me that hospitals would do this to brand new babies and consider it necessary. My baby is only a few days old; I would never have injected her had I had a choice.

I am perplexed about my freedoms and rights. Hospitals seem to be allowed to do all sorts of things to moms and their babies without asking permission, interventions that seem both unnecessary and possibly dangerous. The hospital experiences start me on a confusing path, full of uncertainty, not feeling like my body is really my own or my baby is truly mine, zapping away some of my confidence. I am the mom. Why doesn't that count for something? Why does the "standard of care" override my standards?

Putting protocols above the wishes of patients and parents, the hospital experience left me wondering… Were hospitals their own entity with a different set of rules, just like airplanes and cruise ships? Or did I grant the hospital blanket permission just by walking in? What are our rights, as people, as patients, as American citizens?

CHAPTER 8
LOVE AND LOSS

My little girl had already taken a hold of my heart by the time four tiny fingers wrap themselves around just one of mine. Smoothing my thumb over her precious little hand, I deeply inhale the sweet smell of baby into myself, filling my lungs with a freshness that never stales. My baby lies flat on the floor, her little eyes looking up at me as I kneel over her, straddling her tiny frame, for a routine frenzy of kisses. Leaning in to peck her left cheek, then the right one, I smile, and she smiles back, giggling with sweetness. Grabbing her hands, I pull her two fists together and up to my lips for more kisses.

My belly, constantly full of loving butterflies from the excitement I feel for this tiny person, is the same belly that is padded with comfort as she lays on me like a bed, in our daily ritual of connection. As I lie on my back across the couch, we rest, lying chest to chest, as my baby moves up and down on my tummy with the inflation and deflation of each of my breaths. Her head settles just under my chin, at the top of my chest, with her arms hanging down by my sides. She always turns her head to face my right, lying with her right cheek touching my chest. I caress her head, as

I plant a kiss right on top of her scalp. My other arm touches her back in a loving, peaceful embrace. Gently lifting up and down like a horse on a merry go round, my baby sleeps, and the only spinning is the love in my heart enveloping my baby in the warmth of my adoration.

As time passes, her head rests on my shoulders and my chin nestles in her neck. Her lengthening legs start creeping down my own legs. The weight of her growing body starts to crush my ribs and belly, but I hardly notice. Where limp arms once draped my sides, they now cling to me with my baby's own expression of love. My wonderful child is now hugging back!

Mornings are full of good moods and cuddles when I bring the little one into my bed to cherish the peaceful start of a new day. I love how she pauses to smile at me or grab at my shirt while she eats. I love that she runs her hands through my hair. I love the noises she makes when she is excited. I love her enthusiasm for people and new discoveries in the world around her. I love spending cherished time, sharing days with my dear girl, doing nothing much, other than being in each other's presence and embracing the beautiful moments to memory.

How can one little miracle multiply happiness, elevating joy to heights never imagined? My love for my students brought me Bella, and my love for my Bella brings the desire for even more children. From none to one, I start to have visions of a large family full of little Bellas, because I think that she is the best kid in the whole world, even if the addition of siblings means I will never be able to describe her that way again.

Before Bella joined me in this world, I thought I had everything: a loving husband, a home we could afford, two dogs, and a fulfilling job with students I adored. Life was everything I wanted it to be. My dream of teaching fulfilled my soul and my growing baby filled my belly. I was replete with excitement and anticipation for the new life to come, and I was grateful and appreciative of everything I had. Life was good, and I couldn't imagine being happier.

Then the baby came, and I couldn't imagine being more in love. I thought loving my husband, my pets, and my students was knowing love, but that little girl broke open my heart in a way not yet experienced. Life delivered me this precious child, and she showed me a kind of love I had never known. Now, blessed with a child, I can't imagine life any other way. She is a piece of me, an extension of my heart itself, no longer protected in the shell of my skin, but completely exposed to the outside world.

With my baby completely vulnerable, I am completely vulnerable. My heart and soul seem to escape the containment of my being, as both my exuberance and my vulnerabilities are now on the outside, as my baby lives as my heart outside of my womb. That feeling is an unfamiliar kind of scary.

My new role fills me with such love that I fear loss, having somber thoughts among all the bliss, noticing my own mortality as well as my baby's. The day comes sooner for some and later for others, but it is the lurking truth that most of us don't really like to think about. With the birth of Bella, the realization of mortality knocked on my door, no longer a stranger, but a relevant and real possibility that I began to fear.

This amazing creature grew from near nothingness into our most prized possession, and I am afraid of what her loss might do to my heart. I know I will never forget the good times we share, but I don't want our joyful connection to ever come to an end. Extraordinary love leaves us vulnerable. I know the loss of a child leaves behind an empty hollowness that echoes of tears, and I never want to know firsthand what the heartache of real loss might feel like to a parent.

Fear of loss set in, fears of anything that threatened the blissful happiness I achieved when we welcomed the new member into our family. I had been given a small piece of heaven, and I started to create perceived threats that could steal it all away. I will do anything to keep my baby safe. I just want my new world to stay exactly the same, and I want to protect my child in every way I know how.

I believe we need a pediatrician to help us out. I memorized the appointment schedule in a new baby's life, faithfully obeying the agenda and dutifully booking visits on time. I think I need someone to verify that my girl is growing accordingly, believing the doctor will rejoice with me as we watch my daughter's progression. Maybe, I even think she needs some of those vaccines, even if the idea makes me nervous.

I am anxious by nature, but the pediatrician taught me fear and helplessness in a way I had never even imagined, verbally exposing me to a dangerous world full of invisible predators waiting to attack. He created a vision within me that life itself is some kind of monster ready to swallow my baby and spit on her some deadly disease.

The doctor's horror stories instilled a fear of basic living. Hearing his banter made me wonder how anyone can even keep their children alive, let alone healthy. I didn't have a child to raise her in a bubble, but the pediatrician creates scenarios of paranoia that have us fearing things we never would have considered.

Naturally, he had us fearing germs, fevers to be exact. He told us that if our baby gets a fever in the first six weeks of life she would need to be rushed to the hospital for a spinal tap. My fear of spinal taps is far greater than my fear of fevers or germs, but if one could lead to the other, well then, now I am afraid of both.

With an autumn birthday, during a year of early flu season, we protected our baby the best we knew how, keep her from germs by keeping her away from people. I believed that to avoid the need for medical intervention, we needed to avoid the germs. In our attempts to avoid a spinal tap, we became unusual first time parents. We asked to have no visitors at all for the first six weeks of my baby's life. There were no joyous celebrations, no entertaining, just our new little family enjoying a quiet contentment to ourselves.

We escaped the fever. We escaped the spinal tap. But, sometimes it felt like I couldn't escape my home. The doctor's world was a terrible place that didn't allow for human contact or visits with friends. This was not the kind of place I wanted to live in very long. Holed up in confinement is no way to live. I hoped this isolation period was just until she had all her shots.

CHAPTER 9
DAY OF SHOTS

Fifteen months passed, and my little baby is a growing girl. Fifteen months also happens to be an age that coincides with a routine trip to the pediatrician's office. Bella is completely well for her well visit, and I am so pleased with her development. She started walking solidly, two weeks before her first birthday, and she has been meeting many of the major milestones ahead of schedule. She has been progressing beautifully, from the tiny helpless newborn to this independent toddler that stands before me today.

But why does this little person require so many trips to the doctor simply to confirm that she is well? My naïve little world is good. I am trusting and happy, disillusioned to believe that these well visits are in Bella's best interest. The doctor has us scared to death of germs, but we aren't yet scared of him. I am just doing what I believe is the right thing to do, what I was trained to believe good mothers do for their babies.

Our appointment is scheduled for a Tuesday afternoon in January. My work granted me a personal day, and it is a treat to enjoy morning play with my little girl. I smile watching Bella climb up and down off of our big black reclining chair, dragging her favorite stuffed teddy along. She hides on me, playing peek-a-boo from behind this large chair. Enjoying herself, my little girl delights in trying on hats. Then, I bounce her in my arms as we dance. Goofing off together, we are so happy filling our wait time with wonderful memories of laughter.

Unfortunately, the inevitable arrives, and we must halt our fun. Shoulders slumping, I drag myself to the pediatrician's office with my daughter in my arms, leaving my self-confidence behind. At home, I feel like my daughter is truly my own and I even feel like I might be doing a good job at this parenting thing. But in the office, I am under the controlling eyes of the doctor, and his domineering presence leave me feeling inferior. I am respectful in my manners: polite, non-confrontational, and slightly timid. He only sees my daughter for monthly checkups and isn't doing any of the real parenting work himself, but I am unsure of myself, unsure of my rights, and unsure about all my new fears. He seems to take advantage of my weaknesses.

We chose this pediatrician not necessarily because of an alignment with our own beliefs, but because we didn't seem to have many when it came to babies, and he seemed so confident about his, reciting verbatim from the latest guidelines and publications. Believing that he was "on top of things," I mistakenly mistook confidence for intelligence and rhetoric for knowledge.

At our pre-birth consultations, we were asking about the overuse of antibiotics and not the overuse of vaccines. We didn't even realize there was an overuse of vaccines going on, because we were getting our news from the television. Of course, I looked into vaccines after the surprise at the hospital, but mostly read the stuff that is intended to alleviate a parent's fear along with more assurances of safety. Then I would see something on one of the morning programs and I would believe them. These are the people I wake up to every morning; certainly their familiar smiling faces would be trustworthy...

I am usually full of questions, asking some of the same questions at each visit. Some questions I learned to ask through parenting magazines and pamphlets I picked up right at the obstetrician's office.

One time I asked if there was mercury in the shots. He said, "No." The next time I asked, he said, "Let me check." That discrepancy in responses makes me uncomfortable. I am also uncomfortable about so many shots on one day. I ask what I think are good questions with legitimate concerns about vaccine safety, and additives such as mercury that is supposed to be removed by now.

The clock strikes appointment time. The doctor walks into the exam room, and his first words boldly spout off the orders for the day. He tells me that my daughter will be getting the Hib (haemophilus influenzae type B), MMR (measles, mumps, and rubella), DTaP (diptheria, tetanus, and pertussis), and a pneumococcal conjugate of 7 strains. That is four shots on one day, with multiple illnesses contained in each dose. That is like 14 strains of illnesses he tells me are severe.

Four different shots, seems like too many at one visit, even though another time he gave her five. The doctor doesn't think spacing the shots out is a good idea, because believe me, I asked. The doctor reassures us of vaccine safety, telling me that the human body can handle 100s of shots in one day. But I wonder how he *knows* this? I wonder if someone has ever tried it, or maybe it is just some sort of guess.

Which gets me thinking... how can this be true on one hand, if on the other hand, I am supposed to be afraid of just one illness episode caught the natural way? If the body can actually handle 100s of illnesses at once, what do we need vaccines for? But he is referring to his opinion on how safe he feels the injections are, sharing his thoughts that it is far worse for the child if I have to bring her back for extra appointments to space out injections. His perspective, why upset her so many times?

I am uneasy with his plan. The two shots that bother me are the DTaP and the pneumococcal conjugate. I am not as concerned about the MMR, because I am afraid of the measles, and this will be her first dose. Maybe I think the MMR is still one of those necessary risks, while it seemed that my baby already got enough doses of the others vaccines for it not to be worth the risk of getting more.

In 2005, the pneumococcal series is a four dose series of shots that, according to our doctor, is in such high demand that it often runs short in supply. I was so happy that it had been out of stock at our last visit. Considering that this vaccine offers primary protection until age two, it doesn't make sense to me to give a 4th dose of a shot at 15 months. The closer my daughter gets to age two, the less I feel the need for this shot.

I don't argue my opinion on this one; I keep my thoughts to myself as I swallow my sinking heart. "Out of stock" had been a blessing to my ears. I thought we had already dodged that bullet, but I guess it was merely a delay.

I do remind the doctor of a DTaP reaction with the six month shots. I reiterate the incessant high pitched crying and the inability to fall asleep. I immediately notified him at six months, when this behavior occurred, but he needed more reminding. He wasn't there, so the memories don't imprint so deeply. Even though Bella had several shots at her six month appointment, the doctor attributed the behavior to the DTaP.

I ask permission to do the DTaP by itself, next time. He agrees to appease me by allowing a delay, but the other three shots are a go.

He never asks for permission from me, offering vaccines as a statement rather than a question. "She will be getting these today," he declares as an order, and I sort of sit there and allow it to happen. He never asks me to sign anything, like a clue that would have brought awareness to this procedure being a choice, my choice. My ignorance allows him to steal away my rights. Bella is my baby, yet, the pediatrician treats me as though I am almost irrelevant in this matter.

I have many concerns, but the doctor quickly negates each one and assures me that I am wrong. I don't quite understand all his reasoning, and he confuses me sometimes. Being much too hard on myself, I chalk it up to a mental deficiency on my end rather than his, making the assumption that a doctor must be smarter than me. I believe that he must know better than I do, putting trust in him, the doctor, rather than Him, the God.

I have no training in the office politics of medical practices. Unaware and ignorant, I am looking for honest advice, and I trust the pediatrician to give it to me. I trust the pediatrician has my daughter's best interests in mind and not simply his own. I trust that he is telling me a complete picture of truth. I trust that he knows what he is doing and will be there for us if we need him. I trust him with my baby, when I put her life in his hands.

And in his hands, she meets her fate, in the cold chill of that winter's day.

But he doesn't get his hands dirty. With the day's orders firmly in place, the pediatrician leaves the room and leaves the rest of the job to his nurses. He was merely the salesman of vaccines. Once he closed the deal, his work was through.

Three needles require two nurses and a mom to hold down one protesting toddler. Each nurse grabs a leg and simultaneously thrusts the needles into each of her pudgy thighs. I wish I had yelled, "Stop!" because actions cannot be reversed. My baby screams loudly on impact. As my baby outwardly screams, my insides scream too and release streams of tears. This is awful. This doesn't feel right either. But I have not been listening to my gut; I have been listening to the doctor.

Tasks accomplished, the nurses relax and cover the injection marks with tiny Band-Aids decorated in pleasant childhood themes. The nurses are openly nervous about these bandages, reminding me several times to make sure I remove them before they become a choking hazard. They never once display any anxiety over the shots themselves or explain what a side effect might look like. Their only concern is those tiny bandages. No one is at all concerned about a vaccine reaction, so I don't worry about it either.

I gather my belongings and swoop my baby into my arms, feeling relieved that another "necessary" ordeal is finally over. The only parts I ever feel grateful for are the height and weight measurements I can add to the baby's development calendar.

These "well visits" always leave me feeling sick. "It's for the best," I have always been told. "A few pricks of momentary discomfort are a small price to pay for protection." I am protecting her from something worse I was told. "A few tears of pain can prevent a lifetime of sorrow." These are a bunch of sayings I heard so many times I actually thought they might be true. My head had been trained to these sayings, these memes of the mind, but my body is shaking as though it knows something my brain cannot fathom.

CHAPTER 10
THE SEIZURE

Everything still seems normal when I hold my little one the next morning and barrage her with hugs and kisses before I leave for work. I'm not noticing any hints, any foreshadowing to predict the day ahead or the events to come. Believing that our stressful, routine well visit is behind us, I am still under the cloud of beliefs that convinced me that vaccines are for the best and assured me that nothing would go wrong. But the turning point of our lives had already been injected. Our world is about to collapse, and it will only be a matter of time before I notice.

That assurance was a promise for a positive outcome, and I had faith that the doctor would be correct. But when I come home to find out that my daughter just had a seizure, I am horrified. My little girl had a seizure one day after her 15 month shots. This can't be coincidence. She has never had a seizure before, and she doesn't even have a fever.

I immediately call the pediatrician's office to report the adverse event, but he keeps this information to himself and doesn't report it anywhere. To my next surprise, he doesn't even seem to care. He makes less of the situation, because my caregiver was the witness and not myself.

The reaction witnessed matches the description of a petit mal seizure, but apparently this is up for debate by the doctor who wasn't even there. Instead of being concerned, he is questioning the validity of my claim. Denial. He tries to rewrite my daughter's history with his professional opinion, explaining to me that lay people don't know what they witness because they don't have the proper background to know. Lay people do have the capability to describe exactly what they see, without needing to know the name for it. But the doctor is not offering up any confirmations of the occurrence. Instead, he offers the term "staring episode." Is that another diagnosis altogether, or is he just renaming the seizure to something less scary?

The pediatrician continues to confidently speak all mumble jumbled doctor talk, like a politician attempting to confuse us, trying to discredit the eyes by putting doubt in our heads, forcing us to second guess ourselves, because we aren't full of unwavering confidence like him. I think he is calling us stupid, but I ignore him. The only thing I feel stupid for right now is trusting this man.

When it comes to babies, we're not lay people. We're mothers! Something just went wrong with my baby. I don't really need a label for what happened. I just want to fix it. Actually, I want to make it go away, just like the doctor does. But that won't happen by ignoring it. His disregard is inexcusable, and I am furious. I am angry at the doctor, angry at his nonchalant, uncaring attitude, angry at what happened. He told me that serious reactions don't occur; but they do, for some people. My daughter is the newest victim, and a seizure seems serious enough to me.

Something snapped in me, the part of me I was holding back in order to be polite. Things I wanted to say and ask for *before* this happened, when I didn't realize how serious this could be and I didn't want to make waves. Now, I am in the midst of a storm. The waves have already arrived, and I stir them up some more.

Fierceness came forth from me, the mommy protector within, and I am much more than a little angry. I am in survival mode.

My mind is getting clearer, and I suddenly realize that I am missing huge puzzle pieces of information. I was given only a partial picture of a partial reality. I demand answers, real ones this time. Not ones to allay my fears and concerns, but the truth, answers that will explain what I am seeing, ones that might explain the seizure. I need to go to the source. I ask to have copies of every single package insert from every vaccine the practice had ever given my daughter. The office promises to have them ready the next day. Two days after our well visit, and I can pick up the inserts that might explain sickness instead.

I don't know why I didn't ask to read the inserts before. I was reading the labels of foods and products that I bought, but I never thought to read the labels of an injected substance. Maybe it was because vaccines seemed to come pre-filled, right there in the exam room, without a prescription or a trip to the drug store. Maybe it was because I trusted the doctor and everything he told me. Maybe it was because I didn't classify vaccines as a drug or a chemical, and I was told there was no more mercury to worry about. Maybe vaccines were something special, a magical substance, complete with wishful thinking and the faithful notion that these little injections were our saviors.

I head to work the day after Bella's seizure, a complete wreck, full of worry and anger. I am teaching second grade now, the only position available after my maternity leave. I hold back my frustration until lunch time when I tell my coworkers about my daughter's seizure after receiving her vaccines. At the end of my rant, I blurt out, "She is done with those!" without forethought, but full of truth.

One of my coworkers immediately snaps back, "You can't do that. She needs those vaccines. They're good for her."

Clearly distraught, I am baffled by what feels like an insensitive comment. The teacher's opinion on vaccines has odd timing and is completely unrelated to my personal reality. "Good for her," flew out of her mouth in instantaneous reaction, no thought to what I was feeling, no thought to the seizure, no thought of sensitivity. The words just came out in an immediate reply from years of training, memorized into the unconscious response.

I don't understand the lack of connection. Did she hear me? "My daughter had a seizure." I repeat.

Maybe a seizure is no big deal to her; maybe it's not if it is not your child, but it certainly is a big deal to me, the mom. "Good for her" echoes through my mind. Vaccines don't look like they did my baby any good. In fact, to me, they seem bad for her.

CHAPTER 11

PACKAGE INSERTS

The work day has ended, and I make the drive over to the doctor's office to pick up the package inserts. I expect photocopies, but instead, the receptionist hands over the original paperwork, straight from the cartons. It instantly occurs to me that I am not alone in my ignorance of the inserts. The practice wouldn't have enough originals for everybody.

WTF! This is the exact moment in my lifetime when I begin swearing. What my eyes see written does not match what my ears have been told. I shock into anger with the sharp sting of the words typed across the pages of package inserts. I keep hearing these things are proven safe, and yet it appears to me they didn't even do enough testing to come to this conclusion.

I certainly assumed when they said, "Safe," they knew if vaccines caused cancer. But they didn't even test that? And mutations? They didn't test for those either. They use the terms carcinogenic and mutagenic, but I know what those words mean, and if they haven't tested those factors, how can they be assuring anyone that this stuff is safe? My goodness, not knowing that information might mean vaccines are possibly as bad for people as the radiation I worked so hard to avoid. I might want to be a grandparent one day, but who knows, they didn't study for reproductive harms either.

I avoided radiation, carcinogens and chemicals to avoid cancer and mutations, and my baby is just a baby, I haven't even started thinking about her reproductive system yet. We injected vaccines, under the promise that they were safe, and yet the kind of dangers I am concerned about aren't even tested.

I didn't think to ask if vaccines caused cancer or mutations, because I made the assumption that they didn't when I heard the word "safe." Maybe it's just me, but I think when parents hear the word "safe," they expect with certainty that it will not harm our children in any way. I guess we really shouldn't be making assumptions about anything, because what we think we know might not match reality at all.

Maybe they have rewritten the meaning of the word "safe," changing its very definition, and I just haven't caught on yet. I look up "safe" in the dictionary just to be sure. "Secure from danger, harm, or evil." And I also see "free from risk." Some people are even making the leap from "safe" to "good for her," but there is no implied benefit, only that it will not harm.

What are they testing for then? How do they conclude safety? Why are they calling these things safe, when it seems to me, the best they could possibly say is that they just don't know. Their "protection" might be killing us, because they really don't know.

How useful are studies when they only answer questions we don't even care to know the answers to, while leaving our real concerns unexplored? Did they simply test the new vaccine against an older vaccine to see if the risks were about the same? Were all those side effects just considered "acceptable risks?" What parents find acceptable and what researchers find acceptable might not match. So when studies declare "safe," what was the question? Parents do not necessarily have the same questions as the researchers.

The ingredients are a concoction of chemicals, the same chemicals I've been trying to avoid my whole life, the same chemicals we lock away from our children, chemicals like formaldehyde that I avoided in my shampoos, the very chemical that preserved our science dissection specimens. This is gross. I am familiar with some of the ingredients, and I know they are known carcinogens. I think if we inject a known carcinogen into our body, the side effect might be cancer. But if they don't test for that, the secrets are never revealed.

The side effects are printed, and there are a whole slew of them, risks we took unknowingly, risks we were told did not exist, risks not disclosed by the doctor or listed on any handouts. The MMR insert mentions albumin, a blood component that carries a risk of blood infections. Does this mean that we are giving our kids vaccines for childhood illnesses and now we risked acquiring a real blood born disease like AIDS? I'm not sure, but it is the first thought that comes to my mind.

I check the Vaccine Adverse Event Reporting System, VAERS for short, the government website to record vaccine reactions, the negative events from vaccine administration. On the website, I see lots of reactions being reported. I come to the conclusion that vaccines are certainly not safe for everyone. Someone is suffering those side effects.

Vaccines can cause harm. Somewhere deep inside, I remember this now. I remember hearing the stories of people actually catching polio from the oral vaccine used to prevent it. I remember my mother telling me about "bad lots," batches of vaccines that would get recalled. But this was in my childhood. Surely with our modern technology, they would have perfected these things by now, hadn't they?

Maybe not. With all the additional shots in the schedule, maybe they have created something even more dangerous. So, how does one come to the conclusion that the use of even one shot is safe? Add together a few shots, all with their own package inserts and lists of risks, side effects, and untested potential health hazards, creating a multiplication range of possibilities — and what do parents get? It's a crap shoot really, because we just don't know.

I asked all the wrong questions. I already have so many more, now that I have begun to flip pages into the world of vaccines. Still on the surface, I am just getting started. The depth is yet to come, but I feel sick, as nausea makes its home in the pit of my belly. None of this makes any sense, and it is not because I am stupid. They are lying to us, and the truth is right here, staring at me from these inserts, with unsettling and disturbing information.

I can't believe what we did to our little baby.

CHAPTER 12
THE REACTION CONTINUES

Four days after the shots, three days after the seizure, Saturday brings eruptions of pink spots with light colored pustule centers that start to cover my daughter's belly and then her back. As the speckled rash dots the trunk of her body, Bella's temperature begins to rise. A fever sets in. My baby is sick.

One day shy of one week later, we bring Bella to the pediatrician for a sick visit. The same doctor who ordered the shots made light of a seizure. Will he ignore this too? His first diagnosis: chicken pox.

I think he is crazy as I blurt out my rebuttal, "She just got vaccinated for chicken pox three months ago. How can this be chicken pox? Don't the shots work at all?"

Even though he believes the rash looks like the start of chicken pox, he offers me another possible explanation: a side effect rash from the MMR shot. He tells me there is a 5% possibility to develop a measles type rash with the shot, a harmless side effect, in his opinion, that he didn't previously bother to mention.

He is only the doctor. I am the mom. Who is he to hold back information because he feels I don't need to know? That's not honesty. That's not transparency. And it is certainly not ethical. How can parents have informed consent if we are only given part of the information? Of course we deserve the right to know the risks of routine medical procedures like vaccinations. But he ordered rather than asked, leaving off both information and consent.

We leave with no answers, no proper diagnosis, and our little girl who is no longer well. The doctor who ordered the vaccinations seems to overlook the damage. I am shocked that the reaction is occurring and even more shocked that it is being ignored. He is playing the denial game, refusing to acknowledge the vaccines as the culprit and cause of the severity of her illness, abandoning us when we need him most.

As a frantic mother, panicking for her daughter, I call around to some of the other doctors we had interviewed, begging for a new pediatrician right in the middle of the immediate reaction illness. "Would someone please see my daughter and help her even though she is not an established patient?" I plead.

It is a Wednesday, eight days after Bella's fifteen month shots and we are sitting with another doctor for our first sick appointment in a different practice. I relay the chronology of events to these new ears, words that I will hear myself repeat many times in the years to come. This is the start of our story, lengthening in details as my daughter grows in age. But it always starts the same, unfolding at the exact point in time when this all began, and there we are, right back to the fifteen month shots and the irony of the well visit.

As we speak, the doctor takes lots of handwritten notes. Maybe he is writing his grocery list, but we think he is listening. He looks over my daughter, smells in her diaper, and sends us on our way. There are still no answers.

The fever is still hanging on, clinging to my baby's internal thermometer, kicking the digits up to 105 degrees on our home measuring device. The angry rash has grown into something far more ominous looking, as large blotchier red patches spread from her trunk to her extremities and covering her beautiful face. Her skin is overrun with red rash, no longer hidden beneath her clothes, as the progression claims all the remaining surfaces of her body. The rash is everywhere, from her soft cheeks to her delicate fingers.

Two days later, we are here again, with our sick little girl. It is a Friday, ten days after the shots. We meet another new doctor, a young one at this second pediatric practice. He examines my baby and seems to agree that this looks like a vaccine reaction. Not yet corrupted by the medical system, he doesn't try to negate any of my baby's symptoms or offer up false explanations to protect the shots. He sees my daughter, he hears me, and he shows concern. He warns me about something called Kawasaki disease and tells me to keep watch for the sign of a red tongue.

No one seems to know how to handle a vaccine reaction. So far, the doctors have been clueless or just act that way. Even this new doctor who admits that the symptoms look like a vaccine reaction doesn't really seem to know what to do about it. Not one doctor recommends further care or refers us to the hospital. Buckled into her car seat, my precious baby is sent on her way, carried in my confused arms, leaving our third sick visit of the week without any answers, only the warning about red tongues.

Being a Friday, the work week had passed in my absence as I was busy at home, caring for Bella and taking her to doctor appointments every other day. My sick little girl, exhausted by her illness, has fallen asleep in her portable car seat. Thankful to see her sleeping, I feel grateful that she is achieving a small bit of peace amidst the turmoil. With my baby showing no signs of positive improvement, it looks like I will be absent for at least part of the next week too.

The trip to my school is much easier with a napping baby in the backseat, as I make the drive to drop off my lesson plans and teaching manuals. I am able to pull up right outside the front door to the school, where my classroom aide is expecting me. Prepared to accept my teaching supplies, she meets me, right at my car, so I don't have to bring my sick child into the building.

As I hand off my book bags, we peer through the car window at my sleeping baby. Even though Bella is snuggly covered on this winter day, her face, hands, and ankles are exposed, revealing the telltale patches of red and pink marring the baby soft skin, visible proof that this is all too real.

My healthy baby spent none of my sick days for her care, but with a well visit that has left us in a pool of sickness, my leave time is suddenly being drained. As I watch my work travel away, into the school building, in the arms of another, I realize what those sick days might cost me. But I walk towards the driver's seat, where my precious cargo is strapped in the car, and she is my choice. I know in that moment, my baby needs me more than any of my students will ever need me.

CHAPTER 13

THE LONGEST NIGHT

As the daylight hours come to a close, with a trip to the doctor and a drive to my school behind us, darkness signals the beginning of our nightly routines. My sick baby and I sink into our favorite black chair. Soft leather with pillow puff padding and cushy arms invite us into a welcome coziness. It was less than two weeks ago that Bella played around this chair while awaiting her ill fate. I crank the foot rest into the recline position where my baby and I kick back to relax, snuggling in together. Her head is cradled in my arm, cuddling into my familiar embrace, as I wait for her to fall asleep.

I think tonight might be like any normal night with our nocturnal habit of cuddling at bedtime. But, tonight is not like any other Friday or any other night we had experienced. We have done this pattern so many times, that it is instantly obvious that something is wrong, something more than the fever and rash.

There are unfamiliar behaviors in response to our familiar routine. There is no settling into the crook of my arm and the comfort of the chair. Attempting to fall asleep, she startles from something within herself, instantly awakening with a loud shrill cry and quick movements, throwing her arms into the air and arching her back like she is going to do a flying back bend straight off of the chair.

With each attempt at normalcy, she tries to snuggle into the fold of my arm as usual, but then bursts out in an instant, with an arched back, arms outstretched, and loud shrill cry. Repeating the pattern every few minutes, the cycle continues: settle in, close eyes, arch back and scream, settle in, close eyes, arch back and scream. There is no relaxation, only restlessness. As much as she wants to cozy herself to sleep, her body is fighting. As I hold her writhing body in my arms, I feel the wrongness.

On this night, Bella's body is fully riddled with marks that exploded outward during the course of her illness, progressing from her chest and back, through her arms and legs, onto her face, hands, and feet. This is not the normal spread of a wild measles rash, but she has some manmade invention that can only result from an injected mixture of concoctions with atypical expectations resulting from the possibility of potentials of various combinations. Bella has three different shots encircling her blood, all with various diseases imbedded into their fluids, all with their own package inserts and side effects. How would we know the patterns at which they might react with one another? God only knows the possibilities or how long this could last. The outside looks bad, but what is going on inside my little girl?

I try to remain calm as I run through the mental list of soothing techniques we use when our baby is colicky. I pull out the CDs to play familiar songs she learned in the womb, while I sing to her. I offer more nourishment to ensure a full enough belly. I make sure her diaper is dry, and the clothing is comfortable. But nothing works. Soothing techniques fail to calm my struggling baby.

I spent a few hours exhausting my efforts, trying to comfort my little girl, before I decide to call the doctor. The receiving end of my phone call is accepted by a different pediatrician than the young doctor I had seen earlier in the day. It is late, and he doesn't sound happy to hear from me. Troubling him at night, so soon into the relationship, I wonder if he might be rethinking the office's decision to accept my daughter as a new patient. But I am scared, and I would never bother someone at night unless I felt it were absolutely necessary.

"Is this what encephalitis looks like?" I ask, after describing the exact details of behaviors I am witnessing.

He disregards my idea with a tone that scoffs at ridicule for the suggestion. He reassures me that this experience is not encephalitis and if Bella is having difficulty sleeping, I can give her some Benadryl to calm her down. "Benadryl," he says, will get my baby to sleep. I am a fan of the medicine for its use in allergic reactions, but I had never heard of it being used as a sleeping aid.

To me this episode is more than just "difficulty sleeping." I am used to difficult, but this seems more extreme. I am used to my baby being challenging some nights and her belly being hard to fill. I know those soothing techniques so well, because I get lots of practice. But tonight's behavior is out of the ordinary, out of the range of her normal. I am concerned that this might be more serious than the doctor let on, but my wavering confidence leaves me feeling uncertain.

The pediatrician didn't really alleviate all my fears by making light of what I was seeing, but he had me second guessing myself again. Of course, I don't want this to be encephalitis, so I want to believe every word he said.

We endure as the night marches on, finding an inner stamina to carry on, as I comfort my daughter the best I know how, being fully present to my baby's needs. The long nighttime hours tick slowly in isolation, when my tired arms want to reach out but everyone else is asleep. The quiet of the darkness is pierced with the shrieks of my baby. I await the sunlight, hoping the dawn of a new day will bring change for the better.

My baby's eyes can't stay closed long enough to fall into a real sleep, but I hold her body tightly, preventing her thrashing from throwing herself straight off of the chair into a fall on the floor. Her body's anguish persists for a bit longer before her little body sinks into a deep sleep. One of the longest nights of my life, with memories that will haunt me, the turmoil is suddenly still as my baby collapses into exhaustion.

I make a gentle transfer to the crib so that I can take a break. I am tired too, but not ready for sleep. I need space to think. What is going on here? I didn't see any red tongue, and no one warned me about brain inflammation. I have no medical terms to label what has occurred, and my guess at encephalitis was nearly mocked by the doctor.

Left alone and confused, I am lacking confidence, feeling completely dependent on a medical system that seems to be turning its back to me. Maybe it is called encephalopathy rather than encephalitis, but either way, it was a close call.

CHAPTER 14

WHY US?

Life still feels a bit surreal, as I hold a baby in my arms, a baby that is actually mine, growing up right before my eyes. I am a mother, with full responsibility, no longer limited to a day at work, but an all-encompassing duty caring for another life. When I held my new baby in my arms, I couldn't imagine the weight of such few pounds. I had no problem lifting her 8 pound frame. I had no problem lifting her body with each additional pound, building strength each day, but I had no idea how heavy the magnitude of responsibility would feel when the weight sits on my shoulders.

Decisions in my control that might result in consequences out of my control create a constant struggle within me, with thoughts of what ifs and second guesses. God gifted me with a blessing, and I honor the significance of the charge. Cautious and careful, I thought I knew the difference between right and wrong, but now I am not so sure. And, if I make a mistake, is it considered a sin?

I love that little person more than I ever imagined loving another soul. So precious, ten fingers, ten toes, with qualities shared with other babies alike and all those special features, uniquely hers, like the little crook in her right ear, the reddish patch of skin on her forehead, and her long, skinny feet. I appreciate the gift of life, my baby girl, heaven sent from God Himself, entrusting me with her care. And I messed up. How can I ever make it up to her?

My baby's well-being was destroyed by injections at well visits. The very same injections that were supposed to save her from illness inflicted her with something worse. Needles — so smooth, yet so sharp in their attack, destroying her immune system little by little until the damage was so great we are forced to notice. I wish we were invincible, but unfortunately we were vulnerable to vaccines. And what made it worse, we let them in, like the Trojan horse, under the guise of protection.

At fifteen months old, real fear strikes as my daughter reacts violently to her vaccines, those memorable weeks that will change our personal lives forever. It occurs to me. This is exactly where I didn't want to be when I thought the shots might be a good idea. This exact moment is what I have feared the whole time, believing it would be the germs that would lead me to this unwelcome place. But now, here I am, at the realization of my fears, because of the shots themselves, because I didn't expect vaccines to cause bad outcomes.

I was alert to dangers in public, but in the doctor's office, where I thought we were cared for, I let my guard down. But we were not safe there. Well visits only poked holes into our bubble of contentment, each shot bringing us a little closer to bursting our bliss, shattering our private world into pieces falling down around us.

I thought with the breaking of the fever, we were on the path to recovery, and the usual could be found around a nearby corner. We breathed that big sigh of relief, grateful that my Bella is still alive, but we will never know the normal we once knew. Long term aftershocks continue to wave through my baby's insides, with trembles that reverberate to the outside, shaking up our entire world. The vaccine journey is not over; it is just beginning.

The rash took a long time to go away and in its path left behind some scarring blood vessels at the surface. With each bath, the phantom rash returns, reminding us of the menacing ghost that still lives within. The brain inflammation left behind a physical setback that created clumsiness in Bella's gross motor abilities, and some odd behaviors emerge.

Survival mode kicks into gear with monthly fever episodes, like clockwork, lasting exactly 96 hours each time and always at a fever reaching 105 degrees. Routine illnesses become her vaccine reaction reminders, illnesses that tell us something went wrong and drastically changed this poor girl's immune system.

Why Us? I never felt immune to bad things happening. I always felt that if they can happen to someone, they can happen to us. But we did everything "right." We did everything we thought good parents were supposed to do for their children. No one deserves to have the wrong outcome when choosing to do what we are told is the "right" thing to do. Our little miracle was born so beautiful, so perfect, and so healthy. Vaccine injury wasn't supposed to happen to us. But it did, and I wasn't prepared for that possibility.

Why Us? We were just like any other new parents trying to do what we thought best for our child. We used the soaps and shampoos the hospital suggested. I nursed for a full ten months, resisting the pressure to give bottles of formula. Her mattress was hard, the recommended firmness. Her bedding was crisp and tight, no blankets or toys to crowd out her breaths. We laid her "Back to Sleep" at the campaign's request, as a precaution to prevent SIDS. We followed the advice bestowed upon us by the medical professionals we believed cared for our daughter, assuming they must know better, even when mother knows best.

I wonder if I could have contributed to this in any way, other than being duped. As I comb through my whole life looking for mistakes, reexamining past behaviors and reflecting on lifestyle choices, I can't find anything but clean living and low risk behaviors. But we made the decision to vaccinate, accepting the biggest risk of all, heeding the guidelines of the "experts," following the standard care of mainstream recommendations down the path to destruction. That is precisely *why* this happened to *us*.

Our genes showed no signs of illness, our family histories showed nothing to fear, and our immune systems were powerful at resisting infections. Life filled me with so much contentment that maybe my immune system was naturally boosted with happiness, but we seemed to be blessed with strong immunity, so I was confident this trait would be passed onto my daughter.

Working with school children, I maintained my health even with kids lovingly spreading their germs: sneezing and coughing at me, blowing noses into tissues that landed on the floor, and sharing slimy pencils with me when I helped them with math. Maybe it was the fact that I got sick as a child and my body was familiar with these common germs of childhood. Maybe it was my happiness keeping me healthy, but either way, these weren't bad traits to pass onto my child.

One size seems to fit all, until it doesn't. Then genetics are blamed for not fitting into the shape of conformity. They condemn the families, who fall ill, for some hereditary flaw, trying to convince us that vaccines are infallible, so perfect in their design that the humans must be flawed in some way instead. I am not asked about hereditary histories, genetic differences, or autoimmune diseases that might increase susceptibility to negative consequences, because they don't factor in any of these things when they assume we are all made the same. Genetics only seem to count after a reaction, when parents get blamed.

I blame myself for many things, but not for my unchangeable heredity. I have no control over my genes, and with the one-size-fits-all approach, they don't make any accommodations for differences anyway.

As potential parents, we had our own blood work done to make sure we weren't both carriers of any genetic mutations that might create a defective person, but then nobody ever offered any testing to see if our baby might be susceptible to vaccines or allergic to any of their components. We took the precaution to make sure we didn't conceive a child with something inherently wrong, but then we harm our perfectly healthy baby because we didn't know she would be genetically susceptible to vaccine injury. That makes no sense at all.

Our child may be *genetically susceptible to vaccine injury*, as though there is something natural or acceptable about that thought. We would be better off fighting nature alone, without the intervention of vaccines. When all I watched them do was make my daughter sick, it is blatantly obvious that no one needs that kind of help. We can fend off sickness better when it is our only battle, but now that my daughter has to tackle vaccine damage too, fighting common illness is more challenging. Maybe, we are fit for nature, but unfit for injections.

Doing everything "right" is all wrong. We lost our way by putting our faith in the wrong place. We put our faith in man, rather than God, trusting the words of the doctor, not knowing if he was entwined in the pharmaceutical industry or if he was getting incentive payouts for meeting vaccine quotas. We trusted his words as the truth, even when they conflicted with our own intelligent reasoning. We trusted another man with the life of our child, the child God had entrusted to us. I took risks I wasn't even aware of, jeopardizing everything that is important to me, scarring my blessing with mistakes.

I lived my whole life playing it safe, avoiding risks, watching and learning from the mistakes of others. Then, I go and make the riskiest move ever — vaccinate my child exactly as scheduled. I didn't fully comprehend it was a gamble. If I had known it was so risky, I would never have done it. I hadn't considered that the illnesses we vaccinated for might be less risky than the vaccine itself. I didn't do the cost–benefit analysis. I just had that saying in my mind, "The benefits outweigh the risks."

I think that saying must have been started by the manufacturers, because they reap all of the benefits and haven't had any risks since the government gave them protection from liability. Yes, if I were a vaccine manufacturer, I can see how the "benefits outweigh the risks," by a mile, or maybe by a universe. But as a parent, I'm not finding any truth to that statement.

In awe at the miracle of life and God's intricate design, it should have seemed counterintuitive to mess with perfection, but I was well schooled and faithful obedience to my trainings overruled my faith in God. I had been conditioned to fear, and I was taught the incorrect meaning of protection. I would do anything to keep my baby safe, but maybe I was afraid of the wrong things. Maybe dangers lurked in places I thought were safe. And maybe the germs I had been trained to fear weren't all as life threatening as I had been led to believe.

Maybe sick children don't fit neatly into the work schedule or illness strikes at the most inopportune times, but there is no way to avoid this fact of life, even with vaccines. Catching illness is a natural expectation of life, and our bodies have immune systems for precisely that purpose.

Inflicting illness by injecting toxins into the body, that's the part of life I question. The lingering and widespread effects of vaccine injury were far beyond my wildest expectations. My daughter didn't even have a chance to let wild illnesses catch up to her. Instead, we held her down and pummeled the germs straight into her chubby thighs. These were the same germs and chemicals that I feared, so why would I let them inject them? I expected vaccines to rescue us from illness, not inflict it.

Vaccines changed my expectations about life. Before the reaction, I expected vaccines to keep my baby healthy by rescuing her from childhood illnesses, providing her the opportunity to grow old. I expected that what I was taught would be true, and I expected trips to the pediatrician to be in my daughter's best interest. After the reaction, I genuinely expected people to care. Wrong again.

CHAPTER 15
MY JOB

That vaccine disagreement in the lunchroom was the beginning of the end for me. My second grade team moved on without me. I am not entirely disappointed when they call second grade team meetings and forget to invite me, but I am still under their watchful eyes, always checking in on me, not to see how I am feeling or how my daughter is doing, but to make sure I am still working hard, and leaving my personal problems at home.

The gossip started. It is as though some think my daughter's vaccine injury affected my ability as a teacher. Or that I had changed priorities, even though every working mother still prioritizes her children above the job. Or that somehow I had gone crazy, because now I am questioning vaccines and our whole medical system, even though chicken pox visited my school that year, several cases of the illness in fully vaccinated kids. But that doesn't cause anyone to question their ingrained beliefs. It only causes them to question me.

I know not to mention the vaccine reaction with my students. I know that the only acceptable curriculum is teaching that vaccines are good. Fortunately, there are no such lessons on the science agenda, so I avoid the topic altogether, keeping it all to myself, careful not to cross that line with the kids. I didn't realize that I didn't have the freedom to cross that line with the other teachers either. I mistakenly believed my coworkers might care, but it seems I am not allowed to disparage shots even if they hurt my own child.

With my daughter sick at home, my students are a wonderful comfort, while some of my adult coworkers are less than desirable. One fellow teacher talks down to me in condescending baby talk, communicating with me as though I were a kindergarten child accepting a scolding. This is just her way of sneaky bullying, because she always makes sure to alter her voice back into the adult tone if a parent is to witness. Another time, they tell me I am needed out of my classroom for menial non-essential tasks during an end of year celebration, just as I had pizza delivered for my students, pizza paid for by me, having a substitute fill in to celebrate a successful year with my students, students she doesn't even know.

Adult bullying is more back stabbing and passive aggressive than the way kids do it. This is the other side of teaching, the side no one talks about when we recognize the hard workers and the small pay. It is competitive, and there can be a cutthroat tactics. Immaturity sinks to low levels when adults imitate the worst behaviors of children, but lack the innocence of youth.

I have bigger things to worry about than their behaviors or my job. But they certainly don't make things easy or pleasant for me. Why can't I be left alone to do my job in peace? When life is hard, why do some people feel the need to make it even harder? Instead of some compassion, I am met with something else — and it stinks! There is something rotten going on here, and it makes me feel awful. I know that I am not supposed to let others dictate how I feel about myself, but that takes a really strong person. My muscles are just getting tested, and I have a long way to go at developing thick skin.

Standing in an empty hallway alone, I peer through the window of the music room to see my students singing as I wait for their last few minutes of class to end before I can bring them back to our homeroom. Children singing together create a harmony of sound that hits a note that resonates with love and travels straight to my heart. I delight in the melody of song that emanates from the beautiful voices of young children. The music teacher is wonderful with children, and I enjoy seeing them together.

As I stand there at the door, the principal rushes by, saying nothing to me, only pausing briefly to hand me an envelope. I open it right then to read the letter inside declaring that my contract is not being renewed. Laid off — no explanations, no personal interaction, no human feelings but mine. The news upsets me and I start to cry. I used to work in human resources. This is not how layoffs are supposed to be done.

Was it an accident that the principal had such bad timing? I was quite happy that day, oblivious to the crash that caught me off guard. Laid off, right there in the hallway, with time remaining in the school day. It would have seemed far more appropriate to wait until the children left for the day before inflicting bad news on their teacher. Even though the principal held the responsibility for the decision to let me go, he didn't even have the decency or the guts to tell me in person. He couldn't even look at *me*, how could I possibly expect him to look at the clock.

Shocked and disappointed, I try to compose myself for the children, wiping my eyes and putting on a pretend smile that doesn't fool them for a second. They know something is wrong, because I am not good at playing fake. Being with the kids is bittersweet, cheering me up with their presence, while reinforcing the sadness of my inevitable departure. I don't need much, but I need to teach.

This job means so much more to me than a paycheck. The principal might have known that if he actually watched me teach. He might have known that if he actually took some time to get to know me. He might have known that if he took interest in the compliments of the parents. That might have made getting rid of me a bit more difficult. Had I not taken such a long maternity leave, my tenure would have been secure, but now I am on the way out.

This is a far cry from my previous principal who warmly complimented me, telling me that the children are lucky to have me any time they can get with me, when discussing my maternity leave. Those might have been some of the nicest words I ever heard. But, now, here I am, back from maternity leave, a new school year with a new principal who has entirely different values.

I can only guess at the reasons for my dismissal. Non-tenured teachers are worth an explanation but not required one. Maybe it was my days absent to care for my injured Bella, days that should have been protected by the Family and Medical Leave Law. Or maybe it was my new scary beliefs that he could have only heard about through the grapevine. Or maybe someone knew right from day one that I was not going to make tenure, because for the entire school year, I wasn't able to get a direct phone line like all the other teachers.

Fourth grade teachers want me on their team, while second grade looks happy to see me go. A few fourth grade teachers were part of the interview process when I was hired, and their team trusted me enough to send their graduating fourth graders to my fifth grade care. They request a meeting to try to save my job, doing this in secret from me, never mentioning the kindness of their actions to solicit a thank you. I look to them with immense gratitude, to people who stand up for each other with no benefit to themselves, trying to right injustices. These are the kind of people I admire and appreciate with a million thanks for their efforts.

Unfortunately, someone already had my replacement in mind.

CHAPTER 16

LAST DAY OF WORK

On my last day of work, the last day of the school year, I want to be alone in the last hours in my classroom. The life of the room has left for the day, onto higher grades, family togetherness, and summer break. My students shared in my sense of loss. I am not the kind of teacher that should ever have been let go. But, I know I must move on, pushed out into an unknown future that I must accept even though I don't want to. I have said goodbye to all the people that mattered, leaving shared imprints on each other's hearts. Goodbye to my friends. Goodbye to this building and the school children I love so much. My teaching experience is a blessing. Moving on, I will bring forth the memories of wonderful years.

I still have work to do, some hours left in the day to pack up my things and fill out cumulative record folders for each student. I absorb the surrounding silence of my room to work in quiet reflection of the year that has just passed. But, even in these last moments, I am not left in peace.

My silent contemplation is broken by a rude, noisy woman invading my territory. Barging into my space, moving my things around, and replacing them with hers, this is a current teacher who will be taking over my classroom next year. She doesn't even offer enough courtesy to respect my space and my classroom for the remaining hours that it is still mine.

She has all summer to do this. I only have today. It is the last day of school. She should have plenty to do in her own classroom, but here she is, in mine, moving in before I have even been evicted. Her intrusions distract my focus. She knows I will not be here next year, and she takes it upon herself to help push me out.

Human nature never fails to amaze me with little surprises of inappropriateness each day. Sometimes I don't speak up; I just quietly record every detail to memory as I sit in awe of human behavior. The teacher doesn't seem to recognize her insensitive behavior. She doesn't pause to wonder what her lack of respect and compassion might feel like for me. She doesn't pause to wonder what it might feel like to lose a job that you love and want to cherish your last few hours in the space of a classroom you once called home.

She bullies her way through, with a superior attitude, treating me as irrelevant, domineering the space as though she owns the place. Lacking in common courtesy, she is full of impatience and can't wait until I leave. She is mixing her things up with mine, because she probably doesn't mind if I accidently leave something behind that she can use for her benefit.

Avoiding eye contact, she hardly speaks to me. Her lips utter no apologies, no questions, and of course, no condolences. This woman is rude, inconsiderate, pushy, and condescending with me. But as the school would have it, she is the kind of person who gets to keep her job. I feel badly for the kids.

My favorite rolling chair is wheeled down the hallway to land in the third grade classroom of a friend. The padded red fabric seat was a little luxury that the janitor had found especially for me in my first month of employment, in my first year in fifth grade. My personally owned mini fridge will come home with me, not because I need it, but because there is no way I am leaving behind a tiny perk for this disrespectful woman. She can copy all my ideas that she once had the nerve to ask me for, that I freely shared with her as a colleague. But she isn't me. She can have this empty classroom, but she doesn't have any of the things that made it special.

I was too busy with important things to play the petty work games, but I ended up out of a job, while my coworkers kept theirs. I guess they won. Not much of a victory though, when I was already on the ground, on my knees in prayer. Never once did I ask to save my job. I only begged to save my daughter, and maybe one could not have been possible if I tried to cling to both.

I expected to be a teacher forever. I expected that all those years of hard work in college and employment would have granted me a pay off far longer than this. I expected districts to want to keep successful teachers who love their children. More of my expectations were being shattered. Life doesn't make sense anymore. People I thought were good turned out to be bad, people I thought were supposed to tell the truth had been lying to me, and good teachers were being shoved out the door. From the doctors' offices to our schools, what are they doing to our children?

I am left with a personal rejection I don't quite understand. With no parental complaints and only positive feedback, a sparkling personnel folder and excellent work history, none of it mattered. The job that I loved so much was gone, just like that. I was a hardworking, successful teacher, dedicated to her students — then suddenly, I am not that anymore.

With a sick child, the layoff should feel like a blessing, but instead it feels like another blow to my heart. I lost my daughter's health, and now my teaching job. I had fully realized my fears. And I am devastated by it all.

I just had the two greatest loves of my life, transformed right before my eyes: my baby and my passion, no longer the same.

Everything fell down around me, and there was no herd waiting to break my fall.

Losing the opportunity for career accomplishment and still uncertain of my skills as a mother, I feel like a failure. I was good at my jobs, but as a mom, I already made a mistake far bigger than anything I had ever done wrong at work. So far, my track record was more successful when I worked outside the home, but with no job to go to, I will have to find value elsewhere. I am "just a mom," and I will have to get used to that idea.

CHAPTER 17
WASTED LEARNING

Sickness strikes again. Every pulse of my beating heart sends rhythmic shivers to my throat, choking the air of each breath. Knots of anxiety churn in my belly with fear and apprehension for a situation out of my control. My mind fills with regret for the sequence of events that brought us here. Peripheral noise slips away as my focus grows stronger and stronger on my baby: the rapidly throbbing heart, punching through her chest, her helpless questioning eyes filled with confusion, and her breaths, emanating from her red cracked lips.

Caressing her head, I lean over to give a tender kiss on her burning forehead, with skin so hot I feel the singe on my lips. So innocent, so sick, paying a price she did not consent to sacrifice. My tears roll down my face and drip all over my sick child. My precious little one, what have we done to you?

Bowing down in sadness, defeated, I cry to the holy heavens wishing for the impossible do-over, wishing for God to take away the sins of my mistakes. I pray, like begging, in agonizing cries to make my baby well again. I love her so much. Please don't punish her for my mistakes. I hurt; I can't bear to see my child in so much pain, suffering in the pain of my ignorance, the pain of my responsibility, the pain of my guilt.

Faltering without knowledge, I hold my sickly child in my arms. There is no turning back on the path that brought us here. Some germs catch her and drag her down, while others seem to be internal remnants of the injected bullies that offer continuous reminders of the assault on her system. All I have to give is love, an all-encompassing love, to try to smolder the flames of her illness, as I care for my daughter with tender hands. She is the greatest gift I have ever known. I can't turn back time. I can't undo the crime. I can only wish away the damage.

The pediatric practice offers different practitioners at each sick visit, but they always draw the same conclusion, an uncertain diagnosis of another viral illness. Their assessment is a good guess, although it is not really helpful. I could guess that myself, if I didn't already know that the immune system damage is vaccine related. We never again get lucky enough to see the new doctor, the young one, who said it was vaccine injury, forcing me to wonder if he still has a job.

I want the doctors to look deeper to help me figure out how vaccine injury would bring on all these changes in my child. I keep telling them that my daughter is different, that she is sickly and can't move properly, reminding them that it all started with the vaccine reaction. But that information doesn't seem to be worth investigating to them. Gross motor regression doesn't unnerve them the way it does me. And the illnesses, I don't think they mind seeing her so often.

In my gut, I know they are wrong. In my brain, I know they are wrong too. It was, after all, the doctor "experts" that got us into this mess in the first place. Now, they aren't offering much of anything, except denial of the obvious, denial of vaccine injury. Occasionally, they offer medicine, but usually we leave with that same viral diagnosis that leaves us with nothing.

I visit them anyway, sick visit after sick visit, while exploring alternative help on the outside. I am still hoping that somehow this is a temporary problem that her body will figure out how to fix on its own, because the doctors certainly aren't making much effort. The more I reiterate vaccine injury, the more I am ignored. I find a direct correlation there, even though I don't find much help. How can doctors reverse vaccine damage if they are ignoring that it even exists? Maybe we can't find help among the cause...

The world I once thought I knew seems to be an illusion. I am not sure what I still know anymore, but I still know me, and I don't know if I can ever live with myself if my girl doesn't fully recover. As guilt eats away at my soul, I will do everything in my power to help make this right. If the doctors won't help me, I'll need to help myself and take matters into my own hands. With the loss of my job, God gave me the opportunity to do just that.

A delve into the world of vaccines surrounds me with heaps of new information. Shocking revelations sicken me as I fill myself with reading, devouring a plate full of nauseating disgrace. I don't really need proof; my eyes can see what is crystal clear, we did this to Bella with those shots. I shouldn't need to learn anything more than to just look at my child. But I want an explanation, an admission, an apology — something. And there it is, never uttered through personal vocalizations of the doctors, but in writing, writing that I overlooked when I was trained to only one side of the issue. With Bella's loud shrill cries, God gave me a wakeup call.

A feeling of stupidity permeates me deeply, shaken right to my core, after a lifetime of accolades for my intellectual achievements. I traded away fun times for nights full of studying, memorizing, and homework, earning a top spot in my graduating class, honors distinctions, summa cum laude and a variety of academic awards. My grades and my test scores confirmed for me that I was smart, along with my teachers and my employers, building a major support in the foundation of both my identity and my self-confidence.

I was never boastful or showy, but deep inside, I thought I knew that I was intelligent. And now, I don't feel so sure. I am supposed to be smart, but I certainly don't feel smart anymore.

What does it mean to be smart? Are we still smart if we only know exactly what they want us to know? Intelligence, wisdom and training do not have the same meanings, causing confusion. Maybe I hadn't been smart after all. Maybe instead, I was highly trainable, the same classification we give to good dogs and loyal puppies who obey orders well, memorize commands, and learn new tasks quickly.

I had been well trained to believe fake facts and other things it didn't matter to know anyway. Well trained in the pursuit of false knowledge, believing smarts came from the amount of learning I could amass in a lifetime, collecting information and using my excellent memory to recite it all back. Relying solely on this accumulated data, I forgot to use all my senses. I forgot to use my reasoning skills or pay attention to the clues that didn't sit right in my belly. My brain was full of useless information and good intentions, and my mind always chose what it had been trained to remember.

My investment of precious time into grades, book smarts, and learning the wrong information is worthless in this situation. I valued that knowledge, and now it has no value. In this moment, I can't find a penny of wisdom to pull from those thoughts. My personal stock plummeted into low self-worth, as my investment into a lifetime of educational efforts led me to this unfortunate place, without any security nets to fall back on.

With naiveté, I behaved with a sense of obligation and loyalty to our system, far too innocent to comprehend the imbedded corruption. I had been betrayed: betrayed by beliefs, betrayed by my own education, and betrayed by those whom I trusted were steering me in the right direction. Overcome with a deep feeling of failure, I worry that the biggest mistake of my life could steal the biggest joy I have ever known. That is far too big of a price to pay for my ignorance.

The ideas that were ingrained in my head do not match the reality of my view. My textbook memorizations don't hold the truth of this experience. Here I stand, hovering over my sick daughter, crying, not knowing where to turn or what to do. Lost and confused, I feel helpless, simply helpless. I spent my whole life preparing myself with education, but nothing from my studies prepared me for my daughter's reaction. With a sudden shift in direction, I find myself without a compass, facing a test of real life.

I can't help my daughter in the ways I expect. Good grades have no application. My notes don't hold the correct answers. My academic awards can't buy me any points. I have no teachers to guide the way. We fell outside the closed box of my trainings, and I have no frame of reference to pull from. I prepared myself to provide textbook answers to a memorized course, but my real life is not as I had been trained. My real life is more like an improvisation, full of surprises, and unplanned challenges — and reactions one never expects to have.

There is so much I thought I knew, so much left to learn. I take one step into the world of homeopathic medicine and almost walk myself into a train on the way into the appointment. This is the big city. I'm new here.

CHAPTER 18

GUILT AND REGRET

As I hold my limp, sick daughter, injured from her vaccines, I know that the story is much bigger, deeper, and far uglier than a good, obedient girl could have ever imagined. I can hardly live with myself for making this mistake. A sound of agony emerges from a place within me that touches the trauma in my soul, a primal, guttural scream from my belly, an awful feeling deep in my core.

The good girl doesn't go away. She haunts me at night, with feelings of guilt, the price I was trained to pay for mistakes, reminding me that I had committed the ultimate sin by harming my own daughter. The guilt forces me to hang onto regret, proof that I am truly sorry for what I had done. Guilt makes me feel awful about myself, makes me feel unworthy of good things, and makes me feel like suffering doesn't get to end, ever, in this lifetime.

At night I am weak. At night I cry. Every night I cry. In the day, I am a fighter, and at night, I sink into myself and cry. I cry for everyone. I cry for my poor baby. I cry for me. I cry for all the children and families this atrocity is devastating. I cry for a country that lets it happen. My eyes cry so many tears that I wonder if they will ever stop.

Days fluctuate with feelings, as intense emotions stir within. Some days, I am filled with an infuriating anger at all the people who would knowingly cause this devastation on children for the sake of money. Some days, I can't breathe. The words remain stuck in my throat, choking out room for air. Some days, my heart feels so much pain that I consider the possibility of a heart attack. Other days my heart is weak and faint, its pulse a mere whisper. Aching pain nags at every fiber of my being.

My mind tries to wrap itself around the truth, while it wrestles with regrets. My heart thinks it can help heal my baby with love. My soul is sad. My brain reminds me that I did this to my own child and punishes itself with guilt.

I relive the nightmare frequently, always wishing that I am imagining a work of fiction. I know I should have known better. I listened to the doctor instead of my gut, handing over my baby as though she were a guinea pig. I helped restrain her as she screamed, and they repeatedly poked her several times on the same day. I was more than a witness, but an active participant in holding her down. The thought sickens me with guilt, and a constant nausea moved in, becoming a part of me.

I hurt my own child, and it wasn't even an accident. She was vaccinated on purpose. This mistake is disgraceful, unconscionable, a tragedy, all wrong to the depths of my soul. Parents are not supposed to be the perpetrators of their child's demise, and I am "guilty as sin."

My eyes witnessed what I did to my own daughter. I let her down. I let her get hurt. Every thought I had of myself as being intelligent or thoughtful disappeared in the moment she reacted. Words of insult flooded my brain instead. I was so stupid, so naïve, so foolish. How can I think anything positive or good about myself when I had just done something so wrong, so bad? I should have known better. This is my fault, even though I know I was pushed.

Unlike some of the others, I didn't even hurt anyone on purpose. My sin was an accidental crime, with my personal impact on my own flesh and blood. My whole life spent practicing kindness and teaching empowerment, I didn't even realize that my hands were capable of such sin. Now, I have blood on my hands, my own. I harmed my own baby and that kind of sin feels unforgiveable.

Forgiveness is still a concept, something I learned I am supposed to do to be a good person, but a skill I still haven't been very successful converting into real life application. Forgiveness is not one of my strengths. I guess that makes me a sinner too, because I can't forgive like Jesus, and most of the time, I never even try.

How can I live with myself? I inflict punishment, trapping myself in a prison of guilt. My conscience is always there to remind me of my sins, forcing me to feel badly for my mistakes. I suffer, alongside my child, the child I hurt when I dropped her into the doctor's hands. Guilt is my prison, just as I had imprisoned my daughter's health. When I find the key to recovery, we can both be set free.

CHAPTER 19
SICK TIME

Butterflies filled my belly with excitement. My daughter is precious, an extension of me. Releasing her to another's arms required trust. So, when I hesitatingly passed her off into another's arms, all I could think was, "Don't drop her." Sometimes, I even said it out loud.

But, I was the one who dropped her, straight into the doctor's arms, trusting my baby to his expertise. Unfortunately, his expertise was in medicine, and my goal was to use as little of it as possible. When he broke my trust, I broke her trust, and she fell down into a journey of sickness. Now, the mistakes lay squarely in my hands even though it was his hands that led us here.

The sleepy head is pressed up against my arm. I dare not move for fear of waking my little girl. Sick again. Darkness shadows her watery eyes. Redness fills her hot cheeks, and signs of dehydration crack her red lips. I am careful to keep her warm enough, but not overheated, cool enough, but not chilled, the delicate balance of just right.

Internally, the inferno is blazing; the body is busy fighting battles. But on the outside, it is quiet. The house is still, and we both lay together, as I listen to the breaths and feel the gentle rhythm of the belly as it rolls up and down. I hear her breathing. We connect with the touching of our skin. Nothing in the world feels more important than the need to be here, right now, nothing better to do than be here with my baby. Sleeping is for the best, the time for healing.

Comforting with my presence, I settle in to share my own medicine of love. No distractions when I lie here with her, just me and her, sharing life, sharing space, sharing time. No internet, no checking emails, no phone calls, just tranquil silence of a loving bond. This has become familiar practice for us, pulling out the couch bed where it will remain opened for the next week, snuggling up, cancelling plans, watching lots of television, and taking many naps.

There is an expectation that I will be there. We are reinforcing our bonds, building an intimacy that is uniquely her and I, special in our togetherness. Sometimes I sit and study every delicate detail of her face, her eyelashes, and her ears. Sometimes I cry and ask God for help. Sometimes I think I slip into meditation. I whisper all kinds of loving thoughts and positive affirmations into her ears, hoping they will sink into that magical period of light sleep, when the mind seems fully awake. Touching her in deep connection as though our bodies might join in synchronicity, I hope that through osmosis I can take some of her pain away.

I imagine the injections being replayed in rewind, the needles coming out of her skin followed by all the liquid that was squirted inside, mentally trying to undo history, knowing that it was those concoctions that made her sick and if I can figure out a way to remove them, she would be better. I replay that vision over and over in my mind, the vaccine liquid miraculously coming back out of her legs as though it had never gone in. I imagine sucking the venom out as though her shots were a snake bite. Sometimes I imagine my hands tugging on invisible streams, pulling the chemicals back out.

I am not a magician, but I imagine, imagine that which I hope is possible. I envelop my baby inside my heart, embracing her being within my own, radiating a bubble of warm healing power. Sometimes I believe that love can conquer all, and there is no denying, my love is my strength.

CHAPTER 20
WARNING SIGNS

Warning signs existed, and I missed them. The big business of motherhood lured me in, called out to me with the idea that my baby needed things, along with a bunch of cute irresistible outfits. I walked those aisles of the baby store as though I were a child myself. Mesmerized by all the bright colors and enormous selection of products, I lost some focus. The mundane aspects of life and the little bugs in my ears, slightly nagging, were easily over-looked, because they weren't screaming for attention like all those fun baby products.

Because I truly believed I had freedom, I didn't realize that ba-bies would have medical procedures performed on them without parental permission. It seemed to me that I could worry about healthcare decisions more fully when and if the time came, not realizing the time came as soon as I passed through the doors of a medical institution.

I liked passing through these doors better, the doors to the massive baby story where the rest of the world seemed to stop. I could get lost for hours exploring the colorful terrain. This was much more pleasant than the halls of medicine where children were screaming in pain. The salesmen were helpful enough to lift something into my cart, but not sneaky enough to slip something into the carriage that I didn't want to buy. No one pressured me here at all. In a place I expect to find salesmen, I find help. In places I expect to find help, I find salesmen. Maybe I don't understand this world at all, because it is not run like the ethical one in my head.

Ignorance can be bliss, until it leads to a mistake that tears all the bliss away. I had no idea that our perceived "good guys" would be preying on naiveté and leading us wrong on purpose. I expected that behavior from perceived "bad guys" and put my guard up in their presence. But in the doctor's office, where I believed I was safe, I lost my innocence.

Jarring impact collides into our world, shattering all illusions. Flashbacks to another time recall the whispers of the warning bugs I tossed aside. Now, I hear echoes loudly haunting me, reminding me that I should have seen this coming. There were signs all around, and I was not paying attention. I'm kicking myself, because I can't believe I fell for it all.

Gut wrenching screams from my soul do a good job at waking me up, bringing me into consciousness. I wish there had been an easier way for the light bulb to click on, but when the world came into focus, it showed blatant mistakes and warnings I missed, while distracted by something else.

Warning signs of the past seemed irrelevant to a girl who didn't plan to have children, while warning signs of the present drifted by because I was too focused on all the stuff that didn't matter. Preoccupied thoughts of things filled my mind, new visions of life I anticipated with my new baby. Instead of reading biased magazines and books, I could have just reflected in silence to look back upon my own life. I went looking for information to teach myself, when all I really needed to do was start paying attention to what was right in front of me.

As the excitement of my new baby filled my thoughts, they clouded over memories I should have seen. While I was paying attention to trivial pursuits and the ideas of others, I lost focus on my own past. My own ears held echoes of little bugs and my past held warning signs that could have prevented my daughter's vaccine reaction. But I never paused long enough to land in reflection, only pausing back with regret. I missed the meaning behind these little bugs, little hints that could have prevented lots of heartache.

As good little bugs swarmed my head, I just swatted them away without paying much attention. I was too busy to let myself be bothered by such nuisances. Some of my warning bugs were so large, I should have noticed enough to swat myself on the head to wake up from oblivion. Little critters were all around me, buzzing at me to pay attention, nudging at me to listen. No matter how hard they tried, I just couldn't hear them, until I was bitten with the sharpness of a sting that demands alertness.

I was distracted by the bad bugs. Their ear worms were louder and more powerful. They were distracting me from the quiet nudges to make better choices. Their memes were everywhere, ringing in my ears, drowning out the sounds and memories of my own life. They were distracting me with evil bugs of their own, on purpose, infesting my mind with swarms of fallacies, that I didn't stop to think about, only memorized. Fear bugs build a sense of panic, a sense of urgency, so we forget to think and react out of fear. I let them clutter my mind, so I couldn't see the reflections of my past. I couldn't see my past at all because I was too busy looking forward.

In the mirror of reflection, time passed looks crystal clear. In the mirror of regret, mistakes of the past look like a crash I should have seen coming. Warning signs were right in front of me. How could I have missed them? I was enjoying my life on cloud 9, living with blinders on, when I forgot to remember...

My dog. When I sat with my miniature poodle, and patted her white curly fur, I wasn't remembering her rabies vaccine reaction. I wasn't thinking about the day after the shot when I carried her around because she couldn't walk. How could I forget the lump that grew at the injection site? How could I forget the surgery she needed to remove it? How could I forget the recovery time and the nights I slept on the living room floor sprawled out on blankets because she just couldn't make it up the stairs to the bedroom? A tumor grew in the exact location of the injection site, and I received a form from the vet that told me this reaction was consistent with the administration of the vaccine.

I wasn't thinking about any of that. I wasn't remembering, because my thoughts had been clouded by all those reassurances of safety, those magazine articles, the doctors' words, elevating their positions above my own life experiences, my own life experiences that had lots to teach me.

When my pet reacted, the vet told me I could ask the vaccine manufacturer to reimburse me for my dog's surgery. But then when my child reacted, I had no recourse anywhere. I could report it to the Vaccine Adverse Event Reporting System, the database the government maintains of vaccine injury. But that was really it, because all parties have indemnity.

Parents of vaccine injured children can ask the government for money, but injuries like my daughter's don't count much to them. They count to me of course. They count so much, I count them every day, always remembering to count my little girl. But money is not much of a consolation prize when the health of a child is stolen. Our kids are worth so much more than money. There is just no adequate compensation to make up for them.

Of course money helps pay all those additional bills. And we need money to stay home to care for our sick kids. But money certainly doesn't make us feel any better about making the mistakes that our children pay for every day.

When I flipped through the photo albums, I wasn't remembering the young relative who experienced a seizure after a few vaccines. And when I visited more relatives, I never thought to ask one of their neighbors why they didn't vaccinate their children. Instead of avoiding the topic, I regret not asking. Maybe they knew vaccine injury too. Maybe I could have learned something from them, rather than assuming they had nothing to teach me.

When trying to conceive, I was inundated with articles recommending the flu shot for women who would be in their second and third trimesters during flu season. Not yet pregnant, I was still expecting for it to happen any day, and if that were the case, I would fall into that exact category of women. Never once had a flu shot pierced my skin, and yet there I was, at the doctor's office, asking about getting one. The magazines convinced me I needed one to "protect" my unborn baby. I was willing, and maybe a bit scared.

The shot was brought into the exam room and placed on the counter, while I was given a sheet to read. The piece of paper was a consent form with real information on it. I don't remember all of the details, I wasn't awake yet, but I do remember the sheet saying the flu shot was not recommended for pregnant women. What? I was holding a consent form, and I could not sign it, because I didn't like what it said. I apologized for wasting the shot they had prepared for me, because when I agreed to accept the shot, I didn't know it came with this form of conflicting details. I didn't agree to sign my life away when I agreed to the shot, so I turned it down. Thank you, God.

I was told I had a choice for me, but none of my baby's shots came attached to a consent form. Maybe then, I would have known that I had a choice. I don't sign consent to things very lightly, and I do understand that if they need you to sign a waiver to acknowledge risks, then the shot can't be completely safe for all. That's just common sense.

The false miscarriage diagnosis should have taught me to devalue the words of the doctors, with my knowledge from experience that they can be badly mistaken. It should have taught me to never blindly trust their words over my own instincts. Instead, I should do my own research, read information, get second opinions, and trust myself. No need to obey. Just think, a mistaken D&C and none of this life would have existed.

I feel pretty stupid to have had all these warning signs and still vaccinate, but I put more faith and more trust in the words of her doctor and those words they call science. I lacked the confidence to realize that my own truths were just as valid, just as real, and just as important.

CHAPTER 21

THE PEDIATRIC BATTLEGROUND

Well visits are frequent again with the birth of my second child, a baby boy. He was born two and a half years later than his sister, which is just enough time for one more shot to be added to the standard pediatric schedule. Maybe the shots have mercury, maybe they don't, but they just might have aluminum instead.

Adding up well visits and sick visits, I feel like I live at the doctor's office. I am here out of obligation to my mainstream ways, having each visit documented as my legal assurance, to verify my expected responsibilities of being a good parent. I was told I need to make well visits with a pediatrician to prove I am not being neglectful. I don't understand why all the sick visits and other medical practitioners don't seem to count, but I am certain I'm not the one being neglectful, as pediatrician after pediatrician passes us by. As we ask for help, the pediatricians continue to offer more shots, and that approach isn't helpful at all.

A well visit — what an ironic name for the appointment that always leaves me feeling a little sicker than when I arrive. Quivering with anticipation of the battle up ahead, my body responds stressfully in the appropriate flight-or-fright manner, for these medical meetings that feel like death threats to my children's lives. Dread creeps in days before the appointment. The nerves tick. The body shakes. The mind is sharpened. And the will is firm.

These well visits aren't about wellness, they are about vaccination, and the two ideas do not have the same meaning. Looking for wellness seems to be reserved for the last few minutes, when I am drained from the long condemnations and lectures, and exhausted by my efforts to keep my children comfortable throughout the ordeal. Forty five minutes to pressure me, two minutes to look at my child.

As I struggle to heal my daughter from her vaccine setbacks, I am baffled by the insensitivity, in their lack of senses to see and hear what is going on. There is nothing the doctors can say to convince me that my reality isn't real. There is nothing they can say that will convince me to vaccinate some more, while they sit in denial of the injury that is right in front of them. My first baby is no longer well, and I am trying to protect my second baby from the same fate. But they berate me at every visit, stinging me with their words, never quite letting up, until the closing bell signals the end of the match.

Perplexing rationales spew at me from all different directions, spoken from all different faces, in different voices, from different locations. They are fast talkers, weaving webs of confusion, hoping parents like me get caught in their trap of mumble jumble. The actors keep changing, but mannerisms and tactics remain the same. Sometimes male, sometimes female, but they all feel familiar. I know this character well, because I have met him many times before.

Dr. Q is insistent that I vaccinate my son precisely on schedule because my daughter is so sick. She wants my son fully vaccinated to prevent him from bringing the illnesses home to his sick sister. Her logic confuses me. She wants me to vaccinate my son to prevent him from bringing home the exact same illnesses my daughter is already vaccinated for?

I find no common sense in her reasoning. Do vaccines work or don't they? If vaccines work, how would baby brother make his sister sick if she has her shots? If they don't work, then why do we take them, accepting all of the risks, with none of the benefits?

She can't seem to hear me tell her over and over again that my daughter is sick because of her vaccine reactions. Instead of acknowledging vaccine damage, she tries to sell me more vaccines as false protection for my immune compromised daughter who is already vaccinated. Clearly, we do not understand each other. I hear her pressure to vaccinate as a threat. I think she wants me to care for two very sick kids rather than just one.

Dr. X speaks about her vaccines with a visible animation of enthusiasm as though she genuinely loves vaccines, but she speaks to me in her sweet sounding voice of condescending suspicions. When I refuse her vaccines for my son, she accuses me of coddling him, a snap judgment she makes of me within the first few minutes of our appointment.

I may have been coddling my daughter at this point, clinging to her tightly as her very lifeline to survival. I am not coddling my healthy son at all. I am just trying to protect him, by preventing the doctors from hurting him too.

Ironically, this doctor actually thinks my daughter looks really unhealthy, commenting on her pale complexion and the darkness that encircles her eyes. Even though she believes something is wrong, she is a vaccine fanatic who seems to believe more vaccines are the solution for everything. The reaction didn't happen under her watch, but with rose colored glasses that view vaccines with adoration, she wouldn't be able to see the connection anyway. Her love for shots clouds her mind, leaving nothing but skepticism for those who question.

But she has bigger issues. Controlling ones... She is on top of me, asking me names of every single provider my children have seen for their care, letting me know that she plans to call each of them to verify, with a blatant implication that she is questioning my integrity. She chases me out to the reception desk in the waiting area, to verify that I am indeed scheduling our next appointment. She calls my husband for reinforcement, bothering him at his work number, to tattle on me when I refuse her orders, encouraging him to persuade me on the vaccine issue. That is the best call she could make, because she doesn't realize that my husband and I are on the same team.

Dr. Z is a male pediatrician who tries to rearrange my religion to justify vaccines for me. Warping religion with his own spin on the issue, he tells me that God gave man the intelligence to invent these scientific formulations. His perspective is that vaccines are some sort of gift that God would want us to use. Does he mean the same way we use atomic weapons or chemical warfare? Just because we have the capability to do something, does not mean that we should. Brilliant minds have been working on the wrong side of ethics since the beginning of time. The doctor is free to believe whatever he wants, but I do not have to agree.

"How do you feel about the aborted fetal cells used to create some of the vaccines?" I ask. His face looks confused. He has no words. I don't think that vaccines made with aborted fetuses are talked about much at church.

God gave me senses. I can see what is happening. Inflicting harm on our own offspring with concoctions of manmade shots is pure sacrilege in offense to God. God also gave me children, and He expects me to do right by them, even if it is difficult and unpopular.

As I hold my baby boy, this doctor reminds me that he will need these shots to attend school. School is irrelevant to a newborn, so that argument just gives me plenty of time to decide; no need to consent today. I also know that my state's school requirements are less than what is being pushed in the doctor's office, so I ignore his last attempt at coercion.

I hear everything each pediatrician has to say and write it all down. I hear digs at my intelligence and sob stories about sick children and hospitals. I hear disapproving sounds like that familiar tsk as I am led down the road of imaginary guilt trips that look nothing like the real one I am already on.

Why isn't hurting one child enough collateral damage? Why do they want to hurt my family so badly, trying with all their efforts to claim both children? Why can't they leave us alone, like they have with all the other responsibilities they have already burdened us with?

Sometimes, I hear screaming from the other rooms, reverberating through the walls and vibrating into my own body. The screams bring back the terrors that live inside of me. Screams are the telling sounds of what has just occurred down the hall. They are the reminder of the cries that punctuate the beginning of change, the entry into another life, a new world dealing with the after effects of vaccine injury.

But these doctors are still in this world where they pretend that vaccine injury doesn't exist. Just being here feels all wrong. This is a place of sickness and germs. Well babies don't belong here, and neither do I. It is too painful.

I'm still raw from the first injury, with trauma seeping from my pores. My wounds are never given the opportunity to heal as the insensitive comments dig deeper under my skin, picking off scabs to unendingly re-bleed. Life feels inhumanely cruel, as doctor after doctor judges my decisions, questions my parenting, and treats me like an ignorant fool.

The pressure is stronger now, because I am no longer compliant. My skin tries to thicken, while it shakes with anxiety and fear. But it is resilient and does not cave under the pressure and verbal assaults to my humanity. The fighting wears me out, but I know the outcome is to never surrender.

The doctors don't seem to notice how difficult this is for me. They don't seem to notice my sick child. All they seem to notice is the fresh pure meat they can't wait to prick their needles into. They want their hands on those chubby thighs. They want to pierce that fine delicate skin with their drugs. My new baby is on their "to do" list, and what they want to do —jab that little boy until his checklist is complete. He is not a person to them, but rather a task that needs completing as though God didn't do well enough.

Children wail while getting their shots, moms cry, and doctors have become salesmen. I feel like I have walked into a car dealership instead of a medical practice, but unlike other sales, there is no three day wait period, no leeway to change our minds. If the doctor can convince us, right there on the spot, pressure us into submission, they win the right to jab our children with his drugs. We don't get any do-overs. This is an important decision, and we must live with the consequences, consequences that are very hard to accept.

I don't understand why the doctors can't see my daughter suffering, and just give us a break. Maybe they are so caught up in the memorized procedures that they overlook the obvious, as they continue with the bombardment of pressure, like daggers to the heart. But to me, there is no denying, they are wrong. Doctors are only human, just like everybody else. Fallible doctors are making big mistakes.

I can't imagine they would act this way if they were liable for vaccine injury, if they had some liability for the advice that leads children to demise. But that all stopped in the 1980s when law left vaccines immune from litigation, leaving a government compensation program the only place to turn for injuries. Back then, it would have been obvious that a seizure, brain inflammation, fever, rash, allergies, and regression of physical abilities contraindicated any more shots. Those would be obvious indicators of "those who can't be vaccinated." But today, not so much. As doctors continue to pressure me into more vaccinations for both my children, it is obvious to me that they are not paying attention, they are not listening, and they are not liable.

Those *who **CAN'T** be vaccinated* **ARE** being vaccinated — recklessly!

Sometimes practice doesn't make perfect. Sometimes it just perpetuates mistakes. "Fool me once, shame on you. Fool me twice, shame on me." I've been here before, and I am never going back. I may feel stupid, more stupid than I have ever felt in my whole life, but at least I am smart enough to change.

CHAPTER 22
PROTECTION IS ME

In the midst of the challenges with pediatricians, I find myself in need of a doctor of my own. As I sit in the waiting room, I am grateful for an eye doctor taking patients on the Saturday night of Memorial Day weekend. I realize how committed some doctors are to their profession and how appreciative I feel to be sitting here waiting for care I so desperately need.

As I meet the doctor, he is warm and kind. Doctors' offices have become the battleground of confrontations, but here, I am in a respite from the familiar, and a respite from arguing. I am grateful that he is able to remove a small piece of plastic that had embedded itself into my eye, affecting my vision and causing much pain. Working on a holiday weekend, his caring hands help restore my sight, and I am thankful. What would I have done without him?

With an appointment for me, I am back to having a positive experience with a doctor, reminding me that time in their care wasn't always so bad. He reminds me that even though it may not be my usual experience right now, there are still good doctors out there. But, he is an eye doctor, and my experiences with eye doctors have always been more positive than my interactions with both pediatricians and obstetricians. Unlike them, he helps restore my vision rather than scarring some views about life. It is amazing to me how doctors can put people's lives back together after traumatic accidents and rip people's lives apart with a simple injection.

Times were different when it was only me I had to worry about. Doctors provided advice that I could toss around as I pleased, and disagreements were simply disagreements, not threats on my character. I was never kicked out of a practice for not following orders, and I didn't know any vaccine pushers. I don't go to doctors for myself as much anymore; maybe times have changed all around.

At the pediatrician's office, I am tormented when I make a decision the doctor doesn't like, decisions I was once free to make on my own, without controversy or debate. Disagreements are treated with hostility, as the conversation turns into insults, spoken by the one who wants me to respect his position. He desires an obedient submission to his education and title, when he is the one acting inappropriately childlike, throwing a near tantrum when he doesn't get his way. I sit in a nervous discomfort, while he stands as an obstacle to wellness, rubbing me the wrong way, leaving me feeling irritated and bruised. But I leave, with skin intact and babies in my arms. The choice is still mine. I just have to fight for it.

Genuine warmth can be hard to come by, with cold handshakes and awkward smiles that feel unnaturally forced. I wonder if anyone is hearing me speak, because there is no evidence of listening as he shuffles his papers and avoids eye contact. But he can hear something, because he takes the time to brush off my questions as nonsense and interrupts my words mid-sentence as though the rest of what I have to say is unimportant. Pushing papers eventually progresses to clicking around computer screens, but it is all just a big distraction, allowing the doctors to avoid the real issues.

When I request medical records, I find misrepresentations of events. Good thing I take good notes myself and write everything down. I notice some common practices: adding items that weren't discussed, saying the patient declined part of the exam that was never even offered, or exaggerating the contact time. Never mind what they say about us when they think we won't be reading any of it. I wonder about these practices... Then, I notice other doctors take an opposite approach, by hardly making any notes at all. I think both techniques are to protect themselves from something — and it sure ain't germs.

I can still turn to doctors for advice or help in times of emergency, but for protection, not so much. Their kind of protection only comes through shots. Real protection will have to come from me, drawing forth innate survival skills that I never anticipated I would need, with more dependence on myself, rather than the systems that want us all dependent on them.

I once thought of the everyday protections, like helmets, car seats, and lead free toys. I thought normal protection was about child proofing the home and good supervision in attempt to prevent accidents. I never anticipated protection would entail bucking the very establishments, societal ways, and people we have been trained to trust.

Protection once meant getting shots, but now, protection means avoiding them. Instead of willingly handing over my babies, I cling to them, tightly. Maybe well visits could be renamed *the uncomfortable coercion*, and we just leave our kids at home to protect them. I'm sure the kids could find better things to do than trying to sit still during these long, futile lectures. I'm sure we could all find better things to do with our valuable time.

Doctor after doctor tries different techniques, all with the same goal of having me say yes to their shots. I know they are optional now, so when I am told what my child will be getting today, I say, "No." And with that one little word, the appointment has become a battleground, a battleground of confrontations where we argue to win the life of my child. MY child. The clear winner should already be me, but because I am here, I have to fight.

I am ready to do battle, but I don't like to fight. I am polite as I offer researched information to follow up to each doctor's arguments. I know many of their speeches are just as rehearsed as the questions I had once been trained to ask. I needed to spend time researching for my own understanding, allowing me to have intellectual discussions with the medical profession; not that they think my side is intelligent. Sometimes, it is better to bite my tongue and let them believe that I am just plain dumb. I am not trying to win any arguments. I am just trying to win the battle for my kids.

Why can't the pediatricians hear, why can't they see, why can't they connect? The doctors look for some kind of manipulative mental connection that might get me to comply, while continuing to ignore us. Maybe they could actually make a real connection if they felt a connection, felt something for those hurting in their midst. Maybe if they took the time to listen, rather than speak. Maybe if they offered some empathy, rather than peer pressure. Maybe if they actually looked at us, and made eye contact, rather than judgments. But I have my own connections, to both my daughter and to God, growing stronger every day, giving me the strength to stand in solidarity where bridges had burned.

The battle is worth far more than money to me, far more than meeting quotas and agendas, far more than a test of wills or being the winner in a verbal debate. My children are worth everything to me, and love is my motivator. My children's lives are on the line, and I am the one standing to protect them, not in the way I imagined when my daughter was being vaccinated, but protection from the very people who seemed so willing to hurt her some more. I didn't realize that the decision to decline would matter so much, but with this kind of pressure, it matters a whole lot to somebody. Fortunately, it matters even more to me.

Because I am a loving mom, with selfless interests in my babies, God's perfect creations, entrusted to me. My kids are far too valuable to be sacrificed as victims of these heinous crimes perpetrated by people who aren't paying attention, leading us down the path of destruction to fend for ourselves. I am the protector, not these shots, not these doctors. ME. I'm on the front lines to protect my little soldiers from an involuntary draft in public sacrifice for a herd that isn't even there.

There are no conflicts of interest on my end. I am not earning monetary prizes for meeting vaccine quotas. I am not accepting gifts from pharmaceutical interests. My mind is unencumbered by greed or biased persuasions. My mind is paying full attention, and the only "greater good" I see is for the selfish interests of capitalism.

Why, oh why, did I ever trust these people? The simple act of parents asking questions seems to bring forth the doctor as enemy, instantly transforming pediatric doctors' offices into the pediatric battleground of confrontations. They seem to have one focus, with tunnel vision straight to their agenda, diagnosis as rote memorization, robotic in nature, fulfilling a checklist of one-size-fits-all medicine, treating us like a number to check off on a schedule of another busy day. And if the day's goals are hindered in anyway, they share their anger and frustration with me, at me, because I am the one standing in their way. But that's my job. I am the front line protector of my children.

The threats to my children bring forth something innate, something wild, a fierceness I had been trained to hide. Survival instincts kick in, mothering with an inborn wisdom I hadn't realized I would need. I am done being the good girl, obeying the wishes of others, following orders that aren't right. This is my child. I am in charge here, and I say, "No more." No more listening to doctors who shut us out of their world as soon as we close the door on our appointment. No more following along blindly. No more believing the lies, rhetoric, and propaganda. And no more shots!

Protection is not out there. Protection is ME. I'm it, the fighter and defender of my babies. I may not look strong in appearance, but the shots ignited an inner strength. The front line soldier on this pediatric battleground is me, Mom.

CHAPTER 23

THE GREAT DIVIDE

For some, it was pre-med, but for me, who never wanted to be a doctor, it was simply a love of life that brought me to college as a biology major. Fascinated with the ways living things worked, biology is what I studied by choice, when no one was telling me what to do or grading me on performances. I wanted to teach school, but I liked the idea of a backup plan. The study of biology held possibilities for other career interests, like work in nature or with animals. So, I followed biology for all the reasons other than medicine.

But I didn't like it. When I found myself back in formalized school, life lessons were spoken with such mundane boringness that biology lost its animation. While my focus may have been in the natural world, the university's biology focus was on biotechnology. Maybe a different school would have been a better match, but as an adult, with practical considerations, like my marriage and my home, commuting by car to a state school was the most realistic option, especially since my true focus was teaching.

I couldn't help but imagine myself wearing a white coat, working in a lonely science lab, day in and day out, watching petri dishes incubate, mixing test tube concoctions, and doing lab reports, spending my days doing things that I didn't enjoy. However inaccurate it may have been, that vision was not what I had hoped for myself. I felt discouraged enough to switch my major. If teaching didn't work out so well, a biotechnology job was not the kind of work I ever wanted to fall back on.

Whilst in the midst of my daughter's illnesses, my path crosses with an old friend who chose a life in a field I was hoping to avoid. I gladly pause to talk for a chunk of time. We haven't spoken in years.

He is excited to tell me that he has just joined the medical profession. I congratulate him on his accomplishment. I genuinely want to be proud of him, but I don't even recognize him anymore. His new position comes with an air of arrogance that washes over his interaction with me.

In my head, he is still the silly boy I used to joke with, the classmate that smiled and brought fun to the room. I look past the title for the person I once knew, but beyond his appearance, there are no hints or reminders of that special boy. He has aged, but not in the obvious ways. His face is still boyish and unmarked by wrinkles. I don't notice any extra pounds. Maybe he even stands a bit taller and lighter. But something else had changed, and I am not impressed with his bragging.

He is a new father of his first baby, similar in age to my new son. Even though we think we are having a night on the town, our heads are always filled with our children. We naturally bring them along in our thoughts, adding them to conversation. My turn to share brings about the disclosure of the vaccine reaction that changed my daughter's health for the worse. Maybe I talk about this too much, but it is the life-changing event that consumes me. It is hard not to mention. I often bring up the vaccine reaction to leave that little bug in the ear — if it can happen to my kid, it can happen to yours. I sure wish someone had done that for me.

My long ago friend looks down his nose at me as I relay the story of my daughter. I didn't think there was anything funny to what I had just said, but he laughs at me. I am not embarrassed by his ridicule, but his loud smug laughter does not seem to be the appropriate response. I thought medical professionals were supposed to care about sick people, not laugh at their situation.

Instead of showing concern, he says to me, "You don't really believe that vaccines did that to her, do you?"

"Of course I do," I tell him. "I saw it with my own eyes, and the consequences have been living with us." But he doesn't believe me. I see that he has more loyalty to his new trainings than his old friend.

He can't fully hear what I am saying, because he has already made his own assumptions about me as he scoffs, "You're one of those people who actually believes that the MMR and vaccines cause autism." It is clear that he is saying this as an insult, with an overt tone that his mind has just downgraded me down to the level of village idiot, cementing the gap in our differences.

He holds his head high in arrogant superiority. Still laughing, his parting words are, "Good luck with that," in a condescending chuckle with the added nerve to pat me on the shoulder. He uses sarcasm in his tone, because he is not referring to good fortune in getting my daughter well. He is poking fun at my views.

A man who knew me still couldn't display enough sensitivity to hold back his ridicule. Maybe he remembers my face, but has forgotten who I am. Lacking any emotional connection, he can no longer see the person standing before him. I am now one of "those people," and click, he shuts down his heart.

It must be why he could justify laughing at the mother of a sick child and inflict more pain into a hurting heart. I understand he doesn't get the vaccine connections; he is a product of biased persuasions after all, but to mock someone with a sick child, well that's just sick.

He makes me feel as though I have been instantly transported into another pediatrician's office, where I have become used to the condescending remarks and the rude behavior. But as badly as I had been treated at the pediatrician's office, the one thing I hadn't heard was laughter. Because there really is nothing funny about this issue, and it is sad that someone in charge of people's health would find humor in illness. My life is a joke to him, insult to injury with words falling directly into open wounds and stinging like salt. These are already trying times, and he's making me try hard to control my anger.

He made clear lines of demarcations between *those people* and himself. He doesn't understand that some of *those people* were once just like him, believing all the good lies about vaccines.

Until the day that vaccine injury happens to one of their own. Then it isn't so hard to see the connections between vaccines and autism or vaccines and some other side effects. They don't feel the disconnect to the children because it is one of their own flesh and blood. They don't feel the disconnect to *those people* anymore, because they are now one of those people. They don't have pages of learning blocking their view because the evidence is right there in front of them. Now, they are one of *those people*, one of the unlucky ones with a child hurt by their routine inoculations. To add to their tragedy, they will now have to face constant criticisms from *those people* who like to poke fun at others and laugh at their misfortune.

He is belittling my brain, but I think he has returned from his education fully brainwashed, earning a new superiority complex along with his diploma. Somewhere along the way, he must have felt that he surpassed me, even though in our shared academic histories, I was the one with the better grades. But arrogance has gone to his head. The higher he holds his nose, the faster I lose respect. I know innocent newcomers are trained with the hidden biases lurking in the curriculum, but he is a bit too arrogant to be a total innocent. His mind is closed because his head is already full of himself.

I normally cheer on my friends' accomplishments, and I still value education, but all that training, and he doesn't seem any smarter to me, just meaner, with a cruel sting. Maybe he was infected with some character flaws in graduate school, because he had changed; I couldn't find any hint of my old friend hiding in this new man. Doctors have fallen off my pedestal, one by one, and here is another loss, another casualty of his trainings.

The person he has become saddens me, and I am thankful that my own education never took me to the place his did. We have reached the great divide of beliefs, personalities, and attitudes, and there is no turning back to reconnection.

Vaccine injury. How does this life experience create the deepest of chasms that can never be crossed? It is a dangerous move, the fine line that gets traversed through the tip of a needle, creating an abyss that divides people into distinct camps.

Could I have become *one of them*? Surrounded by pre-med students in my biology major, I was in the presence of peers. There was no animosity, only friendliness. When did sides separate, part ways, and become so disrespectful of one another? When did we forget to feel and empathize? Did I miss something when I was busy taking care of my sick daughter? Because, we're all just people.

The vaccine debate brings out the ugliness in people, and the repulsion pushes us away from each other, when we don't like what we see. My old friend and I are in two opposing worlds now, and maybe his biology is just different than mine. Besides, I already have my own special M.D. in my mother–daughter bond.

CHAPTER 24
I'M ONE OF *THOSE PEOPLE*

S hit! I'm one of *those people*. What does that mean? That I can't have friends? That I will be discriminated against for the rest of my life? That I am destined for a lifetime of ridicule? I feel like I have been blacklisted from my own life, living in an upside down world as a pariah among a herd that doesn't seem to accept *those people* who don't handle shots so well.

New revelations are a shock to my mainstream American system, but the journey to the "other" side is a bumpy ride, because we aren't exactly welcomed with open arms. My herd has left me, but to the other side, I am still a sheep, and some insult me for my decisions too. To some, I am just another stupid mom, who didn't do her research, blindly following along.

Now, I am "lucky that she didn't die," you fool. Sure am, I know that. "That's nothing," because my daughter hadn't died wasn't really the compassionate response to interject into a discussion between a few moms sharing stories of vaccine setbacks in their children. I am taken aback by the rudeness interrupting our conversation with insensitivity. This mom has been on the other side since her birth, one of the ones who knew better, right from the start and let me know it in less than compassionate words. Moms like her didn't make the same mistakes I had. I think they are making different ones.

Neither side seems to understand the pain of vaccine injury firsthand. Both sides just have judgments about it. One side can't seem to see it, while the other already "knew better." Sure, they know vaccine injury is a risk of vaccinating, but they don't know what it feels like to make that mistake. They haven't internalized the pain and the guilt, and they have healthy kids, so they don't understand my life at all. At least that is the way it feels to me when I hear some of their harsh comments. The extreme sides of the debate don't get me at all. They have polar opposite approaches to life, but some of the same treatments to those who are different.

Maybe I am just becoming overly sensitive because life is beginning to wear me down, with expectations of bliss morphed into real life hardship. I am so physically tired from all the care giving and the studying, the battles with doctors and the search for answers, feeling drained by all those people who sucked some life out of me before parting ways. My herd immunity is wearing thin because I am not immune to the insults of the herd. Every insensitive remark is a direct shot at my heart, and every harsh judgment burns my ears.

I don't feel like I fit in anywhere, being stuck in the middle somewhere, teetering for steady ground, while being lumped, molded and conformed into labels. On one side, I lost my "herd" and on the other side, I am still a "sheep." Maybe, I need to find my way somewhere in between. I know that we need to make changes, but I am not ready to give up my entire world of familiarity for a new one I am not sure I want to be a part of either. The great divide isn't just with doctors; it is everywhere.

I expected everyone to think like me. I thought they would share my horror and outrage. I thought they would show compassion and care about my daughter. I thought they would see my pain and care about me. I guess I thought wrong about a lot of things.

Because no one wants to hear about my problems, I am told, "Tell me what I want to hear," because of course, the feel-good lie sounds a whole lot better. I thought she might want to hear my truth, but as she repeats, "Tell me what I want to hear," I know that's not true. Hearing the easy lie means she doesn't have to get embedded into my crap, making an easy get away from connection.

I am not a surface kind of person, and the real me doesn't care for pretend relationships where I am only allowed to say what someone wants to hear. My thoughts go to all kinds of places, the places that many aren't willing to talk about — at least not out loud.

I am tempted to say, "We're fine." Go about unencumbered by our burden. But I let her have it with the sucky truth because I can't hold back the pain. The truth is too difficult for her, she says, because she doesn't want to be bothered by any of this. She doesn't want to be saddled with my problems or visit any dark places or try to understand what I am feeling. She'll just pity me from the outside without the empathy of entwined lives. Besides, she loves her vaccines more than she loves me, so I offend her with the suggestion.

If she wants a different reality, she needs to talk to a different person. "Tell me what I want to hear," really means, don't remind me about the vaccine injury. Haven't you moved on from that yet? No, my baby is still sick, and I can't get over something I live with every day. Good thing she doesn't have to live with it, if just hearing the truth is an inconvenience.

What do I want to hear? How have you been? This must be awful. How can I help? Do you want some company? These would be some nice words to hear. Even small children know how to comfort someone who is upset, even if they have no understanding of the problem or pain. They hug. They bring tissues and wipe away tears. They do something silly to bring smiles. Maybe adults have lots to learn from small children.

What do I want to hear? I want to hear the laughter of my little girl. I want to hear the doorbell ringing for some company to play with. I want to hear an acknowledgment and some apologies for the wrongs committed to my child. I want to hear peaceful words of compassion rather than the judgmental words of scorn. I want to hear the truth, even when it is painful or difficult. I want to hear the workings of miracles to heal all the injured children. I want to hear that vaccine injuries have stopped.

In another ear, I hear another familiar voice... I'm sure she must be talking about vaccines being controversial and not my daughter's reaction to them. My own friend pretends it didn't happen because she has a problem with that reality. Good thing for her that her reality didn't get altered. She just wants me to stop talking about my daughter because it doesn't fit nicely into her established beliefs over the topic. If we just avoid the conversation, she can pretend the world is exactly the same.

But I can't pretend. I have a new reality now, one in which vaccine injury is very real. While she may be sleeping soundly at night, I'm up making sure my baby is still breathing. I'm reading everything I can get my hands on, learning possible ways to get my baby better. I'm crying over my computer screen for all the other children, just like my own. My very ordinary life is now full of scandal and controversy, not an accurate picture of reality, but it never is, from the outside. But I am pressured to keep it all to myself.

I guess it is not socially acceptable to discuss vaccine reactions even if they happen to your own child. But meanwhile, the pro-vaccination agenda is allowed to say whatever they want, without criticisms, but applause, handed microphones on television. They don't shut their mouths. They are still all over the news and advertisements proclaiming that vaccines are safe, while parents like me are back home living the alternate reality, trying to clean up the mess their words have dragged us into.

Where did the herd go? They seemed to have left me alone to figure out the damage myself. They seemed to have left me alone without compassion for our situation. They seemed to have left me alone, without support, to care for my little girl. They seemed to have left me alone when I cry myself to sleep every night. They seemed to have left me alone when I drain our savings for medical care. But, they don't leave me alone when I speak up. Then, they pick on me. Why is that?

I find that to be an interesting perspective, to look beyond our own eyes, our own hearts, to ignore our own senses, to search out studies to negate the reality that presents itself, denying damage. This is not what they want to see, not what they want to hear, not what they already believe, so they look to manipulated data and warped statistics to tell them what they already "know," that vaccine injury doesn't exist, even though in truth, it does.

Sometimes beliefs are solid, blocking the absorption of new ideas. Instead, thoughts get warped and transformed into something that fits, not a true understanding, but a communication challenge. My reality doesn't fit their understandings about life, so they try to create a new reality for me, one that fits what they already know. If the belief is "vaccines are good," well then, the shots can't be the problem. It must be my "bad genes" instead. Instead of considering what might be wrong with vaccines, it becomes, what's wrong with you. They have already decided what side of the debate they are on, and it is not mine.

With suggestions that maybe it wasn't the vaccines, or maybe it was my genetics, or something wrong with my parenting — but no one ever asks me if there is something wrong with my eyesight, because everything is clear as day in my view. When I start questioning the foundations of our beliefs, tearing into the seeds of our knowledge, and exposing the roots of our thinking, I realize that most people don't want to be shaken to their cores if their own lives haven't personally been hit by an earthquake.

It is okay to question the foundations of my beliefs, but not everyone else's. And it is okay to have my world come crashing down, as long as I don't take anyone with me. And it is okay to question vaccines, as long as in the end, I decide I am still for them.

To maintain relationships as they were, I have to pretend like nothing has happened, to go on acting like life is exactly the same, keeping conversation superficial at best. I live frustrated, because I can't pretend. To me, vaccine injury has been the biggest eye opening shift in reality that I have ever experienced. I am forever changed, and I can't go on like nothing has happened.

Where are my friends? Where is all the emotional support I thought might be there for me in a time of need? My whole world has collapsed, and I stand in the ruins while everyone passes by, ignoring the fact that we are hurting and life is in disarray. They don't understand, because to them, the world is exactly the way it was before, and they don't quite see that I have fallen off the edge and am no longer there.

We're all in this together, right? But sadly, I think that might only be the title of a song. We're on our own. Good thing we have each other.

CHAPTER 25
SOCIAL BUTTERFLY IS GROUNDED

B ella doesn't always have her health, but she always has me, her constant companion, planting seeds of stability, with roots that intertwine, growing unbreakable bonds between us. I'll always cherish the closeness we share in our indestructible link between mother and child. With a young child completely dependent on me for her survival, I am truly needed.

At our place of employment, we are often reminded that we can easily be replaced, but at home, our shoes are not so easily filled in our roles as parents to our children. My job as mother to Bella could only be filled by a unique me, as the two of us share interconnected lives, beating together. We have each other, and she is loved, receiving one hundred percent of my focus each time she is ill.

We both need to pull from our inner strengths to find the power to navigate through these new waves of difficulty. Even though she is so young, Bella has a drive for independence and determination, always pushing herself to accomplish the next milestone by herself, like trying to stand on the day she learned to sit or feeding herself without help, even when she clearly needed it. But, stubbornness is an asset when it refuses to give up. Her health may be injured, but not her spirit.

My baby needs me, but what I really need is a support group. But instead, I face those judgments and criticisms in a world where all I have ever tried to do was the "right" thing. Sure, we can live peacefully isolated in our home, but I am not going to punish my happy, social baby by keeping her prisoner in her own home when she isn't sick. Isolation sucks, and I am not tolerating this lack of acceptance very well.

We leave the house, and I face the cruel world with my kids by my side. I start to become quieter and more reserved so that I can blend in better. There is nothing to pick on if people just don't know those controversial stances, so I decide to keep it all inside for a while, to make life a little easier, a little less controversial. I still can't believe the kind of reception our little heroes are getting as they fall ill doing battle with vaccines to protect the herd, but I suppose the country has done it to real soldiers returning from war, so it shouldn't come as any surprise.

Stop talking about my daughter. That thought more than baffles and offends me, but the pressure got to me, so I stop talking for a little bit, because life is very difficult when I speak up about these "controversial things," like my daughter. I need a break from the hostility, but elephants never forget, and I will one day honor my baby.

In my silence, my social daughter is cheering for people, constantly watching the windows and listening for sounds outside. I have never seen a young child so friendly and excited to see others. Whenever she hears signs of life close by, a car door slamming, familiar voices, the delivery truck, or the bounce of a basketball, she runs to the front door, screaming with excitement. She waits to pounce, not wanting to miss a single opportunity to visit her "friends." My little girl loves people.

Happy little Bella makes pals all over the place, without discrimination, including a broad spectrum of people with varying ages. Neighbors, the mailman, a person walking her dog, these are all potential friends, and Bella looks to me with full expectation that I will take her outside to chaperone her visits. Bringing her outside to see neighbors when she feels well is a small favor that brings joy to her life. Sometimes, I reluctantly acquiesce, but as my baby's jubilance spreads, I soon become infected by her enthusiasm.

Seeing people makes Bella so excited, which makes her illnesses even sadder, as my outgoing social butterfly has to spend many sick days as a hermit, cooped up in a small house, with me. I hate seeing her sick. I feel badly that she is not living in the way I had hoped she would be enjoying her young childhood. My sick butterfly can't spread her wings and fly when the weight of illness keeps her down.

Two to three weeks might pass before a fever strikes again. Long, hard illnesses, once to twice a month, mean missing out on many childhood activities. But I still get her out of the house for some fun, attending activities like story hours at the library and gym classes to work on her lagging physical abilities. Trying to live a normal life, I want to take advantage of every good day, because I never know when illness will knock us back into bed. We can't waste the days of wellness. We need to go live them, outside of the house.

But to my dismay, other parents bring sick kids to childhood events. Sick kids bring contagion to mine, leaving us with more bad days and more bad illnesses, because we never seem to get anything minor.

Winters in New England elicit copious amounts of mucus production along with the snowfall, but Bella doesn't get the normal common colds like the rest of the kids. It doesn't look like the common cold when the illness erupts in my girl. It looks like the immune-compromised version with high fevers and alternating periods of listless, lifeless behavior or uncontrollable crying. She gets a frightfully uncommon version that wipes her out for a week, raging in temperature rather than mucus. But all it takes is a little bit of that slime, touched to my poor little Bella, and she slips into another fever episode.

"It is just a cold," people say — maybe to justify their decision, maybe to convince me I shouldn't be worried. But my child has a compromised immune system, and the common cold is a big deal.

I learn to scout out places for visible signs of illness, hoping to protect my baby from an unfortunate meeting with friendly children goopy with germs. Eyes open, I scan for mucus monsters with noses oozing of thick gobs of greenish slime hanging out from both nostrils, ready to be lapped up by an awaiting tongue. I search for the Cyclops carrying conjunctivitis, with red, watery pink eye. I listen for suspicious coughs. Pale skin and dark circles are everywhere, so that is just the normal unhealthy look, but nothing to fear. Searching for signs of contagion, I am looking for potential threats to my injured baby. We try to do the normal things that kids do for fun, but whatever the event, there is usually someone who comes sick to ruin it for us.

Kids are just being kids. They don't always think to wash their hands before they grab onto each other. They don't know that boogers aren't for sharing when they admire the little surprises they pull from their noses. Coughing warm wind into each other's faces is a game. And they think it is fully appropriate to slather a toy with a kiss before handing it off to a friend. This is just how kids play together, sharing fun times along with their germs. None of this is their fault; they are just being kids.

But I expected more courtesy from the adults. "Sick kids stay home," is a saying I heard many times, but I think they only meant if the kids were from my family. There is a sense of entitlement in the air, along with the germs, a sense that some parents feel they have more of a right to be here, even though at the moment, it is their child who is sick. Their infections are dangerous to my baby, but no one seems to care. Inconsiderate parents don't want to catch sickness from others, but are more than happy to let their own child spread some germs.

I understand the inner turmoil that working parents face, but some parents aren't playing fairly, bringing sick children for fun, and not necessity. Justifications are no excuse, because there is no good reason why sick kids need to come to play. We miss enough because of my baby's own illnesses, but we have to miss out for other people's sickness too, and that doesn't feel fair at all.

Sometimes, we stay, and I become hyper vigilant and extra clingy, physically guarding my baby from the damaging touch of mucus-filled fingers innocently awaiting to smear my daughter with harm. Holding my baby in a loving grip is my best tactic for avoidance if we decide to stay. Sometimes my parenting takes on the helicopter effect, always on guard, gently guiding my baby away from the sick ones, or grabbing dirty hands quickly before they make their way to her face.

Sometimes, we have to leave when someone else brings sickness and chases us out the door. Sometimes the only defense I know is to pull my baby out from the situation. I don't worry if I offend anyone by my abrupt behavior, because I am not the one who did anything wrong. I am just trying to protect my baby, my immune compromised baby, who I vaccinated so I wouldn't have to worry about these things. But now, I find myself deathly afraid of the common cold and surrounded by people willing to spread it.

Life isn't supposed to be this way. I thought we vaccinated so I wouldn't have to worry about my kid playing with other kids, but the vaccines ruined her immune system so much that she can't always enjoy that simple pleasure. We took all of the risks, can't see any benefits, and experience the continued suffering of unintended consequences. Vaccination certainly isn't doing us any good.

Vaccination status seems pointless when sick kids come out to play. As long as people don't bring their visibly, obviously, unmistakably sick children around mine, then I don't really care if they are vaccinated or unvaccinated. Just don't bring them when they are sick!

But of course, the "unvaccinated" are blamed for all childhood illness, because a vaccinated mucus spreader won't get anyone sick, even though, in real life, they do. Many parents are bringing their children out visibly sick, masking fevers with medicine and making false assurances that deny contagion. But it won't be those parents who will be blamed if someone catches something "preventable." It will be the people like me who question or refuse vaccines, even if sickness never walks outside our house.

I don't think we made a good trade at all. Twenty plus shots, multiplied by multiple diseases filled into each vial, causing us only harm. Something at least as bad as measles is visiting my house at least once a month, and the common cold takes the life out of my baby much worse than some of those childhood illnesses we thought we could prevent. But we don't vaccinate for the common cold, so I guess I can't blame all those sick kids who got my kid sick so many times, with preventable illness that would have been preventable if they just stayed home.

CHAPTER 26
THE PHARMACY

I drive into the next town to pick up a prescription for Bella. Usually the pharmacy a half mile up the street has what we need, but this time I am in an unfamiliar pharmacy about a fifteen minute drive from home, where some medicine is waiting for me.

Everything seems normal when I pay and accept the small white paper bag. This prescription is not generic, and it is not dispensed from some larger bottle. It is a brand name in its original box, and I toss it on the front seat as I drive away. Riding home, I am mentally preparing my scientific brain, getting ready to read those inserts.

My mind is fully alert as I open up the prescription box, to find — surprise — nothing! Yes, the medicine is still there, but not that important paperwork that goes with it. The inserts are missing! I paid for this prescription. What right did the pharmacy have to steal away my package inserts?

I immediately call the pharmacy to complain about this dilemma, and I ask for the inserts. Although I don't want to, I am willing to drive back to get them. I don't know the laws on this or standard policies state to state, but this pharmacy told me they threw them away. Something so valuable to me and they just "threw them away," tossing them right into the trash.

She continues to tell me that they do not have an obligation to give inserts to patients. They are "supposed to throw them away because the inserts are not intended for the patients themselves, unless the patient specifically asks for them." I didn't think to ask for them specifically, because I didn't think anyone was going to be opening my brand new product for me and deciding what parts of it I get to keep. I'm trying to be an educated consumer, making an informed consent to use the product, but they are stealing the educational information right out of the package. Why?

I didn't realize I had to ask for things that should rightfully be mine. It comes with it. Why would I need to ask to keep them together? I don't ask stores to keep the tags attached to the clothing I buy. I don't ask them not to tear off the logos. They just don't because they are part of the product. They just come that way, a part of the whole, the total package.

Something is going on here, and it isn't good. Seems a bit fishy to me, but she isn't going to fish them back out of the trash. I have to go online to get them, and I don't even like being on the computer. They always seem to be adding those extra steps that most of us won't make, making it harder and less convenient to get the answers. Some of us will not take those extra steps into the darkness. They are counting on that to keep us in the dark.

Those inserts are my right to know. They are the part of the information I need to make informed consent. And they just steal it from an item I paid for because I didn't ask for it ahead of time. I don't give over-the-counter products without reading the labels, yet for this prescription that is exactly what the pharmacist expects me to do.

Kind of like the vaccines that seem to come prefilled and ready to go at the pediatrician's office, neatly laid out in a row on the counter, ready for immediate use. They were dispensed as one-size-fits-all, with the doctor's preference as to brands, type, and vial type. The vaccines don't seem to come with any labels for parents to read either, just those printouts given to me after the fact.

I didn't get to watch who filled the syringes or if they shook the bottles. I didn't get to check the expiration dates or the ingredients. I didn't even get to double check if the vaccines my girl was supposed to get were actually in the vials she did get. I didn't get to see the process with my own eyes to watch every move from beginning to end. I just trusted that the office was looking out for us and took care of all these details I usually do for myself.

These are the details I prefer to trust myself with, because I am extremely careful with important tasks of this magnitude, double and triple checking things in hopes of avoiding any errors. I can only hope they took the same care with these things as I would have, because my baby's life was in their hands, and I trusted them with my heart.

I am trying to be an educated consumer, yet they don't want me to educate myself with real information. Sometimes inserts are watered down into "patient friendly" documents. Sometimes they offer me the abridged version filtered through their own minds and spun into convincing words that flow smoothly from the lips. One doctor told me that learning from the internet was stupid, and then told me to go to the CDC's website. I can't help but giggle.

Another doctor told me that I wouldn't be able to take any medicine if I read the inserts. Well, maybe that is the point. Maybe I don't want to take just any medicine or have it injected into my children. Maybe I should get the decision to evaluate if the risks are worth the benefits. That is not the kind of decision to leave in the hands of another. And because he is not me, he is not the one taking the risks, I am. Let me decide if the benefits are worth the personal risks. Without the inserts, I have nothing to go on but "doctor's orders."

It seems to me none of us are being given a real informed consent. If we want a full picture, we have to paint the other half ourselves, researching those forbidden places they like to tell us aren't science — because it is not *their* science. All it takes is one night at the television to be inundated with advertisements for medicines with their side effects back to back with advertisements from lawyers to fight for those with medical harm. Add two and two together and there is a bigger picture.

CHAPTER 27
KNOWLEDGE ALLEVIATES FEAR

The house is sleeping. Slumped over the keyboard, my eyes are fixated on the screen in front of me. My face, propped up by my hands, starts to sink from its heaviness. My head bobs and eyelids droop as the day's weariness longs to rest in peaceful slumber where the worries at hand will part ways until the rising of tomorrow's sun.

In my little world, I am all alone, but in the larger world, I am one of many, silently connected to all those other parents out there, clicking on keyboards and studying weary eyed throughout the night, other parents just like me, struggling with guilt and wrestling new fears, mothers and fathers full of perseverance to make things right.

As the medical professionals move on with their lives, we the parents are left hanging on a string, ready to break at any moment. We are left alone to find the pieces, pick up the pieces, and put the puzzle together ourselves. We live lives we never imagined. We speak new languages. We lose friends and family who just don't understand us anymore. We are changed. Our kids changed. We did that with the needle, but that injection has far reaching consequences, well beyond the confines of the body.

I thrust myself into a world of unfamiliar healthcare that has options far beyond what I have been told by the competition. Maybe there are answers hiding in the unexplored territory of the alternatives, and I will venture to overturn every holistic stone I can find. Where can I find the hidden gems of the past, healing techniques intentionally covered up with our nation's allopathic ways, and good traditions that got ignored in favor of all things modern? The answers have to be hiding somewhere, and the journey has to begin with me.

I have no idea what tools I will need for survival, because I learned dependency and obedience along with all those pages of memorized textbooks. I was never taught the true meanings of healthcare. Instead, I was trained to run to a doctor for help, leaving me feeling a bit helpless in the dependency. I was trained to run to the doctors for answers, and they were waiting for me with the wrong ones. I was trained to run to the doctor with my baby in my arms, seeking wellness with a shot of "protection." I was trained to be needy.

Sometimes they offer more harm than help, by offering what they have been trained to prescribe. Sometimes I think, maybe I'm not the incompetent one here. Sometimes all I can think of is, "First, do no harm," and all I can see is the very harm doctors commit, surrounding me everywhere. It is time to build my own skills. I don't want to rely on doctors before myself, and I don't want to be dependent when I can be competent.

My bookcases start to fill with homeopathic, naturopathic, and vaccination literature at the time when my file cabinet is becoming stuffed with medical records. My home is transforming into a research library, with reference manuals ready to pull in an instant. My medicine cabinet is shifting from the traditional standards of over-the-counter care products to new remedies, a homeopathic assortment, flower essences, and some various herbs.

I use the books found in the colleges that train naturopathic doctors, the NDs of the world, instead of the MDs. I have these on hand for herbal preparations and natural, simple home ideas for comforting children through their illnesses and aiding their recovery. I want to learn a variety of healing modalities to have at my disposal to call upon myself when the time arises. And I memorize homeopathic medicine, because that might be the one new learning that elicits some passion.

I still like textbooks, those big oversized college ones with a thousand pages full of illustrations and diagrams. I am old fashioned that way, enjoying a tangible book and the turn of a page. The computer is a great resource to tap into real information, but sometimes I find all our modern gadgets a big distraction from paying attention to life. Sometimes, life is the most important teacher of all, because sometimes science gets lost in translation when it would have been so simple to focus on observation.

I learn about autism too, because maybe my daughter's problems aren't so different. I think a lot of clues are hiding there, clues to my daughter's healing, clues to the world, holding secrets to our future, making healing discoveries that the rest of us just might want to know about.

I learn about illnesses and diseases, creating a database in my mind with symptoms and treatment options memorized. Learning about childhood illnesses is a good thing. They don't scare me as much as the media scared me or as much as the doctor scared me. Learning brings less fear, not more, because in the words of the textbooks, in the numbers of the statistics, the data just doesn't seem to match the hype, so learning the facts helps me calm down. Knowledge alleviates fear.

I can know the answers. I can have the skills. Sometimes I can do this, all by myself. Maybe those are some thoughts to consider when evaluating the worth of an education. I take back some control, claim some independence, and open my mind to another world of healing possibilities. I put some power back into my scared, hesitant hands, convincing myself that with my new found knowledge and wisdom, I can handle much more than I previously thought. My hands are competent, capable healers.

My gut stopped churning with the uneasiness of all those past medical decisions that just felt wrong. I feel more competent and less fearful, needing less dependency on others for the routine sick care I can do myself. I probably fear unnecessary doctor intervention most of all, and the less I need doctors, the better I feel. Maybe being a parent involves facing fears and learning to trust myself. I can do this.

After I learned, the test arrives. Real life rings the phone. My heart sinks, drops right into my stomach, as the woman tells me about confirmed whooping cough at the gym we attend twice a week. She found out a week ago, and is only calling to let us know because the health department intervened in the situation. I look down at my six-month-old son and start to worry about his fate. He is young enough to be in the exact age range where they tell us that whooping cough can be deadly.

At the time, I am having the worst cough of my life, with uncontrollable coughing fits that last longer than expected and hack up sputum. I probably wouldn't have even thought to consider whooping cough had it not been for the confirmed case at the gym. Besides the periodic coughing spasms, I am able to go about my day normally.

My baby son starts to cough. I start sleeping in his room at night, knowing that any noise he makes will wake my light sleep. When he wakes in the night to cough, I hear a tiny gasp at the end. I am uncertain if this is the whoop I expect to hear because his cough is not as extreme as I imagined and the gasp not so scary. I have heard the horror stories, but our experience doesn't seem so horrible.

He sleeps on his organic mattress and fills his tummy with breast milk. I watch him sleep peacefully from the couch near his crib. I await his coughs, ready to intervene if necessary. I am prepared to sleep sitting, holding my baby upright on my chest if necessary. I am prepared to do whatever work necessary to help him. He looks like he has a cold, but otherwise, most of the day, he acts his normal.

With our exposure to whooping cough, my son and I get coughs. My daughter and husband have no symptoms of a cough. My husband didn't go to the gym like the rest of us did. My daughter was vaccinated, maybe it worked. Or maybe, she was never exposed. She wasn't in the habit of tasting the toys anymore or putting odd things in her mouth. I was exhausted from the stress, a known immune drainer. I had my vaccine for that one, but they don't last forever, like real immunity.

So, when I think whooping cough has joined our household, I expect to stay up on night vigils. I expect to hold my baby upright and catch mucus at the end of a cough. I expect us to get through this, because certainly I believe this is easier than tackling vaccine injury. I am determined. Certainly, I can do this for six weeks if necessary.

To me, any illness that has an end in sight is something I can muster the strength to tackle. It is the chronic illnesses that frighten me. That is a true endurance test, so to swap one for the other doesn't seem like a good trade. Whooping cough comes and goes through our household, without leaving a single harm behind.

The fear monsters scare us into familiar corners, but now I have new places to turn. I have new knowledge and new skills. My education misled me in the wrong direction, imbedding me with faulty traditions that I would have naturally passed onto my own children if not injected by change. Now, I have no natural immunity to share with my babies, but I can pass on a wider perspective of the world, a more complete picture of healthcare, and some skills of their own.

CHAPTER 28
THE AWFUL ALTERNATIVE

I hear numerous tsk sounds to welcome us to the initial appointment, as the health practitioner counts up the shots on Bella's vaccination record. This woman does have a respected mainstream professional title, but she also considers herself a medical intuitive. Regardless, she comes to my mind as the awful alternative.

Bringing me on a journey through her own past, the practitioner explains her own son's vaccine reaction to the MMR. This is an appropriate connection, and it even clarifies her current job choice. She is a proud mom who brought her son to full recovery, and she feels the need to progress through the chronicles of her life as well as the life of her son. She needs to write her own book one day, because she clearly has lots to say.

I don't mind listening to her story, but she is expensive; I want her to focus every minute on my child. But, she feels we need to go on her journey, with her own child, before we can get to mine. Her son is about my age by now, a full adult who could have growing kids of his own, and she is still talking about his vaccine reaction. That's how hard it is to "let it go." Vaccine injury stays with us, maybe forever. But as we pay her by the hour, and I am by no means wealthy, I watch the clock tick away lots of precious minutes while I wait to arrive at what we came here for — help for my daughter.

I am here with lots of concerns. There are still some lingering vaccine effects to deal with, like those fevers. But I have new concerns now too, because I am not just trying to fix immediate vaccine damage anymore. I want to prevent the long term damage too, hoping to resolve the issues before they cause future harm.

Bella's measles titer is so frightfully high; I am concerned about excess antibodies attacking her organs, causing cancer or autoimmune disease later in life. Besides the excess antibodies, she had two doses of the Hepatitis B vaccine made by the manufacturer that had a link to multiple sclerosis. Now that eye doctors are finding multiple sclerosis in children, this is a very real concern.

I am hoping to prevent further damage from all those antibodies. How do we get rid of excess antibodies? How do we get rid of the very thing that they want us to have to "prove immunity?" But she shuts me down, ignoring this theory, my concerns, saying that "it is only the additives of the vaccines that are bad." I do not agree. So, we disagree on whether it is just the toxins in the shots that cause harm or the diseases themselves that do damage too.

After providing her the courtesy to speak, about herself, through more than half the appointment, she isn't interested in discussing my daughter's vaccine reaction or allowing me to describe how Bella's health has improved with age. She doesn't want to hear all the ways we have already helped. She doesn't want to hear about our diet; she just made the assumption that it is bad. Because my daughter was vaccinated, she lumps me into a category with every other American parent she finds distasteful. She can't hear me either, because to her, I am a parent of the herd, and she has her own judgments about what that means.

I want to know if she knows something we can do differently that might get my daughter better. I am looking for help, expecting her to know more than me, especially considering she is charging for her services. All that talk about her son's vaccine reaction, and she wants to blame Bella's immune problems on a yeast overgrowth and a parasite that Bella supposedly picked up around the age of 2 ½ years old. That doesn't really explain the missing sick time between 15 months to 2 ½ years…

But she comes to this conclusion, with no medical testing, no listening to my concerns, just her intuition to guide the way. But I don't trust her intuition the way she does. She wants me to listen to her intuition when I am still having trouble trusting my own.

She might trust her intuition, but she wants me to trust her intuition too, on complete blind faith. But she is a mere stranger, and I don't even trust her. How could I possibly trust *her* intuition to work for *me*? I will not obey, and I know her powers are not strong enough to make me.

When I am not keen on accepting her assessments, she makes some harsh comments. First, she suggests that there are lots of people who don't actually want to get better, because they identify with their illnesses. Then, she plays her own guilt trip and accuses me of not wanting to get to the cause. I have been trying for years, but since she doesn't want to hear about our lives, she wouldn't know that. She is snippy, because she wants me to get the root of the problem by blinding following her judgment to an inaccurate time frame. To her, finding the cause is using her magic finger to pinpoint it. But if she stops at age 2 ½, she hasn't dug deep enough into history to reach the roots.

The practitioner is very critical of who she calls "parents nowadays," as she dumps me into her classification. She tells me that I need to be the parent and force Bella to do things, like drink her water, criticizing my decision to give juice with her fevers, in our attempts simply to get fluids into that little body.

She continues, "Not having a bowel movement for three weeks is not normal, but parents come in and tell me this. They say their pediatrician tells them it is normal, but it's not normal." I am not even here about bowel habits, but she throws that crap at me anyway.

Then, she makes a comment about what parents let their kids watch on television. She said parents want to medicate their kids because it is the "easy way out." "Medicate and plop them in front of the TV," she says. She speaks with frustration in her voice, criticizing modern parents as though they are the bane of her existence, when it appears to me, that they just might be a source of her livelihood.

I emphasize that she doesn't know our history or what we've been through, only to bring her back to talking about her life and what she has been through. But our experiences are not identical, and I am one of those "parents nowadays" that she can't stand. She is missing many points, because she has no idea who we are or she wouldn't be making up all these inaccurate assessments of our parenting style. I don't like the way she is treating us. I don't like the way she talks about "parents nowadays," and I don't like the way she dismisses any opinion but her own.

I ask more advanced questions than the minimal knowledge she assumes I have. I don't think she was prepared, getting a bit defensive, with her shut me up kind of replies. I wasn't trying to offend her, I just gave her undo credit for knowing more than I do, and maybe she just doesn't.

I don't agree with her answers. As I listen, I don't think she realizes that I caught an inaccuracy. Her child couldn't possibly have reacted to the MMR at the age she quoted, because it wasn't even in existence yet. I am not denying that her son suffered vaccine injury, I would never deny her that, but it was probably from the measles vaccine instead. I don't know if it is intentional or just a mistake, but I pick up on these little things and lose trust. But she probably thinks I am just one of those parents who won't know the difference anyway.

In her mind, she must be right, or I wouldn't be here "needing her help." Looking for help doesn't exactly make one needy, but paying for it from this woman might be a lost avenue on the road to recovery. She helps herself to our money while using me as both her therapist and her punching bag. I think she still has anger issues over her own child's vaccine injury so many years ago, because among these disagreements, that is the part of her that I can understand. That is something I don't blame her for, because I wasn't judging her for her mistakes the way she judged me for mine.

CHAPTER 29

AWAKE

The nighttime is always the longest part of sick days, when time ticks on slowly, and the silence is punctuated by the moaning and crying of my child. Entire nights spent awake, with sporadic moments of dozing. Standing guard, I watch my baby cope with her misery, able to supply comfort, love, and support. My arms are ready for hugs, or bringing drinks, or simultaneously catching vomit in the bucket while holding her in my grasp. Being the arm to lay on, I am the constant companion of my sick little girl. My baby touches me, skin to skin, the constant reassurance that I will always be there.

I want to go back to sleep. Life is too painful this way. I want to go back to sleep to the days before vaccine injury, to the days full of health, happiness, and fun. I want to go back to the days of ignorant bliss, back to the days when I was well liked and well respected. But I must stay awake.

My baby lies across my arms. She is sick again, in the most unnatural way. Illness inflicted by the very needles touted to preserve health by preventing illness, and here she lie, her health devastated by those needles I was told would keep her well.

Another night spent fully awake in constant vigil as the minutes tick into hours and then days. I am familiar with lack of sleep and long nights studying for exams, but I am awake in a new sense. I am not sleepy, but awake — fully present to my baby's every breath.

Awakened by the shrill cries of good intentions gone horribly wrong, I have awakened to a new reality and a new future unlike anything I could have predicted for myself and my family, awakened into an unfamiliar world where familiar images flash through my mind, reflections of my own life and the experiences and the beliefs that led me here. I am awake and on guard to protect my children. Blissful ignorance has ended.

I am awake, and as tiring and stressful as my new life has become, I have to fight the urge not to go back to sleep. My baby needs me awake and alert — paying attention and learning from the signs that are all around. Something was stolen from us, when healthy days morphed into sick ones. My enthusiastic idealism turned into mistrust and skepticism. My baby turned from vibrant and healthy to pale and sickly. But to everyone else around me, the world had stayed exactly the same.

When I wake up and there is no one to talk to, it gets tempting to fall back asleep. Igniting the candle at both ends, I am burning out quickly in my full time role as a caregiver. But it is important to stay awake. I've got work to do, and there is no giving up on my daughter.

I want to cry. I want to cry with someone I know will understand. I want to cry with someone who gets all this in a world that tries really hard not to. I want to cry with someone who knows those round the clock vigils, so they can be there in spirit with me the next time I have to go it alone. I want to cry with someone whose heart has been ripped open from the pain we share alongside our children, from the pain of betrayal from those we trusted, from the pain of emptying out our brains and making room to start over. I want to cry with someone who knows what it feels like to be stuck, to hit a wall and not know where the next punch or the next ray of light is going to come from. I don't want to feel alone in this anymore.

I need to talk with someone about shared experiences, a comfortable conversation with families who understand each other, away from those who deny vaccine damage. I need to discuss mutual experiences, to share healing advice along with our stories, to share on a deeply emotional level that digs deep into the heart of the guilt, the sadness, and the anger. I need support from someone living in the same world, and that kind of support cannot be found in a therapist's office. True understanding lies in the hearts and souls of moms and dads just like me.

I sure need a friend, but I don't reach out for me. I only reach out for my daughter's health, putting all of her needs way above my own, jeopardizing my physical health by not attending to my emotional health, not truly understanding how one could impact the other, not fully realizing that suffering in isolation and being bombarded with constant stresses of life would impact physical health too. It seems only natural to take care of my baby first, but I am fading, fading away in the darkest of days and the longest of nights. I am still running on adrenaline. I have some fight left in me, and I use it to fight for Bella's health and not mine. I am fading into my own oblivion, losing bits and pieces of myself each day; my only identity is that of a mom, and it seems my only friends are my kids themselves.

CHAPTER 30
DOCTOR DILEMMAS

N ot quite two years after the vaccine reaction and we are at the pediatrician's office for an annual well visit. I find irony in the title *well visit*, the kind of appointment that landed us into a pool of sickness and has us returning frequently for sick visits. The appointment feels like an obligation where I am offered no sharp points except that of a needle, which by now, is pointless.

Too many sick visits have the office feeling like familiar territory. The waiting rooms are a child's delight with colorful walls and playful decals. Toys and books are everywhere, and a popular cartoon plays on the television. There are two waiting rooms, one for sick visits and the other for the well visits, but they both share the same hallways and the same checkout desk, allowing the germs to intermingle even though the children do not.

We are quickly whisked from this pleasure zone into a room of pain. The temperature of the room is uncomfortably chilly. Everything feels so cold: the hard plastic chairs, a grungy table covered in thin noisy paper, instruments on the wall, and vaccine sheets displayed on the counter. This is a typical exam room in a pediatric office. The nurse hastily performs the standard tasks of height, weight, and temperature measurements before she closes the door to commence our long wait.

Forty-five extra minutes trying to keep two children quiet and well-behaved in an exam room is challenging even for the most patient of souls. I struggle to keep my daughter from falling off of the exam table as she sits there, completely naked. There are no paper robes for children, so we swipe her brother's baby blanket for some warmth.

Bella is three, and sitting is not her favorite thing to do when she is feeling well. Controlling a child's curiosity among all these gadgets begging to be touched is nearly impossible. Reaching, she wants to handle all the medical tools hanging on the wall. Trying to keep her bottom off of the unlined parts of the exam table has me stressed about germs.

Forty-five minutes is a long time to wait in here when they have such a welcoming child-friendly area just outside the door. I wonder if this is a tactic too — to have parents exhausted before the appointment even begins, to wear us out so we are not up for a fight. A frazzled mom will be much easier to bowl over.

My watch keeps ticking away as we await the familiar knock on the door, notifying us of the doctor's imminent entry. Our appointment this day is scheduled with the exact same doctor who took my nighttime call and offered Benadryl as the solution for brain inflammation. He barely steps foot in the room before he is back out again asking the nurse for Bella's vaccination card. There are no greetings and no apologies for his late arrival.

He flips through Bella's medical folder and surprisingly, the first thing he wants to discuss is iron. He asks me if I give Bella iron.

"Yes, but not every day." I remind him that it had been his office who instructed me to supplement with iron.

He finds the notes. Then, he tells me to stop. I think he just realized that Bella would have been overdosed by now based on his office's recommendations.

My girl tested borderline anemic, but I know that there has been no overdose. If I followed instructions exactly, she would have been. But I pay attention and double check recommendations, reading labels and inserts, because I know no one else is doing that for me. Bella has fewer fevers when we keep up with the iron drops, which has been the most positive result we have seen to date. The doctor says there is no connection, just coincidence, but I have heard that line many times before, and I am not convinced this time either.

I ask, "Can we do blood work to recheck Bella's iron levels?"

He refuses my request, indicating that it "isn't necessary."

I see. It is not necessary to him, because he probably doesn't want actual proof of an iron overdose, so he prevents that possibility with a simple, "No."

"Why should we put her through that for no reason?" he says.

I can think of plenty of reasons why this test would be valuable, but moms don't have any legal rights to order blood work on their own, so a doctor's word is the final say.

"Why should we put her through that for no reason?" he says, when referring to a blood draw, but he is more than happy to pump her full of a few more shots. My concerns about her sickness are not on the doctor's agenda. Inflicting more needles is his goal of the day. I feel like we have practically lived here the past two years, but sick visits don't require vaccines, instead it contraindicates them.

How could he forget this little baby when she was fully reacting at just over a year old? How could he forget that we spent Bella's entire age-two exam discussing the serious reactions from the 15 months shots? How could he forget that we are here all the time, and he is holding her medical folder to prove it? How could he have forgotten her? His memory is clearly not as vivid as my own, and his connection to my daughter not as personal.

His first push is for the DTaP, so I remind him of her reaction at six months. To appease me, he offers the DT as an alternative, but I bring it to his attention that he cannot offer that one without the added mercury.

There is no reply to negate my comment. Instead, he proceeds to tell me, "Tetanus is prevalent, and people die from it." He tells me people die from diphtheria too, but tetanus is more widespread. He avoids the whooping cough speech, because he has already offered the shot that lacks this portion of germs.

"How can you not want to protect her?" he asks, failing to mention any of the risks that walk hand in hand with vaccination.

I remind him of the risks. I repeatedly remind him of Bella's past vaccine reactions and her continuing struggles. My sickly child has debilitating high fevers every month. I reiterate the gross motor regressions and delays. To exhibit one of my concerns, I ask Bella to try to jump for him, but he doesn't even look up. He won't even look at her, avoiding any possible connection to this little life in his exam room.

He is trying hard not to hear me, and I am trying hard to get him to see. I point out all the tiny capillaries on Bella's face and back, the little red and purples lines that surfaced with the vaccine reaction rash, never to dive beneath the skin again. Instead of taking a good look, he tells me that skin thickens with age, which will make the colors less visible. As my words fall to the floor, a sinking feeling drops into my belly.

Why are we here again? I find this a completely useless waste of time and money as I continue a conversation with heartfelt words that reach no heart. I beg him to look at my daughter, continuously reminding him of the vaccine reactions and the residual health problems. But he keeps bringing the conversation back to where he is comfortable, pressuring for more shots.

He tries to sell me the flu shot with a story about children getting complications from the flu, while completely ignoring complications from the flu vaccine. I don't understand how a flu shot is even relevant to anything I have just said, but he keeps going back to the vaccine issue regardless. He really wants to sell me one of them.

He will not give up easily. He really wants to stick it to her today, before I have more time to think about it. But this is what I think about, day in and day out. Vaccines consume my mind, filling me with sickness rather than protection, and the guilt of unintended consequences of harming my own daughter. I no longer have soft beliefs that the doctor can mold. I have hardened into someone not so malleable with his tactics.

He continues with his pressure telling me he really "wants to help Bella." I know these are empty words as he has had plenty of opportunities at her numerous sick visits.

"By giving her more shots?" I explode, but I keep the second part, "Are you crazy?" to myself.

I waited for 45 minutes for his arrival, and now I have been under another 45 minutes of pressure, with two children still in my care. My tone is not quite as polite as I respond, but I control my emotions enough to prevent screaming at him. I tell him that I did everything the doctors told me to until 15 months. Then, we had a reaction and no one seemed to care. Then, I researched. Now, I'm done.

I point out the fact that he wants parents to sign accepting responsibility for the shots. He says that "doctors are more responsible." Really? How exactly? There is no legal recourse for parents, and no liabilities to the vaccine pushers. I don't see how it is possible that doctors have more responsibility, because it seems to me that it is the parents who have all of the responsibility.

His hands are washed clean while mine are left holding the sickness that overtakes my child. It is my heart that breaks. As I get stuck, completely frozen, traumatized and paralyzed by the pain, he will continue going to work as though nothing wrong has ever happened, inflicting more shots on unsuspecting children and families. He doesn't hold my hand to lift me up and prevent me from falling toward my own demise. He doesn't open his pocketbook to help pay for additional expenses. He won't share his salary to help compensate for the one that I lost to be with my sick child. He doesn't spend sleepless nights with me, full of worry. And he certainly isn't helping me do any of the care giving. I can't see how he is responsible at all.

He decides we might have a problem, when I tell him that a naturopathic doctor is helping. He offers up a referral to the children's hospital when Bella is not even sick, to the infectious disease unit, no less, a unit with the very germs that just might kill her, in a hospital that just might steal her away or use her as some guinea pig for test procedures in their research. I can't decide if I think he is nuts, or very dangerous, but after ignoring the damage for nearly two years, he does not exactly hold the opinion I can trust.

He has his own agenda. If I bring the topic where he doesn't want it to be, he just ignores and moves on, with no acknowledgment of my concerns, forcing me to revisit the haunting vaccine issue with him over and over again. He repeats that he "is just trying to help her."

"By giving her another shot? How does that help her? We haven't even fixed the other issues yet." I snap back.

He says he is trying to "help her," but he won't even order the blood work for her borderline anemia. His idea of helping is pushing more shots on a child who has already reacted badly to them.

I think he is trying to help himself instead. It seems conflicts of interest guide his actions and not my daughter's best interests. I see his recognition plaque on the wall honoring his nearly perfect vaccine compliance level. Maybe it even came with some matching green backs to line his pockets. I think he'd like to keep his plaque, so instead he decides to get rid of us.

"The staff has already warned me that if I didn't agree to the vaccines today that my children would be kicked out of the practice," I inform the doctor.

Since I am not intentionally trying to be a doctor hopper, I ask him for a letter stating his intentions. I also ask him to keep my daughter as a patient for now. She is vaccinated, but she is the one who gets sick all the time and needs someone. I don't find the practice much help, but I don't yet have another pediatrician. But Bella is not worth anything to him when I am not compliant. As he closes the door to end our appointment, he shuts us out of his practice.

While still in the exam room, I instinctively squeeze my children in a tight hug. I cling to my children when confronted by the enemy willing to steal them from me with the guise of care. These are MY children! The crying breaks free from its containment as my frustration, anger, and pain pours down my face.

When we settle into the confines of my car, I pause before leaving to cry some more. Feeling disgusted with the practice of medicine. Feeling sick at the way we are treated and ignored. This feels like some alternate reality nightmare that I can't believe is real. Why so much pressure for a medical procedure that carries real risk? I'm green with the thoughts that the root of this insanity is money. That sickens me enough to vomit.

He tosses us on the street, the sly, backhanded way, with a polite phone call from one of his staff asking where they should send the medical records. "I don't have another pediatrician," I remind her. As she confirms that we are no longer welcome there, I tell her, "I'll have to come pick up the records. I don't have another doctor to send them to."

And there we go; they only want us when we comply. It doesn't matter that my girl accepted over 20. It was the one I said no to that mattered to him more. He rejected my sick little girl without even a thank you for her sacrifice for the herd. That is not love. That is not compassionate care. This is something else entirely. Something like discrimination. My little girl has just been rejected and abandoned by another pediatrician. And he tells me "he cares." Yeah right.

CHAPTER 31
OBEDIENCE TO FAITH

I wasn't prepared for the vultures hanging over me, waiting for the chance to steal a piece of my baby girl. I didn't have the right education to prepare me to tackle the beast; I had the kind of education that made me the perfect prey. I thought I was prepared, but I was too naïve and trusting to realize the forces I was up against. They had been trained, trained in persuasive tactics and manipulation. I had been trained in obedience, an easy target.

This is not what I envisioned when I thought the world was bad. This is far scarier, because evil is hidden in places we trust. I wasn't unprepared for my baby's arrival, but I was unprepared for a world waiting to mold her before I even had my own hands on her, a world with hungry eyes ready to snatch her from me as soon as I got pregnant.

I never even heard the term before my pregnancy, but with some training, I knew exactly what the term *well visit* meant to a new mother: doctor's visits for baby. I took the complimentary parenting magazines and brochures from the obstetrician's office. Free parenting books showed up at my door. I left the hospital with not only my baby, but a diaper bag filled with formula and another book. Little notes in the mailbox seemed like thoughtful reminders, making me believe I was part of a village that cared.

I thought I was learning all this great information, from generous companies, but I'm pretty sure I was being set up. They were luring me straight into their traps, with little gifts, the same way real kidnappers and molesters lure children. I was easy prey, because I was unaware of the ulterior motives, never once putting my guard up against the outside persuasions dropping on doorsteps, enticing their way inside my home. I was an easy target, because I didn't want to believe people would be this bad, even though our whole economy seems to be built on tricking people to become consumers. Mothering comes from within, but external influences work their way inside, slanting instincts that were perfectly straight, damming an effortless flow of innate wisdom.

Pregnant women are happy. We are thrilled that others seem to be sharing in our joy. Because we have announced to the world, "We're pregnant," we have just been placed on their radar. They don't need to see our growing bellies. They just want our addresses, our email, our phone numbers, our identities, so they can add us to their giant databases. The hospital collects a whole bunch of data on us too, when we apply for the social security numbers right through them, when they record birth records and that first shot, our fingerprints, and our child's DNA when they swipe some of that umbilical cord.

No, I wasn't prepared for any of that. I was preparing to play house with my little girl in my own little world, where people would never hurt babies on purpose. In my own little world, where people are good and I am good, where I couldn't imagine the worst in others or how bad bad can truly be.

Peer pressure never got to me when it was from my peers, but when it was from a doctor, I fell for it. I weighed doctors' words heavier than most, dragging my baby straight into harm. The pediatrician risked my baby girl's life without even warning me of the dangers, because if he had warned me, I wouldn't have handed her over so willingly. I had my warning signs stowed away in the back of my head. My mind forgot, but my gut didn't.

Obeying his command, I handed over my most prized possession, and I didn't get her back in quite the same condition. He dropped my little girl, the beating life from my life, soft and vulnerable; her only armor was the protection from me, her loving mother, and I let her down with my foolish trust of a doctor's misleading words. He broke my trust, and he broke my little girl. He didn't take good care of her like I do.

I didn't know that I was part of a game, and my daughter was just a toy. The world of medicine was a tricky place for my naivety. I was being set up by all the propaganda on the outside, to willingly surrender my baby at the doctor's seducing reassurances of safety. I knew that doctors weren't always right, but I never expected the calculated manipulations or the tactics used to trick parents into compliance. They weasel their way into our kind, sweet natures, beguiling us into obedience, taking advantage of innocence, lack of confidence, and fear.

Because how many new moms feel completely secure in their new role? We are full of doubts and lacking sleep. We are often without makeup and wearing casual clothes. No, most of us do not go to these early appointments with our game face on, because if we knew it was a game, we wouldn't be there in the first place. Maybe if we wore our business suits and brought our lawyers, maybe then, they wouldn't dick around with us.

I thought bringing a baby into this world might require a dusting off of the home economics skills. In an ideal world, I already had the perfect skills to be a good mom. But with the outside influences trying to break down my family, I needed new skills, skills I didn't have. I didn't need book smarts, I needed street smarts. I needed survival skills, and powerful muscles to stand strong and upright in the presence of forces trying to bowl me over. I never expected that becoming a mom would make me a warrior, fighting for my children's lives. I just thought it made me a mom, a mom that could trust a doctor.

At school, I learned obedience and a wavering confidence that depended on grades and a teacher's judgment of me. I was taught to look outside myself for the answers. Good girls like me didn't question authority or talk back in defiance. Rebellion for the sake of rebellion didn't make sense. I was a strong student, building a reputation rather than a life.

Being trained for obedience messed me up at the doctor's office. I put doctors on pedestals, valuing the higher education, and I looked to them for answers. Not one for confrontations, I acquiesced to the orders. I asked lots of questions, but I didn't ask if I had a choice in this matter, because it certainly wasn't presented to me that way. I wasn't thinking about God's laws at the time, only some faulty traditions put in place by man, and obedience to the human hierarchy seemed to have been brainwashed into me.

In reflection, I remember that mistakes of obedience have perpetrated some of the most brutal crimes throughout history. Historical pasts reveal obvious displays of times when following orders were clearly the wrong decision. But in the mass hysteria of the time period, it wasn't obvious to everyone, not as obvious as it looks in hindsight. We need to think for ourselves, when following orders is not even an acceptable defense in our criminal system.

As a child, I believed obedience was a form of integrity. Now, it is clear that obedience led to my downfall. I forgot to remember that I am not a child anymore, and I have no obligations to obey. I look at this situation with new eyes, not the naïve little girl with eyes looking up at another human ready to comply with willing obedience. This time, I look past the human man standing taller than me, all the way up to the heavens. What would God's perspective be on all of this?

I promised Him back when He saved my daughter, that I would not make that same mistake a second time. I promised that I would not fall back asleep to be led astray, that I would stay awake and protect my baby, protect life, protect God's gift to me. The accepted protocols are hurting kids, and I am not going to sit by being the good girl while they continue to make my baby girl the ultimate victim. My eyes are open now, and they are not going to steal her under my watch.

So, I said, "No!" and I created enemies, simply by changing my mind. I defied traditions and customs we had always done without question. I trusted less and questioned more and spoke my mind regardless of consequence. I went from being a good girl to a gentle rebel, following an inner guidance I felt as though directly from God.

Even in church, I had been trained to obey. But when I look to God, it is not obedience that is the virtue; it is having the strength to do what is right, no matter the cost. I know that He isn't asking me to listen or obey anyone but myself. I already know His answers. Now, I just need the strength to fight for them, because the right way is not always the popular way.

I once put my trust in the wrong place because I didn't yet understand a deep faith, a genuine personal relationship with God. I knew a set of rules and the places of heaven and hell. I thought I was being good simply for believing and behaving. I learned to fear, and I learned to obey. And if I ever messed up, I learned that my conscious would punish me with guilt. I studied religion the same way I studied my other subjects — memorization. I believed in God because I wanted Him to be real and not because I actually felt His presence. Faith was an abstract concept I didn't fully comprehend because I had not yet experienced the connection.

But that is all before the reaction, before I knew the experience of deep faith. When I stopped believing that He might exist, to truly knowing that He does. When the only place to turn is to the heavens and prayers are answered by Him. I lost some faith in man, but gained leaps of faith in Christ. Rather than my boss, I feel He is my friend.

CHAPTER 32
THE HOMEOPATHIC BLESSING

I grab the mysterious option from my medicine closet, offering up the homeopathic remedy I have on hand. I own a whole bunch of them even though I am still afraid to use them. I feel scared while I wait for God's medicine to work. Within hours, a transformation occurs; a tiny miracle awakens my Bella from the sickly stupor that had overtaken her body. She is on her way to recovery in record time, with the precision of the remedy working beautifully in restoring her health. In homeopathy, like cures like, and it works!

I get so excited about my new experiences that I want to share them in the world of conversation. But with a foreign word in a stubborn land, I hear "Homeo what?" The teacher in me begins to explain when my words get brushed aside in declaration, "Oh, that herbal stuff," as though he already knows the details. Homeopathic medicines and herbal supplements are not the same thing. I try to clarify the common confusion, but he isn't interested in hearing that. He is already walking away.

As for me, I keep walking towards my new found old technique of healing. As I learn and as I experience, I am intrigued. I am amazed. The remedies are inexpensive, and they are as back to basics as the earth. It is my kind of medicine, and I appreciate a solution that digs deeper than the surface symptoms. Thank you, God!

Then, I make that first appointment with a new homeopathic M.D. We tried the other one once before, but I just wasn't ready. Now I am ready. I think I understand.

I expect him to examine my daughter in the half ass way I am used to pediatricians looking past her. He takes the time to look at her instead, making a real connection. He is actually interested in her, and not all those gadgets to poke and prod her with. I feel a bit confused — in a good way. He is shattering expectations from my training, from my allopathic model where I expect doctors to behave a certain way, and then he just doesn't. Because my experiences with pediatricians have been so bad, that is a really good thing.

He isn't interested in examining my girl with the familiar tools. She is not "female, typical child, age 3." She is my Bella, my little girl, made differently, and the "standard of care" doesn't fit. Instead of pushing her away like some pediatricians, he connects. He is a homeopathic M.D. and one-size-fits-all is not his specialty. He is interested in the differences to create custom made help. He connects by being a genuine, compassionate human being interested in all the qualities that make Bella special. And that makes him extra special in my eyes.

But, can he help make my daughter better, can he restore her wellness? He makes no false promises like the other doctors; he only says he will try his best. His genuine honesty is a breath of fresh air and shows worth far more than worthless promises. Someone trying his best is really the best anyone can hope for. I think my baby is finally in the right hands, good smart hands full of integrity.

When I ask questions, he takes no offense. He answers me in a calm, mild mannered voice, without any derogatory comments or insults to my intelligence. His answers make a lot of sense, and he doesn't treat me like I am not smart enough to understand. I am smart enough to understand, or I wouldn't have such complicated questions in the first place. Yes, I have put lots of thought into these questions, with a mind that is always working, always thinking, and this is the first person I meet who might actually know some real answers.

He has an Ivy League education, a medical degree of prestige, and yet he flaunts none of it. He doesn't pretend to be perfect. When he offers advice, he doesn't force me to take it. He doesn't demand my obedience. He doesn't demand anything. He is a wise, modest adviser. He's not threatening. He is not intimidating. He just IS — brilliant. I think he is the smartest doctor I have ever met, yet one of the most unassumingly humble.

His biology knowledge is way above mine, but he allows me to join him as an equal in an intelligent, respectful conversation. He doesn't disregard the parent's input like the familiar pediatricians. My input is imperative to him. Good thing, because I am the one who knows Bella the best. I am the one who spends my days and nights in vigil. I am the one who has been watching her since the day she was born, and no one knows her life history better than I do. I pay attention to the details, and now they finally matter to someone besides me.

He wants to know Bella, seeing her with eyes that care. He wants to know everything that makes her unique. The details will help him decide the course of treatment. I have been treated so poorly up until now, that I can't believe he is letting me speak and actually listening. He takes handwritten notes; he pays attention to every word, asking questions to learn the specifics, not passing over a thing.

We are finally in the presence of a caring doctor who is paying attention, a caring doctor who listens to me, a caring doctor who wants to know the little details and quirks, a caring doctor who wants to know the very things that make my girl different, rather than categorizing her and fitting into some uncomfortable mold. Wow, what a relief.

He practices medicine, homeopathic medicine, and he has a beautiful wood apothecary cabinet where he stores all his vials. Maybe I need to rethink my thoughts about medicine. Maybe I just need some new remedy choices with real historical safety records. Around the world, homeopathy is the second used healing medicine, while what Americans think of as conventional medicine is the fourth used medicine. Even Prince Charles speaks highly of the benefits of homeopathy. Homeopathic medicine isn't outdated. It is time tested, and they work, without harm.

I am so grateful. I think this man is near perfect. He is kind, he has manners, he listens, he genuinely seems to care, and he is a great doctor. I am so appreciative that I want to keep complementing him, praising him, loving him with gratitude, hoping he doesn't see it as false flattery. But after the time we've had so far, meeting this doctor has been the biggest blessing.

He is a ray of light that brings hope into our world, a beautiful soul working in a profession I have grown to dislike. But I like *him* so much, maybe I'll change my mind. I know not all doctors are bad. I also know that most doctors aren't this good. He is one of the best, and we have just been lucky enough to meet him.

He may be out of network, but he is still part of healthcare, here in America. I found something different, I found someone different, and it is the exact kind of different that I admire. Life would be so much easier with more people like him in the world, but he is his own original, a once in a lifetime, a one in a trillion kind of man. He is far rarer than those vaccine reactions I plan to tell him about. With him, I get to talk about all those lingering vaccine effects that no one else wants to hear about.

I lost all respect for a man called doc, and then the next man called doc, and a few more called doc. Finally, I find someone who is awake, someone who recognizes the existence of vaccine damage, someone who helps, and he is also called doc. He is different. He is special, and I love him for it. If he makes me cry, it is not because of frustrations, it is because I feel safe enough to feel. I was finally led to exactly the right place, a safe haven in an old Victorian building, in a new world of healthcare, where good things from the past are still working great.

CHAPTER 33

THE ALLERGIST

B ella is on the uphill climb, doing much better, with fevers breaking quicker or actually acquiring a real cold with a running nose rather than a running fever. I thank that man, that wonderful man working as a homeopathic doctor, looking up to him with the deepest respect and admiration.

His efforts help snap my daughter out of her constant fever cycles, giving her a childhood back, because all my baby ever wanted to do was be with other people and play with other kids. He made her life better where no one had succeeded before, or genuinely cared enough to make an effort. He touched our lives with his goodness and wisdom, bringing sunny days back into our world. Some doctors earn not only respect, but a place in my heart. He is the way it should be everywhere.

With his thoughtful honesty, the homeopathic doctor admits Bella has some lingering effects he hasn't figured out yet. Our search continues, looking beyond his care, in search of solutions for the problems that remain.

My daughter's skin is full of blemishes. Little pimples dot her upper lip and the sides of her nose. I try to read the message written across her face. What are her symptoms trying to tell me? I don't believe a four year old body is asking for acne medications and antibiotic creams, even though that is what one medical professional suggests we should use. The symptoms are not looking to be masked, they are crying out for healing. I think my little girl is showing signs of allergies.

We take one step back when we climb the stairs to the allergist's office. This is the first time Bella will be seeing an allergist. As I walk up to the entrance door, I see that our doctor has both an M.D. and a Ph.D. after her name. Once again, impressed by credentials, I feel like maybe we are in intelligent hands. She must be really well trained...

The unfinished personal questionnaire is still in my lap as the allergist enters the exam room. She offers to help complete it together and then offers up her judgments of my parenting choices. Nothing I say pleases her, and she makes no efforts to understand when she doesn't agree. There is no yelling or emotional rise in volume, just a steady stream of disapproval through her comments and tsk sounds. The appointment is already one big argument, because she doesn't like the way I answer her questionnaire.

The real conversation starts with a direct question that asks what I think Bella might be allergic to. I proceed to explain the instances when the ingestion of certain foods brings immediate red, blotchy patches around Bella's lips and cheeks, while pimples get worse.

As I explain the pasta meal that caused this first reaction, the doctor interjects a question, "Does Bella have an Epipen?"

I answer, "No."

The allergist follows with a firm reply, "She does now."

Bella also had the same kind of reaction to orange flavored toothpaste, so I brought the tube with me and hand it to the allergist. The doctor scrutinizes the tube, squints to read the small print, and then, frustratingly hands it back to me as she asks me to read the ingredients. I think she forgot her glasses, but there are no ingredients listed on the toothpaste's label. I can only assume they were discarded with the box it came in, but she grows impatient when I can't find any ingredients.

The doctor doesn't like the looks of this unfamiliar toothpaste and has me explain why I am using natural toothpaste without any fluoride. We knew about fluoride long before we knew about vaccines, but my explanation doesn't matter to her anyway. She disregards my statement and proceeds to say, "Well, if she is not getting any fluoride in her drinking water, you need to be getting her fluoride for her teeth." This is said in a tone conveying a direct order to me, although I don't see how our lack of fluoride use is even relevant to the allergist, unless of course, Bella is allergic to it.

Next, I try to explain all the health problems we have been working on fixing since the vaccine reaction. At the mention of "vaccine reaction," the doctor loudly huffs at me, in immature fashion. I just don't understand people's insensitive reactions when I tell them this truth, but the doctor's behavior is a strangely familiar response.

She could thank us for the business, because if it wasn't for those damn vaccines, we probably wouldn't be here. Without any further questions on the topic, her loud huff ceases that part of the conversation as she carries her irate tone swiftly into the next question. "Who's her primary care doctor?"

I tell the allergist that we had some behavioral reactions, two of the times after eating homemade chicken soup. To which she replies, "We do not believe food allergies cause behavior problems."

When she said "we," I'm not sure if she was referring to her practice or some allergy medical group in general. Our first pediatrician often recited guidelines, following along because he was part of the club. Maybe allergists have a club of their own. Well, I do believe that food allergies can cause behavior problems, and I am not the only parent to notice.

The doctor repeatedly tells me that it wasn't my chicken soup, so I explain how I made it, using a boxed organic, gluten free chicken broth as the base. That is all she needs to hear. My soup wasn't actually homemade at all. She tells me that I had "used a processed food and added water to it." Not exactly, but I still considered it to be homemade when I included all the fresh chicken, fresh vegetables, and rice.

Even the most holistic parents I know use cans and broths sometimes. Not everyone soaks their own beans or brews their own soup bases. No one is perfect. I tell the doctor that I suspect MSG, but she says we "can't allergy test things like MSG, just foods," and then she adds rice to the list to be tested.

I have to admit that I was getting worried about this appointment before today. I started worrying if the allergens they test are in any sort of preservatives, like the vaccines. Are they like drugs? Are they dangerous in some non-obvious way? So, I start asking the doctor these types of questions. "What exactly is the scratch test? Can you explain it to me? Can I see the package inserts and the package they come in? Are there any preservatives?"

My questions seem to have pissed her off. She is not doing a good job hiding her disdain, with her facial expressions and the tones in her voice. She isn't trying to hide her disapproval or her annoyances. No, she is very open about her judgments.

Instead of responding to any of my questions, she retorts back, "They're all FDA approved and safe." In my head, I hear that worried laugh, because this is the doctor talking. Some FDA approved products get recalled, and some have court cases for harmful damages. Instead of answering my questions, she suggests I blindly trust the government. My questions seem so simple that I don't understand why she won't answer any of them for me. Maybe she doesn't know the answers. Or — what is hiding in those inserts that she won't let me see them?

I reiterate that I would like to see how the scratch material comes packaged, and I want to read the package inserts. She denies my request, arrogantly telling me that I will not be able to understand them. I would "need to have a Ph.D. in biochemistry," she tells me.

I wonder if *her* Ph.D. is in biochemistry. I don't know why she assumes that I don't have a Ph.D. in biochemistry, because I am certain that she did not ask me about my education status when I walked in. I wasn't asked to bring my college diploma when I scheduled the appointment.

I pause in silence, still in shock that I have just heard these words aloud. This was a direct statement, pointed squarely at my intelligence. I play the thought back through my head... she won't let me see a package insert, because she thinks I am not smart enough to understand it. That is a pretty harsh judgment to make upon someone she doesn't even know. I wonder if this is how most doctors feel about their patients — that we are all just too stupid to understand, so they save us the trouble and withhold helpful, important information.

I stopped paying attention the moment she insulted me, as I stand, stupefied, in shock at her rudeness. I can't see a package insert for my own daughter, because I am not smart enough to read it anyway, said from a woman who has no idea about my intelligence level or academic history. I feel the need to call her on her comment before she continues to lose her words to the wall she has just built up between us. I tell her that her remarks were condescending and unfair, but she offers no apologies or comments to reword for clarification. No, she meant what she said, exactly as she said it.

As a matter of argument, maybe I do have a degree in biochemistry; but it is all irrelevant anyway. It is just another tactic the "experts" use to make parents feel inferior, to have us bow down in obedience to their pretend educational authority. What does having a degree have to do with someone's intelligence level or ability to read? Brains come with us at birth; we don't earn them along-side degrees. We just need to remember to use them, along with some common sense. My master's degree doesn't exactly make me stupid, but it just might make me a bit less trained.

The doctor proclaims that, "Unless you can pinpoint what Bella is allergic to, I won't know what to test for." If I knew exactly what was causing the problems, what would I need an allergist or testing for? I guess, to prove that I am right?

The doctor is clearly not interested in showing me the scratch test, so she huffs, "Fine then, we'll do the RAST test, but that is not really accurate at all. It has a 10% error rate, both positive and negative, and the scratch test is really the gold standard." I do not know the accuracy of her direct quote. A brief pause fills her voice with anger, "If you don't want to do the test, why are you here then?"

"To learn about the test, to learn about options, but you won't let me," I reply with my own frustration. "Look at her face," I plead as I place my hand under Bella's chin and turn her head to face the doctor. "Clearly there is something going on," I continue.

But the doctor hadn't even looked at her yet to notice. Until I turn Bella face to face with this woman, she hadn't really seen her.

Actually, now I don't know why I am here. I want information that the doctor won't give me, and I already need to know what my daughter is allergic to or she won't know what allergens to test. If I knew that, well then, I wouldn't need to be here. What do I need an allergist for if I need to produce the answers in order for her to do her job?

My tongue is numb from my constant bites in attempt to hold back my words. I offer to check with Bella's other doctors for their suggestions. My strong negative vibes want to repel her as visions of running out the door fill my head. I use some wind to blow her off. "No, I do not want to do the testing today." As she makes her way out of the room, the allergist tells me she needs to write a prescription for the EpiPen and the blood work; then the nurse will be right in.

CHAPTER 34

TRICKED

A few minutes later, the nurse walks in with a scratch test kit. Words flow as she explains what she is "going to do." Her demeanor is much more comforting and pleasant, but I am overtaken by surprise, and I can't control my pounding heart. As the nurse is talking, I blurt out, "Wait! I didn't agree to any of this!"

I had just said, "No." Does the doctor not understand that simple word? Or is she so evil as to tell the nurse to go in like normal to pressure me into the testing? The allergist wants me to believe she understands all those big technical words she claims I won't be able to understand, but then she can't even seem to remember the meaning of the word NO.

I want to walk away, no package inserts, no treatment. I want to say, "We're done here," but the part of me that is trained is waiting for the doctor to conclude the appointment. I imagine my arms scooping up my daughter and running out of the room, but I am afraid that behavior might precipitate a call to someone other than my husband. I want to reaffirm, "No," but my mind thinks she is playing a very serious game with me, and I just might lose. Parents are supposed to have parental rights, but sometimes they get stolen.

The nurse shows me the scratching tool and its package insert, but not the one for the allergens. She tells me that she puts the testing liquid on the surface of the skin, nothing gets inside. I know that skin can absorb topical substances, but she makes the procedure sound gentle. I did not intend to agree, but I don't even know what just happened here. The nurse manages to calm my insides enough to alleviate some of my conflicted thoughts, even though my anger at the doctor is boiling.

As nervous chills shake my insides, a part of me still believes that my daughter needs allergy testing. And we are here already. I am not sure how to read the doctor's behavior. Her arrogant snobbery really annoys me, but I find her frightening at the same time. Is she a real threat or just obnoxiously arrogant and condescending? As I comply out of fear, I wonder... Is it okay to give a little so they don't take a lot?

I quickly learn that it is called a scratch test for a reason. The multi prong tool looks like a board of white plastic with a handle on one side and rows of scratchy tips on the other. Each tip is dipped into separate compartments of allergens, testing many potential triggers at the same time, one allergen per prong to be scratched like a chalkboard eraser across my daughter's back, roughly. The nurse told me it was a surface procedure, but she abrades the skin hard, to get the allergens good and in, making rows of tiny marks of irritation from the scratching itself. It seems to hurt. Bella is crying, and I feel awful. I let her down again.

The liquid compartments are separated on the idea of an ice cube tray, one prong to dip in one tiny pool of liquid, that way many allergens can be tested at once. It is this liquid that concerns me, liquid that gets used over and over, patient to patient, with repeated dipping. Seems to me they might have some thimerosal in there to preserve them. Lots of over-the-counter liquid products that look like water have thimerosal in them, products like some nose drops and some eye products. Maybe the package inserts confirm my suspicion which is precisely why she wouldn't let me see them.

My little girl and I are left alone to wait in the exam room, while the clock ticks in anticipation of the results to appear on my baby's skin. My daughter is clutched in my lap, both of us crying together in embrace. She is in pain, and I am feeling tricked once again, upset with myself for letting this happen.

Except for the positive control, the results are all negative. The doctor returns, bringing with her the prescription for the EpiPen and the blood work order. I notice that "orange" is on the blood work when it had just come back negative on the scratch test. If scratch testing is the "gold standard" in her opinion, why would she test it with blood too? If the doctor can't explain the difference between skin testing and blood testing for allergies, then why should I be expected to know? I mean she doesn't even think I am smart enough to read the inserts.

The blood work request is written on a prescription pad. She says that I can add to the blood testing list if I find the ingredient on the chicken stock. She says I can just "write it in." She just told me that I could alter the prescription, which I'm pretty sure is illegal. Of course I would never comply. Following her orders could get me arrested, but then again, I should just trust her, right? Because she has that Ph.D. Well, it is certainly not in law.

As a last thought, I blurt out, "Oh, can we test for bees? My mother is allergic to bees, so I've always worried that Bella might be allergic too."

She firmly says, "No. This is not a fishing expedition. There is no hereditary connection."

See, I think this is a fishing expedition until we figure it all out. But needing her permission and receiving a "No," means I have to go fishing with someone else.

She says I need to meet up again "at my convenience, in about a month. Blood work takes about three weeks to come back." We end there. I already know that one appointment is one too many.

CHAPTER 35

THE SEARCH FOR ANSWERS

I know Bella has allergies, so we went to the allergist. But I didn't know what to test for, so the allergist couldn't help. That is good, because I am glad to never have to see her again. Parting ways, it is for the best sometimes, freeing us up for someone better.

I search for answers. I search for solutions. I search within myself. How did I get here? I am on a fishing expedition after all, and I don't even know how to cast a line.

I am still worried about those potential long term effects, and I am still worried about those obvious allergies screaming across Bella's face. Knowing that there are some lingering effects that we still have not overcome, the homeopath refers us to another great man who happens to be working as a doctor.

As I widen my search, I cover more ground, traveling an hour to see the specialist. There are no pleasantries on the initial appointment as the doctor walks in, leaving his bedside manner behind. He asks gruffly, "What do you expect me to do for you?"

I don't know. Help us. What can you do for me? For my daughter? I don't know all of the options. Tell me. And he does help, so I overlook the first impression.

When he keeps talking, he quickly warms up his softer side hiding beneath the tough exterior, and it turns out he's not so bad. He is a wise man, a mixture of old school values meeting the challenges of modern health problems. He is not love at first sight, but with a little polishing and polite conversation, he shines, earning every bit of respect. He is definitely one of the good guys, but I couldn't have seen that on a quick first look.

He tells me that by using Avogadro's number there are .003 parts per million of mercury, enough for 200 atoms of mercury per nerve cell — and that is only in one shot. That sounds like science to me. It just might be that bio-chemistry the allergist mentioned. He tells me to look back to traditional time tested 3000 year old practices, mentioning Bible sections like Leviticus and Genesis, and leprosy. Hey, leprosy? I didn't think that was around anymore… I keep learning new things every day.

He is quite capable of allergy testing, and I value his second opinion much higher. After a few visits, we leave with pages of blood work results. My baby is riddled with allergies and sensitivities that seem to indicate a leaky gut. Eating has just taken on a whole new meaning.

We venture out to try another doctor, an M.D. specializing in natural medicines. Bella is the patient, but he hands me a tiny white envelope with a remedy for me. I didn't ask for it, he didn't charge for it, he just gave it, sensing maybe I need something too. Then, he tells me about his favorite book about God, and it isn't the Bible. He teaches me the difference between whole milk, skim milk, and all the percentages in between. He explains the difference between raw milk and pasteurized milk, while introducing me to the name Weston Price. Even though watching television seems like the appropriate activity for feverish times, I leave with a tiny criticism about the TV. I don't quite understand the problem.

Sometimes I learn the most from the waiting rooms as I look around in the extra minutes to occupy the time. I pick up a magazine entitled *Healthy Children*, put out by the American Academy of Pediatrics. I see a red bar across the bottom of the front cover that declares it is "sponsored by Merck." I pause to think about that connection very carefully.

In another waiting room I peruse through the library of books and come across one about sensory processing disorder, and realize I have just hit a match. Issues with clothing stand out the most prominently: hollering in agony over a seem in the sock, pulling the shoes off in an urgent fashion as though a panic attack were manifesting inside, pants always "choking my belly," Bella yells to me. Sensitive to the feel of clothing, fabric in a bunch or crooked socks is more than a tiny inconvenience.

Sometimes, pharmaceutical salesmen show up unannounced, pushing themselves to the front of the line, barging ahead of all the patients who are waiting patiently in the waiting room, peddling products the doctors will push onto us.

There are so many things I am learning, all on my own, simply by paying attention. The *why us* question starts to resurface as I pick up tidbits of information everywhere. They don't call this science, but I have been quite the researcher, amassing a whole bunch of information, little clues revealing themselves with each stone overturned.

In the exploration for answers, I may have uncovered some hidden risk factors. Birth control pills may have disrupted my body balance for each and every year I took them and continue right on through a lifetime. Those antibiotics they said were necessary may have been a silent culprit creating a breeding ground of weakness lurking in my gut, having a devastating effect on the good flora that I needed to pass along to my daughter. I thought I had a decent diet, but maybe it was a bit on the SAD side, when I included white breads and sugars, further disrupting the delicate microscopic balance of internal life forms living among us. Maybe there was even some systemic yeast in my system. But who knows? These aren't the things that most pediatricians concern themselves with when they prescribe vaccines for all.

I had a big eczema rash on my left leg during my pregnancy with Bella, fully exposed in my summertime shorts. Not one person said, "You have eczema there. Maybe you should think twice before vaccinating your baby." This was when I was going to the doctors for frequent pregnancy appointments. No one should have missed this autoimmune symptom, except for me, the layman.

With medical mistakes being a leading cause of death, maybe none of the medical interventions are as safe as we all think, including those unnecessary ultrasounds. And we start the shots so young, when they might not even work because of the mother's antibodies still floating around; so young, when the blood–brain barrier isn't fully developed, and toxins can pass freely into the brain. Maybe we take the risks for nothing, merely practicing coming to pediatric appointments for the benefits of the doctor.

I may have fortuitously forgotten to give the fever reducing medications in combination with vaccination. I had no idea what glutathione was at the time, but it just never made sense to me to give meds to a kid who wasn't sick. If the vaccines are harmless, as they say, why would my child need medicine to combat them? One mistake turns out to be a good mistake. Maybe "right" isn't "right" after all.

CHAPTER 36

THE AUTISM COMMUNITY

My panic reignites along with my guilt as I watch a bubble beneath Bella's eye begin to grow. We have seen so much improvement in both behavior and health, but this giant chalazion seems like a setback. Eye doctors recommend hot compresses several times a day along with squeezing to try to get it to pop, squeezing right along the skin of the delicate eyeball. If that doesn't work, we have the option of minor surgery, to pop it with a knife.

What is still going wrong in that body of hers? With the little pimples that will not budge, and now this eye bulge, I feel stuck. I face constant visual reminders that leave me feeling horrible for all this harm to my little girl. I just want my baby to stop having to pay for my mistakes. Every health problem until the day she dies could very well be my fault now that I had damaged the very way her body is supposed to work.

In my search for answers, I finally hit a wall. I reach out when my daughter's eye looks like it will bust, when my heart feels like it will burst from the ever expanding guilt festering inside. This is when I start reaching out for help, sending feelers out online to holistic groups, when I start to swing tentacles far beyond the doctors into the world of parents, parents who might understand all of this, parents who understand vaccine injury. I hear some parents are even finding solutions to problems inflicted by vaccines.

I put aside my own judgments, my own assumptions about *those people*, and I reach out. I have long felt a silent connection, so I make an actual connection, contacting my local Generation Rescue angel. I am reaching out for help from the autism community.

This puzzle is not yet complete, and I have a feeling they might know more about the health complications than I do. I don't think our vaccine side effects cross over into autism territory, so I am not sure if we belong. I just know that I am still a mess for making a mess of my daughter's immune system, and I plead for advice.

Will they help me with our problems without any autism diagnosis to speak of? Do I belong, or are they too busy? Is there any room for someone who maybe doesn't quite fit? I believed that families dealing with autism would be so exhausted from their own lives that they simply wouldn't have the time or the energy for someone not directly affected by autism. How could they possibly find the time for somebody who maybe didn't have it quite so hard? They need help themselves, how could they possibly have anything left in them to help me? I made assumptions about their busy lives, with some gratitude that felt maybe I had it a little bit better.

I do not pretend to know all the hardships, but I know this, many families of autism had stories that started out just like mine, and now we face our various endings. Our journeys are lovingly intertwined in silent connection to one another, in a world that feels so isolating.

Fortunately, I receive a response from a woman freely offering up helpful information and her time in a genuine and caring way. There is a fire in her belly too, but she's not taking it out on me. I feel a connection, like we know each other, even though we don't. Vaccine injury is one of their own. It doesn't matter if I have a label or a diagnosis. It doesn't matter if we are a fit. It only matters that we need help, and the rescue angel is there for me.

She invites me to an autism support group meeting. I'm not even sure I know autism, and I am being included like I belong. We are strangers meeting for the first time; the only connection is our angel, with wings that welcome us all.

The energy in the room is not negativity, but a mixture of hopeful optimism combined with weary sadness and strength. Three hours pass as we discuss our experiences, sharing stories and ideas. I went with notebook in hand, ready to capture words of wisdom from the air. I feel so burnt out that I don't think I can be much support to anybody, so I am surprised that others find my experiences helpful. Sharing my personal experiences, that is the kind of support I can offer, and it is good enough.

The mother seated directly across from me is grappling with the death of her partner right alongside her son's autism diagnosis. Her spirit still seems hopeful and optimistic among her world of whirlwinds, as she struggles with grief, parenting alone, and now an autism diagnosis. She reveals that her son had multiple ear infections and now has tubes in his ears. She came for information too and asks me lots of questions about my experiences with homeopathy.

Another mom is a single mother with no father in sight. He seems like he may have been one of those parents who don't take the autism diagnosis so well and splits, leaving the mom to find the impossible strength to carry his weight too. As the sole provider, the mom has to work, but her son's daycare has just kicked him out; they can't handle the behaviors of his autism. She has no idea where to put her son so that she can continue working. And the father, he is off living the easy way out, in his own world where just hearing the word autism is too difficult for his selfish ears.

This mother mentions that her son lost words after his twelve month shots, then regressed more after his fifteen month shots, and then she totally lost him with the eighteen month shots. I don't understand why the doctor would keep giving vaccines when the boy was having such strong side effects to them. But I didn't understand the behavior when the pediatricians were pressuring me to give Bella more shots either.

Her lifetime of heartache will be so much greater now that she won't have to deal with a few acute "vaccine preventable" illnesses. She'll pay for the rest of her life for the doctor's mistakes, while the doctor's life gets to go on exactly the same. "Life's not fair," I hear, but these weren't the kind of situations I imagined when I learned this saying.

CHAPTER 37

MAKING CONNECTIONS

I don't see families with autism as separate from me. I see myself as getting a lucky break from a more difficult fate. I see all
those parents that vaccinated their children with no perceived ill
effects as the luckiest of us all. By no means do I relate any of these
fates to our intelligence or our scientific backgrounds. One group
is not better or worse than the other. We are all the same, unknowingly playing Russian roulette with our children's lives, and some
of us are just turning out luckier than others.

It upsets me when people toss aside their stories, a part of our
human story, tearing their pages out of the books of humanity,
when they are all of us, living different consequences for the exact
same actions. And I am one of them, with a daughter, the victim
of vaccine injury, with harm that just manifested in a different way.
Many of us make the same mistakes; some of us just happen to
have harsher consequences. We are all so close to different outcomes, yet so far from another reality.

Vaccine injured families are not like the pro-vaccine machine
would have people believe with their derogatory condemnations
and labels, as they name call us insults like "a bunch of anti-vax
foolish parents practicing junk science and creating fear." Nope,

we were all once just like everyone else, before we became the outcasts, the scapegoats of medical blunders gone wrong.

They don't even prove themselves right, they just disparage and ridicule the people bringing the messages they don't like, the messages that disagree with their agenda. But we're just people, everyday people with injured children, and for some reasons, they just don't want you to know the truth about us. Good thing smart people know to look deeper than the surface gossip.

An opinion from the outside will never match the experience of what is inside, of what the eyes have seen and the heart has felt. No one knows what it is like to have a vaccine injured child until you are holding your very own.

Why do I believe that vaccines are linked to autism? Because I believe all those parents just like me, telling their stories. I believe them, because I know. I faced the haters and the naysayers. I've been denied or blamed for my genetics. I've argued with pediatricians about reality, our reality. I know, because I've been there. Even though my baby's reactions expressed differently than autism, I believe, because I believe the parents. I believe the mothers and the fathers who boldly share their stories even though they face retaliation. I believe, because I am one of them. They know without a doubt it was the shots that got their kids sick, just as I know without a doubt that it was the shots that harmed mine.

They injected change into their children, the same way I injected change into mine. Is there a way out of this mess we injected ourselves into? Well, I heard for some, there is. I also heard doctors deny that "cures" exist too, which seems remarkably cruel to me, to deny the very life they harmed, and then deny that there is anything we can do to fix the damage. But some doctors are just living in denial, while we are living injected by change.

Some doctors will say that they are just better at diagnosing autism nowadays. I don't know if they mean to insult the doctors of the past, but that philosophy sounds like pure arrogance to me. In one breath, they will say that they really don't know what is causing autism, while in the next breath, vehemently claim that there is no link between vaccines and autism. I think this is because they do know — that there IS. But denial is so much easier than admitting wrongdoing.

How much proof and heartache is tucked away along with thousands of journals, photographs, and home videos sitting on shelves and inside closets around the country? How much proof is tucked inside a medical file that expands along with the ever growing vaccine schedule? The evidence is there; it is as simple as before and after, night and day. Some took their children in for well visits, never to see a well-child again.

Sometimes, all that proof doesn't seem to count, because those words, those hurtful words have already done their secondary damage, denying the truth that exists, denying life. With those words of denial, the propaganda experts have magically turned our lives into a sham and magically created an entire population of people that believe *them*, not us, not us parents who have real children with stories to tell.

It feels like magic, because I can't believe it. I can't believe this can happen, and I can't believe that people believe *them*, before us. Because of course, mainstream media are the people to trust in this world, with public relation campaigns years in the making and all that fake science they tell us exists. Meanwhile, they continue to bash our lives, pounding our stories into oblivion.

There are all sorts of denial. Some people take the direct approach, look us squarely in the eyes, and tell us that this is not caused by vaccines, even though they have no clue, because they just weren't there. Sometimes, they try repetition, repeating the same fallacies over and over again, until it sounds like it might even be true. Sometimes, they take the sneaky approach and brainwash our children when we aren't there to protect them, sneaking ideas into their books or into their heads. Sometimes, they even bring vaccines into school, so they can sneak them into little bodies.

Sometimes, they take the loud approach on television, making claims that the vaccine link to autism has been "debunked," while they toss around some poor guy's reputation. Sometimes, they take the threatening approach, calling for loss of licenses for doctors who are brave enough to speak out. Sometimes, they threaten anyone who speaks out, because their side is the only side that gets to control the microphones.

Others take the passive aggressive approach, trolling the internet from obscurity, writing hate speeches and threats to all those "anti-vaxers" out there in some alternate reality. Sometimes, we are called "science deniers." Whatever they say, they usually make up some sort of insulting names for those of us with vaccine injured children. If we are bold enough to confront them directly, they may even say, "I don't mean you anti-vaxers, I mean the other ones, the other anti-vaxers who haven't hurt their own kids yet. They're the ones we are after."

This group of anti-vaxers is already lost to them. It is not going to be those of us with injured children who will ever voluntarily change our minds back into the cycle that hurt our families. They want to capture the ones who maybe just heard about people like us, without the deepest of sincere convictions, that this is wrong. They want to trick the ones who still might waiver in faith just enough to be persuaded. Those are the people they are trying to sway back to the points they are concocting.

Maybe if they can produce a fear greater than the shots themselves, they will have more takers. Or maybe they'll just go lobby for some more laws to make them mandatory for everyone, which would blanket encompass all the children already hurt by vaccines, along with the siblings we were hoping to protect from the same fate.

They'll have the public believe that the children who need medical waivers will get them if they are one of those special children who can't be vaccinated, but when families need those waivers to be written by doctors who can't seem to see damage and believe in vaccination to the death — well then, "Good luck with that," because pediatricians seem more than happy to waive that right for us. And they seem more than happy to keep on injuring our children, if we, the parents, weren't in the way, stopping them.

The pro-vaccination agenda comes from various angles, trying nearly every approach possible to deny the existence of an autism–vaccine link. The only approach they haven't seemed to try — connection. Aha. Maybe if they could connect vaccines and autism, maybe that could get them to stop ignoring a whole group of very important people in our society. Maybe if they could connect vaccines to injury, they could see a problem so much bigger than their broken link to autism. Maybe they could see the links all over the place. Maybe they could connect, person to person, link by link, building a chain of connection. Maybe we could all stop being in denial of the obvious. We don't deny our children, and we don't deny each other.

CHAPTER 38

VACCINE REFUSAL

The doctor is a kind face when I no longer believed I could find such a face on a pediatrician, when I believed that the words *good* and *pediatrician* used together described someone who didn't exist. The new practice exposes us to new experiences with a pediatrician who listens, shows thoughtful care, and treats my family the way I expected to be treated before my expectations were lowered.

When I decline the offer of fluoride, she looks at me a bit blank eyed, but she doesn't say anything. She is a non-confrontational doctor, so I feel no need to explain. I thought to ask, "Why would I give my child a known carcinogen?" but I don't. Then, I could have spouted off the history of fluoride and why it is even in our water in the first place. But I don't. I like this doctor, and I am not burning this bridge. I keep my heated words to myself, especially since fluoride has not been the fighting issue for me. I'm tired anyway, tired of trying to explain myself all the time. So I let differences remain differences with no feelings whatsoever of the need to justify my position — at least not on this day. I need to save this conversation for the dentist.

She is aware of our vaccine reaction and promises never to pressure us about vaccines, even though I think she may believe in them. I think she also believes me. Finally, we have found some acceptance in the conventional pediatric world. I am more than grateful. There are no more tactics of intimidation, just respectful communication and kindness. She is conventional in her treatments, but she doesn't feel threatened by our use of homeopathic medicine or second opinions. We may not see eye to eye, but we try to understand each other.

As I am packing our stuff together to leave, the doctor comes back into the room with a vaccine decline form. I was hoping to make a clean break from an easy appointment, a well visit without the typical pressure to get a shot or two or five. But the doctor is back with the ever present nuisance that just will not go away. I suppose it might if I would just sign the damn thing, but then it might come back to haunt me.

I don't agree with the wording, the implications, and the technique. I know who wrote it, and it is not written in my best interest. This seems like a contract, and we don't have a meeting of the minds. The form makes no mention of the risks of vaccines or the consequences of the vaccines themselves hurting children. It is a one sided agreement meant to make one side look bad, and that side just happens to be vaccine refusing parents like me. The form passes the buck of responsibility right onto the parents, even if it is a defective vaccine or vaccine shedding that actually gets someone sick. It is just another too good to be true deal, FOR THEM. All I see is more scapegoating blame that always ends up right back in. a parent's lap.

We don't get to add our own explanation why we might choose otherwise. I cannot sign this, based on principle, that if all the risks of not vaccinating are listed, then I want all the real risks of vaccinating listed too. Why don't they just staple the package inserts right on there too and stop giving me those darn CDC sheets.

They only want my signature acknowledging their biased perspective as though it were truth. I bet they had lawyers represent their interests when writing it, but I am here alone, without any legal experts to back me up. Well, if I don't want to sign this one, I can always sign the other one, the one authorizing a vaccine. That is choosing between what we have to offer, and I choose none of the above.

I know this technique from the television. I've seen it in interviews. "How does it feel to knowingly put others at risk with your decision not to vaccinate?" I heard a question to this effect, spoken by someone claiming to be a journalist. But there is bias in the very question itself, so when I hear that question with my mind, I think… I don't understand the question.

Then, I hear, "Just answer the question." And I think I don't know how, because I don't agree with the implication. I don't agree with anything they have just said. It is a leading question, leading conscientious objectors into a trap. I wait for a lawyer to yell, "I object!" But they are usually not invited to represent the interviewee.

One look at that piece of paper and it slashes through my layers, making my eyes start to water as though I am cutting an onion. The touch of the paper makes me quiver and shake. This form isn't really between me and the doctor. She didn't write it, but it still feels like a setup, a trap. I will not sign it, and I cannot sign it because my hands are shaking so uncontrollably they cannot hold a pen. And I let those frustrations vocalize, the frustrations with the other pediatricians and the authors of this form, even though I am here with her.

She mentions the sheets they give to their patients, referring to the handouts that are given for each vaccine. I explain to her that the numbers of reactions on those sheets are inaccurate because doctors don't report the injuries. She assures me that her practice reports them. Then, I spout off every child I know who has had a vaccine reaction, and the only one reported was mine, not because of a helpful doctor, but because of me.

The doctor explains that the practice needs the form for audits, to show why some kids do not have all the recommended shots. I don't need to argue with this pediatrician. She is not forcing anything on me. She is just trying to prove that she offers vaccines.

That is the part of her job that I get, because another doctor told me, "Big brother is watching." Doctors have rules to follow to stay in business, rules that include record keeping requirements that I completely understand from my days in the office. It is the criminal coercions that I don't understand, and I have seen none of that here. I think she is one of the good guys. But nothing ever seems easy at the pediatrician's office, even when the doctor is trying to be as easygoing as possible.

We talk, and she understands. This "scary" form isn't good from a parent's perspective, so the office decides to write a "kinder" version of their own. How cool is that! Sometimes people can offer us another choice, if we ask. The worst they can say is, "No."

CHAPTER 39

THE HOLISTIC MOMS CONFERENCE

A conference is coming up, a yearly convention calling for my attendance. It is in New Jersey this year, and I can't imagine taking that drive all by myself. I try to lose the thought even though I have this nagging feeling I am meant to be there, a nagging feeling that won't go away.

Then, I receive a genuine invitation too good to refuse. A local mom offers me a ride and a place to stay so I can accompany her to the conference. With excited thanks, I accept.

We are heading out, two friendly moms on a long drive with plenty of time to talk. Four hours of highway straight into New Jersey leads us to more than our location. We learn a lot about each other on the journey, further developing our friendship through shared stories. I admire the qualities that I believe make her different from me: her independence, her confidence, and her ability to take risks.

My throat gets sore telling it, but she is the first person outside my immediate family who actually wants to hear our whole story. She doesn't tell me to stop talking about my daughter. She wants to know more, not less, and I feel grateful that she really wants to listen. Releasing the weight off my chest with her ears, she is there for me, a captive audience in a moving vehicle, but she would be there for me anyway. She is a new friend, walking towards me after old friends walked away.

We arrive a day early, with plenty of time to rest and enjoy the scenery. It is beautiful here. Gorgeous nature fills in a scenic backdrop. Beautiful views of rolling hills are truly breathtaking on this crisp autumn day. Good thing I didn't judge the whole state based upon some bad jokes and a short trek across the Jersey Turnpike.

We are staying at the home of my friend's mom. Her residence is a convenient 30 minute drive to the convention center. She is a lovely woman who welcomes me into her home for a place to stay and treats me to some much needed kindness and generosity. New Jersey is beautiful, and Mom is too.

The conference takes place on a Saturday at a large hotel that overlooks mountains colored with the changing leaves of fall. Maybe they are giant hills, but they seem vast like mountains to this newcomer who is pleasantly surprised by the visions. Outdoors is beautiful, but we walk inside to the vast foyer where we are directed to the wing of the main floor dedicated to our group.

The space is filled with vendors and free samples on table after table. There are even separate rooms for childcare, more vendors, and a silent auction. There is plenty of baby stuff, but my growing children no longer qualify for that label even though they will always be my babies.

We have time to peruse the offerings before the start of the presentations. There are so many freebies, so much to grab. Just before we move on, into the lecture hall, I swipe my free goody bag along with coupons, samples, and magazines. This is like a buffet of freebies, and it is still hard for me to resist a good magazine.

Chairs fill the lecture room, and we arrive early enough to select seats near the front. We are waiting to hear Barbara Loe Fisher speak. The day's keynote speaker is the founder of the National Vaccine Information Center, an organization she started after her own young son was vaccine injured in the early 1980s. For me, she is the main attraction of the weekend. She may not be a huge celebrity in movie land, but here in the vaccine world, she is one of the greatest role models I know. She is the reason I am here, right alongside my friend who drove us.

The room quiets down for the customary greetings, the welcome bit of pleasantries, before Miss Barbara herself steps to the podium in the front of the crowded room. The lights dim, music begins. I recognize the song lyrics of Bryan Adams. The mood is instantly transformed when images of children begin playing across a large video screen next to the podium.

These are the memories and photographs of children who have suffered, suffered after their routine vaccinations, making life look nothing like the expected. The music plays on as child after child flashes upon the screen. There are boys like her own son, girls like my own daughter.

The film is painful to watch. It ignites trauma, but I force myself to pay attention to respect and honor every life in my view. These are our children, a nation full of children negatively affected by vaccines.

The photographs are so upsetting to me that hysterical sobbing erupts, an emotional outpouring far too loud for the quiet room, far too noticeable for my reserved inclinations. But I can't control myself. The face of each child hits home as though he is my own. I have a hard time with this.

I have a hard time looking at healthy babies now too, because I imagine the piercing of that soft smelling skin, the harming of precious life with every poke that injects risks, risks I worry about for them. Trauma does that to a person.

Some tissues are placed into my hand by a kind soul sitting to my left. "Thank you," might have been too difficult to utter, but I think she knows. Sometimes no words are necessary.

Every cell shakes with uncomfortable familiarity, shakes with the pain of uneasy heartache, shakes with the urge to bolt straight out of the room. I lived this already. It is too real; it is too painful. But these aren't my children, and I force myself to stay out of respect. I need to be there for them, for me, for my baby, with a reserve of inner strength that anchors me to my seat. With my presence, I can honor the stories and lives of these children. It is my duty. It is the duty of us all. Vaccine injured children need to be seen, heard, and felt. Because when it is hard to watch, it is even harder to live.

Mere minutes of attention with focus is all those images are asking, while the parents of these children were involuntary signed up for a lifetime of this very same pain, yet deeper: deeper in love, deeper in connection, deeper than anyone from the outside dares to go. At the end of the film, Barbara states that every child in the video suffered vaccine injury or died after being vaccinated. Yet, we already knew this. No words are necessary to an audience full of tears. There is no denial here. Touched by fellow mothers who know the truth, this is all too real.

There have been billions of dollars paid out in vaccine injury compensation. That is a lot of money considering that most vaccine injured families don't get any money at all. Yet people still pretend that the injured don't exist. All those suffering children, all those suffering parents are denied their lives, denied their existence. Well, the people here today don't deny. "They get it," I am told, by Ms. Fisher herself.

Life can be so sad. I never anticipated having such an emotional outpouring within the first hour of my day. My daughter, my baby, my tears — love spills out of me like song lyrics of deep meaning. *(Everything I Do) I Do It for You* — with love and kindness and only the best of intentions. Thank you, Bryan Adams, for your eloquent words that could be the mantra of mothers everywhere and not just those with me today. As parents, we know we'll never give up fighting for our children.

Then, just as quickly as I became saddened, I am uplifted, uplifted by the words to end the presentation, words that indicate Barbara's son has been with us, working behind the camera. He's okay! He's alive, standing there, looking outwardly healthy. Seeing him represents hope, hope for all vaccine injured children, and hope for my daughter. I am rooting for these kids.

The sight of him makes my heart jump with excitement. My arms want to wrap his body in a big bear hug. Once again, I need to restrain myself to the seat, so I don't rush him with my enthusiasm. What a surprise! I am so happy to see him. He is only slightly younger than me, but I love him, love him like a mom.

———⊱⊰———

Bumping into her, crossing paths at the restroom door, I am hoping for the opportunity to speak with Ms. Fisher, but not this way. I want the chance to share some words, but I know a bathroom is not a place for that, so I mind my manners and leave her in peace. I show respect for her privacy with the restraint of my words. I'm holding back a lot today, even while letting go of so much.

It is in the hallway where I meet up with her son, Chris. I am still feeling joy in discovering that he is okay. Not knowing what became of his life after vaccine injury to seeing him standing before me, appearing to be in health. I know that most people seem fine, on the outside, and because I don't know him, I don't pry my way into the inside with questions about chronic conditions or pains. I am just so happy to see him, beautiful and alive.

After conversation with him, he brings me over and introduces me to his mother. Overwhelmed with emotions, I know the feelings more than the words, but I tell her that she has been such a wonderful role model for mothers. I tell her that I am so happy that her son is okay. I tell her about my daughter, who is vaccine injured too, explaining that as soon as we get our kids better, no one believes they were ever even sick. I tell her about the skin problems and the allergies. I tell her that I can only imagine how difficult her fight must have been, because it is so difficult, even now.

At one point, cameras obtrusively join our conversation. Putting my hand out in gesture to get away, I do not want to be on television. This private person doesn't want fifteen minutes of fame. I just want to talk, mother to mother, in private, a validation of my experiences with someone I admire who truly understands what it is like to be a mother of a vaccine injured child.

With tears in both our eyes, we connect. After all these years of fighting, she is strong, but not hardened. Her heart is not numb to the feelings, emotions, and pain. It still hurts, because our kids are real.

I give Barbara and her son some hugs, before we take a picture. Speaking to Barbara and her son, Chris, is an extremely emotional moment for me, as years of built up feelings, frustration, and sadness come flooding out of my soul.

As I am leaving for the day, I stop for one last goodbye, leaving behind some good sentiment and some last words, "You made my whole weekend." But to me, it is really so much more.

Then, a crisis hits, starting immediately upon our departure from the convention. I think it is a healing crisis, a catharsis. First the experiences with my new friend and then, meeting a special role model and her lovely son. It is a lot to absorb in two short days. It is a lot to release in two short days. There are a lot of positive and negative energies being swapped around.

People were nice to me. People could understand. Burdens were lifting from my soul. But it doesn't happen eloquently, like visions of weights flying away. Instead, I am heaped over the toilet in her mom's bathroom, dry heaving and vomiting. My head is dizzy and my nose is clogged. I'm not sick; I am letting go, and sometimes we face turbulence and blockages along the way. For me, wonders were worked that day, a day I shall never forget.

Thank you my friend for bringing me here. I needed this. As we say goodbye for our journey home, I leave behind some painful baggage. But I still take a mountain home with me.

CHAPTER 40

OFF TO SCHOOL

As much as I reiterate my concerns about the playground to the principal, she has no understanding of our past, and writes me off as just another nervous parent. I can tell by the eyes that roll and her words that shift into another topic. We look out the glass together towards the playground, and she assures me that things will be alright. I hope so, but I have heard that line before, and it no longer brings me comfort.

I hope Bella's physical abilities have improved enough to enjoy the days without an accident. Her movements still lack some fluidity and at times she is clumsy, nothing overtly noticeable to someone not looking for it. But she is my child, and I can see. I worry about recess, with fears of the jungle gym, with climbing bars and stairs to the slide where impatient children push slower kids out of the way. I can't help but worry about the indoor stairs she will need to walk up and down several times each day as she makes her way about the school.

This is a major milestone, and she is crossing this path at precisely the right time. I drop Bella off every morning and wait in the cafeteria with her until her classroom is called. This is a small private school, and I try to reassure myself that she will be fine in her class size of thirteen.

My relationship with my daughter reminds of those best friend necklaces, the ones with a heart broken in two, each friend wearing half of the other's heart. My daughter has become my BFF and now here she is, heading off to school, taking half my heart with her. It is hard to say goodbye each day, even though I make it look easy. With a big smile on my face and a great big hug, I let my baby cross the bridge into a classroom. I am so happy in love with her that I want her to enjoy the day, but it is still hard to separate from the little girl who was nearly taken from me twice.

This growing girl is still my baby, and I am fearful to let her go. For years, I have stood under every attempt to climb with open arms ready to catch my daughter in a fall, and here she is, in a new school and in a new play yard, her first time alone without a net. I've joined her into the system. I hope she is ready.

Memories flood my brain on the drive to school. Traffic forces me to slow down, and the thoughts start pouring in. Private Christian school is about 15 minutes away, but needs 45 minutes of driving leeway with the flow of the rush hour commute.

I use these long drives full of traffic to reflect, while the kids giggle in the backseat. Traffic forces a pause with lots of stopping and starting on a busy highway full of commuters. I like this drive, more than I anticipated. I'm not trapped very long, but just long enough to pause in reflection as we sit waiting. I write notes as soon as we hit the parking lot. I write in the afternoon while I wait for dismissal.

I think about traffic situations that connect to my vaccine dilemmas.

I think about denial, denying the existence. It makes me think about cars that want to cut into the traffic. If we make eye contact, if we acknowledge each other, we get favorable responses. But if we refuse to see, if we pretend we don't see, we don't let them in. We don't let them into the traffic or into our hearts. I wish people would look at our children, and stop turning away, stop believing they don't exist.

I think of peer pressure. When a driver honks the horn and makes the front driver nervous, pressuring him into a move he is not comfortable making. Then, the front driver crashes in an accident, while the honking driver keeps driving by, moving on with his life as though his actions weren't relevant. The car that beeped, who bullied, is off on his way as though nothing ever happened. Because nothing did happen — to him. Kind of like the pressures from doctors who move on without us, while we parents pick up the pieces from the crash they left behind.

I look into the other cars, and I see so many people on their cell phones. Some don't even seem to look up at the road at all. I wonder if some of those people are more worried about germs than the statistic that car accidents are a leading cause of death for the entire age range of childhood. Most of us drive every day, but some of us focus more on germs and gadgets than the roadway.

I look forward to seeing some of the moms each morning. It feels like a community here, and that is a nice feeling. There is a great group of families that come here, not wealthy families, but families making other sacrifices to afford the religious educational experience. Tiny houses seem to be a common way to afford the tuition. Some have only two bedrooms, just like us. I value the religious education too, but we are here for a different reason. Their private rules are more accommodating to Bella's personal needs, and I value that even more.

The holidays seem to bring up the questions. At Christmastime, Bella's questions have nothing to do with Santa. As soft Christmas music plays in the background of our morning drive, she gently asks,

"Why did you get me shots?" She is old enough to understand that her experiences are connected to her shots in some way. She has started school, but the doctors' appointments have not ended. Some weeks she goes twice afterschool, some weeks it is Saturday morning.

Her immune system is still compromised as her recovery from illness takes longer than other kids. She accumulates a whole week of absences each time she gets sick. Hiding in her records are little hints of history, allergies on her medical form and sick days adding up on her attendance. Otherwise, her injury is now imperceptible to others, except for those little pimples lining her nose and lips. She doesn't stand out as being injured; she stands out for being special.

She seems to have the power to read my mind, because I am always thinking the same exact question. The thought brings water to my eyes, but my response today is simple, "Because we didn't know better. I'm so sorry."

All that schooling, and we didn't know better. All that schooling, and the doctors didn't know better either. All that schooling, and we are still listening for the directions from some higher human authority. That is not smart at all.

One day, Bella brings home a can that is labeled an "Obey Jar." Oh no, they are training my daughter to be obedient, just like I was at her age. It is plastered with a quote, "All wrongdoing is sin," a simple sentence that is quite complicated.

What exactly constitutes wrongdoing? It would have seemed obvious before, when I thought the meaning of wrongdoing was so simple. Yet, living is showing me that there is no black and white, only muddy tones of grey where good and bad aren't so cut and dry. I am having some difficulty determining right from wrong when my daughter got hurt doing what we thought was right. I was a sinner, when I didn't even realize my crime. If I can't neatly classify what constitutes wrongdoing, I'm not sure kids can either. I like my daughter incorporating God into the school day, but sometimes I do disagree with the lessons.

At Easter, Bella jumps into the car and shows me her new poem, "The Jelly Bean Prayer." The neatly typed words are enclosed in a small plastic sandwich baggie along with some jelly beans, each a different color to symbolically represent the importance of Jesus and Easter. She looks up at me with her hazel eyes, smiles a crooked smile, and lets out her comment. "Mommy, I think you should eat the black one. The black one stands for sin and sins mean bad choices, and you made a bad choice when you got me shots."

She reaches to hand me the black jelly bean. Thanks, my love. I'll take the black one, and she gives it to me, right alongside that second helping of guilt. I might have cried, but instead I chuckle at her comment and say, "I think you're right. Maybe I should eat the black one."

It is a sweet gesture with thoughtfulness from a child. There are no black ones left for Dad. She gave the only one to me, and I took it all for myself. Then she adds, "But I forgive you. You're the best mom ever." With the innocence of a child, she eats her way right into my heart.

CHAPTER 41
WARPED FOUNDATIONS OF EDUCATION

One morning, after the school drop off, I decide to explore a new market nearby. There are no aisles jammed with people. Instead, they are full of unique grocery items that I do not know. I walk up and down every aisle, curious to the selections of products they carry, looking to discover a new item or brand I can't get back at the usual market. I'm losing myself in the moment, savoring the quiet peace of having a full grocery store all to myself.

Perusing the international food section, I come across a clear glass jar of pacaya in brine. At first, I walk right by, but feel the urge to back up my cart to take a second look. I pull out my notebook, certain I have to jot down this new discovery and look it up later. What is this exactly? I have no idea, so I take a closer look trying to figure it out, but I can only guess.

I use my eyes to look through the glass. I see something that looks like textured fat cooked spaghetti, similar in coloring, all held together in a clump by some thicker chunk at the top. Maybe it looks like baby octopus legs with little circles down each strand reminding me of the suction parts of an octopus. I think it might be some sort of vegetable.

I am not curious enough to buy it, but curious enough to take that second look. Because I have no teacher, no one to explain this item to me, I fear it a little. I am certainly not going to try it without knowing what it is. What does it taste like? How do I use it? Does it need to be cooked? What exactly would I be eating? Where does it come from? I have lots of questions about my new discovery that has probably been around for a long time.

Then, it occurs to me, this is the exact same feeling I had when we ventured into the world of homeopathic medicine and alternative therapies. It felt just like this at first. Foreign. Unfamiliar. Scary. Had I grown up in a family where I was exposed and had familiarity, there wouldn't have been hesitancy, but to start with me, I took steps slowly. We were the guinea pigs for my newly acquired knowledge, even though people across the globe have successfully treated themselves and have been enjoying the benefits for years.

Trust required a leap of faith into unfamiliar territory where the old time tested methods of healing live. Homeopathic medicine lives here, in this category of off limits healing, because it has been put down too, with comparisons to placebos and the sugar pill effect.

I had been trained to beware. The foundations of my education were built long ago, back when I was a small child reading storybooks and watching cartoons. Then in my progression through schools, I learned about the noble profession of doctors, got my own shots, and was taught the "miracles of modern medicine." It is hard to get that kind of programming out of my head. Maybe I didn't need it all to leave, but certainly some alterations were in order.

I knew no one to lead the way, and my training bred caution and keep out signs, trained that anything off of the mainstream path was bad. So I didn't pay much attention to the other stuff, because I was trained that this was the kind of information that was off limits or the fodder of the foolish or came from conspiracy nuts. And they labeled all the people on the other side of their own with awful names like this, so I wouldn't be tempted to join them.

Why ruin a perfectly good reputation intermingling with "those people?" Why would I want to voluntarily join a group of outcasts and get called horrible names too? The mainstream path needed to be more tempting to stay more popular, so they ridiculed the other side into oblivion, so that the rest of us would stay away and not go looking for information among the "quacks."

I never used any of those names myself or looked down on people who lived life differently than me, but there was still that block in my head that made alternatives feel off limits, scary somehow, maybe even wrong — so I practiced avoidance. Completely unintentional on my part, but that sounds something like prejudice. Maybe they were teaching us prejudice when they taught us that their side was better and the other side was filled with losers.

When I had been tricked, I suddenly realized that the *other* side had information that could have helped us all along. The ways of my training let me down, crashing on the road of abandonment. Survival forces me to break down those walls separating the allopathic from everything else. What is right for me may not be what is most popular, but it just might fit perfectly. It might be exactly the path I am looking for.

But sometimes they are not very welcoming to the newcomers, because after all, they have been picked on for years, and it is hard to distinguish the nice guys from the meanies who have been insulting them. Some judge harshly for being a "stupid sheep," but there are many that welcome with open arms and hands ready to help, thankful that you finally see some of their light.

I cross over, without commitment, sort of straddling two different worlds, wondering if I can live in harmony among both. The people are still enduring all the harsh name calling and judgment, because the mainstream side is too scared to listen to what they have to say, too scared to identify with those who get teased, too scared at what they might find. And now that I am a part of them, I get it too.

I think they started teaching prejudice back to the country's warped foundations in the early 1900s, when some rich families decided that their methods should be the only methods taught in the medical schools, pushing all others aside, which eventually progressed to all this ridicule. Many alternative healing modalities along with homeopathic medicine have longer histories and safety records than the allopathic medicine model we have become familiar with, but we still fear what we do not know, and they would like to keep it that way.

Time passes, and generations grow up under a new paradigm, but it is the only one we know, it is the only one we are taught, and we believe it must be right, because it is science after all. At least that is what they tell us.

We build on these warped foundations through the years, picking and choosing the knowledge that already fits our schema of the world and discarding all the rest, adding more stones to our already warped foundations, making the structures of our reasoning skills a bit off balance, skewing our beliefs, perceptions, and molding our opinions into the ones we firmly hold as right. The habits and understandings that ingrained the deepest mold and shape our beliefs about everything else that we encounter. But we learned and we believed and now this is who we are.

Teachers are everywhere, teaching us the wrong things. The wrong education can lead us down the wrong roads — getting us lost on a path of mistakes. That is in addition to all the conflicts of interests embedded into people who are teaching us wrong on purpose. Beware of your teachers. Make sure you are not memorizing the slogans of the enemy.

When I started to question my intelligence, I began to question everyone else's too. What if everything we thought we knew turned out to be wrong? What if we were intentionally misled by everything we had been trained to believe? What if the people in charge have it all wrong and are enforcing rules on us based on their own ignorance, or worse, their greed? It *IS* possible to learn too much if we are being steered in the wrong direction. What do we really know if we don't know the truth?

It is hard to undo all that learning, all those habits, all that tradition. It is hard to accept that a lifetime of learning can lead us in the wrong direction. It is hard to accept the truth, that some of our beliefs were just founded on lies. It is hard to break through the stubborn wall of a closed mind. And it is hard to start all over again.

CHAPTER 42
TRAUMA

At fifteen months, tragedy strikes and by kindergarten, the injury is imperceptible to others. Bella makes friends and quickly rises to the top of her class. The world should feel wonderful. I have my daughter alive and well, and I thought that was really all that mattered.

I am so proud of her, proud of her strength and endurance, so proud of her achievements and her efforts. I am so proud of *her*, but still so upset with myself. The pain, guilt, and trauma still lives within me. My baby had become successful at overcoming her past, but I had not.

I thought I would have a break when my little girl took off for school. I wasn't expecting a break down. As I worked to put her life back together, mine had fallen apart. I hadn't noticed because I was too busy fighting, studying, taking care of people, and trying to right past mistakes. While I was busy fighting for someone else, I had a purpose, a mission, a determination that I would get my baby well. Now here, with my own life to deal with, I seem to lack all of these qualities. I have no fight left for me.

I never gave up on my daughter, but I made no such commitment to myself. She is better. I am worse. Without her by my side,

I don't need to be strong, and I melt into a mushy mess of vulnerability. I see crystal clear flashes of horrible moments imprinted in my mind's eye. I am broken and injured too. I just didn't notice, until I slow down and relive the pain.

Flipping through photo albums reveals more than snapshots. The months of sadness have far fewer pictures. My depression is directly linked to my daughter's suffering and my inability to forgive myself for letting it happen. I think it might also be linked to a bunch of other people who are mean to me about it all. I never expected life to be easy, but I didn't expect others to make things harder for me on purpose.

There is a breaking point, when I am forced to me knees, forced into reflection, forced to take a break. I have been on the stressed out offensive and defensive for years, until one day, I collapse on the field, unexpectedly falling to the kitchen floor, not fainted, not unconscious, not hurt. My legs just sort of folded up on me and brought me down.

Making no immediate efforts to get up, I lie and rest, right on the cold hard floor. I feel no rush to move, pausing life right there, in that moment, for stillness. I notice a kitchen that needs some attention: the tiny splash marks on the wall from a drink that didn't get completely wiped up, the gritty feel of linoleum that needs sweeping, the dust bunnies accumulating under the dishwasher, the little details of a home that get neglected when worries become much greater than having a spotless house. My home needs some attention, and so do I.

A deep sadness has been growing within me, with a life of its own overcoming my own life. An empty feeling takes root, choking out all of the energy I have left. Day after day, I fall apart more and more. I thought I had already gotten through the bad stuff. I thought I had already lived my darkest hours. But dark days resurface, and grow blacker. My heart starts slowing down. I am falling, slipping into another side, crossing over into the darkness and pits of despair.

The doctor seems to know that something is wrong even though my words try to hint otherwise. She starts prying a little here and a little there and before I know it, I'm in tears. My emotions are still as raw as the days the reaction first cut through our lives, when it sliced off and stole a piece of my heart.

I am able to tell her how doctors let me down. How these people I had always believed were good and there to help had let me down. They abandoned us in our time of need and denied that vaccines could hurt children. I am still in tears as I recount my daughter's reaction. I'm still hurting inside. My caring doctor comforts me, and she confirms to me that vaccines can sometimes harm people. She says she is sorry for what we have had to endure.

Then she compliments me, saying she trusts that because my daughter is in my hands, she will be okay. As I cry, she asks me, "Who do you let this out to? Who do you talk to about these things?"

I silently shrug, because I am not sure who I talk to anymore, except my husband. My basic needs are met, but emotionally, I feel abandoned, isolated, and alone. Other people just don't seem to understand, or they feel I should have moved on by now. Either way, I'm not welcome to talk about it, so my husband gets it all, even if he doesn't want it.

My doctor tells me that when something this traumatic, this painful, this life changing happens, I could break down in tears over it for my whole lifetime, when touched by the right triggers. She also said she thinks I feel things on a very deep level, more deeply than most. This is her professional opinion, but I think she seems right.

I can't believe that just when I thought I had done so much healing, all this old pain resurfaces, pain I thought I had dealt with. But it turns out, I hadn't done anything with the pain yet, I just pushed it inside, and let it fester there. While I was working on healing my baby, I never realized the depths of my own wounds.

I cry every day, and yet the tears haven't wiped away the pain. Suffering continues. Heavy consequences rolled over what was once my life, destroying everything in its path, leaving behind a hostile and unfamiliar world I really don't know how to live in. I feel a shadow of my former self, completely recognizable on the outside, but the inside is full of truths and turmoil pushing their way out.

The pain is the silent resident that moved into our home, the silent resident that reminds me of hurt, the ghost of the past that moved in to haunt, the elephant in the room that brings heaviness, adding weight upon my shoulders and branding my heart. No, he's never moving out. He is a part of me, crushing my life into new form. He is here to stay, the unwelcome guest who invites me to change.

CHAPTER 43
PHILADELPHIA

By the time we take our first family vacation, my daughter is nearing kindergarten graduation. We hadn't planned a vacation earlier in life, because it was too risky to play the odds, putting up so much money for a good chance we might lose to sickness. Sickness struck far too often to plan ahead.

I was all set to go on a trip of my own, to attend a medical conference on healing ailments like vaccine injuries, taught by doctors who had boldly broken away from their peers with the courage to think differently and take a stand where it matters to me. Because my daughter matters so much to me, my mind wanted to go and see what more I could learn, but something within felt otherwise.

In the process of booking my plans, I just couldn't get myself to click the last computer strokes to finalize the details for my on-line reservations. My body was demanding some rest, while my mind might have difficulty processing new information added to the current overload. What I really needed was a vacation, and so did the rest of my family.

We used the money set aside for the healing seminar, kept the location the same, and drove just over six hours to arrive at our first family vacation. Here we are, in Philadelphia, where some fun might be good for everyone.

Our internet special is a beautiful hotel downtown. As a complementary Mother's Day surprise, the hotel upgrades my stay to enjoy concierge privileges at the lounge. I am immensely grateful for this gift, a special treat for a stressed out mom in desperate need of some pampering. Riding the elevator to the top of the building to enjoy fresh fruits and chocolate covered strawberries each night is the type of luxurious perk I have never experienced.

The hotel is located within walking distance to nearly everywhere we plan to go. My husband and I take turns pushing the double stroller. The streets are neatly lined up in grid like fashion and lead us to the numerous attractions the city has to offer: museums, gardens, historical sites, the zoo, duck boats, and a bus tour. When driving is necessary, the traffic isn't nearly as bad as the traffic we know in our area.

A trip into the city is not really where I expected to take little kids, but they are in wonder at all the hustle and bustle that abounds. Pushing elevator buttons and a view from the top is enough excitement to win them over. It is a good week, free from illness and bad weather, and no emergency trips to the children's hospital. My kids, ages 5 and 3, label Philadelphia "the best trip ever." Of course, it has been their only trip ever, but the special hotel in a special city will spoil them for years to come.

The city is full of symbolism for American freedoms and ideals. History lives here: Independence Hall, the Betsy Ross house and flag, Benjamin Franklin immortalized in statue. The Liberty Bell is a symbol of freedom too, even though people are not allowed to touch it.

On foot, we walk right up to a sign declaring land as the original site of the Homeopathic Medical College of Pennsylvania, founded on April 8, 1848. I knew this place had great historical significance to our country, but here it has some historical significance to the study of medicine as well.

I pause in gratitude for the discovery of homeopathic medicine, with some sadness that the college is no longer here, just this sign. Homeopathic medicine, this wonderful, energetic medicine that helped my daughter was once unknown to me, but here in Philadelphia it has historical foundations and a sign commemorating its presence. Nearby, a store sells homeopathic healing remedies.

Sitting at the Hard Rock Café, my favorite place to eat in the city, I read an Elton John quote on the wall, words from his song *Philadelphia Freedom.* There is something inspiring about this city, and in this moment, I can feel that sentiment. As I enjoy my hamburger after a busy day, I feel casually relaxed, a freeing feeling from the stresses back home. My heart is filled with warmth for a place I never expected to visit.

I have been roaming around a city rich in the history of our founding ideals, but it isn't until our visit to the National Constitution Center when it connects with me deeply. As we sit in theater chairs to view a beautiful presentation, pictures of our idealized nation float across the screen, one image after another, reminding me of our country's greatness.

Flashing images ignite my heart. This is the America I learned about in school. This is the America that gave me big dreams and hope for a future full of unlimited potentials. This is the America I long for. This is the good footage, historical flashbacks that build pride, appreciation, and all the love.

Mixed feelings erupt as I focus intently on the beauty of the people and times in our nation's history. I remember that hope inside me, the promise of our great land, the American dream I believed in as a little girl. I feel that inner patriotism rise from within, my pride in this great nation. On a dry day, the images on the screens touch me in ways that spur tears to fall.

Then, disconnect arises, with an edgy feeling of discomfort, the cognitive dissonance when *what is* and *what should be* do not match. There is a great gap between the ideal and what is real, in a country not living up to the beliefs set forth in our foundations. Yes, there is the country I believe in, floating across the screen. But where is this country in real life? Did it ever exist, or has it changed so much that it is now unrecognizable?

What is happening to our country? Maybe it has always been happening, and I just didn't see it before. Maybe I was blinded by the ideal visions I picked up at school through those rose colored glasses. Maybe I was too naïve to see the dark side. As I watch her deteriorate quickly with my open eyes, the downward shift seems to be spiraling out of control, a land barely teetering on our foundations. Surely this wasn't the image the forefathers pictured for this great nation. The symbolism for our independence and freedoms are everywhere, but instead, we create a system of dependence, and far too many rules.

I want to live in the America shown to me across the screens, but somehow, I ended up in a different reality within the same country. The country I live in lets children face harm, because it protects the interests of manufacturers before the interests of its people. I see a country that writes laws alongside the businesses benefitting from those laws. I see crimes against humanity and conflicts of interest, a government bought, and freedoms stripped away. The America I know makes me sad, makes me disappointed, and makes me worry about survival. I don't feel safe or protected at all, and I certainly don't feel free.

I care for my country enough to examine her, faults and all, to see the truth, looking for weaknesses, room for improvements, and opportunities for growth. America needs its people loving her enough to examine mistakes and imperfections, and finding a will to change.

⊷┼┾

To me, Philadelphia is great. Brotherly love shows itself in many friendly faces willing to exchange cameras to capture photographic memories for each other, tourists here for a visit and locals sharing their favorite things to do. I'm not naturally a city person, but I feel comfortable here.

Philadelphia brings out the patriot in me. Maybe, I could move here one day — or maybe not, because in this city of freedom and independence, a man works threatening to steal it all, a man in power who stands in opposition to my dreams of complete healthcare freedom and parents' right to choose. Oh, he's not menacing like a real monster, he is just a doctor. But he believes himself to be an expert on vaccines because of course, he promotes them.

He is a threat to parents like me, to children like mine, to all of us really, because he doesn't seem to want us to have rights to decide medical treatments for ourselves. He only wants doctors like him to get to decide, doctors that have patents in vaccines. I think he would probably like to take away my homeopathic medicine and our supplements too, because well, I read his books.

Fear and feelings of threats — because of one man. But, I remember one other important detail to this great city. Philadelphia is home to Rocky Balboa, and here he is far more than a character in a movie. He is the David to the Goliath and symbolizes the heart of Philadelphia. The giant Rocky statue sits at the bottom of the steps to the Philadelphia Museum of Art.

I climbed those stairs like the thousands of tourists before me, holding back an exuberant jubilee with my reserved nature. The massive staircase to the entryway symbolizes the struggle, the climb, and the success of the underdog. Each step is a small victory, triumphant against the odds, overcoming each obstacle placed in his way on his journey to the top. Rocky, the hero, a boxer in a lengthy fight, reminds me that there is hope and possibility, that we can win, united for freedom, united for humanity, because divided we fall.

I am in another man's land here in Philadelphia. But it doesn't feel like his land, it feels like my land, with the history of homeopathy embedded into its foundation, Rocky to represent the powerful underdog of success, a glorious art museum, a legacy of great Americans, and a history of the fight for freedom. There is so much symbolism here that it is hard not to take notice. A favorite song of school children pops into my mind, *This Land is Your Land.* But that's just the title; the rest we know by heart. Thank you, Woody Guthrie, for the reminder.

CHAPTER 44

HEART TROUBLES

I am desperate and on her table. She has been my doctor for nearly twenty years, and this may be the first time she has seen me really sick. I am confused in her explanation because I am near collapse, not in physical pain, but a frail weakness that leaves me feeling like my whole body will just give up at any moment.

The doctor says something about my heart and my blood pressure, my pulse working in an opposite way to which it should be responding. She gives me two choices, calling my husband to take me to the emergency room, or calling an ambulance to drive me. When both options lead to the hospital, I know that is not a real choice. But I like this doctor. I may even trust her.

My doctor called in my arrival, and the hospital staff is waiting, ushering me in with a wheelchair, pushing me ahead of the waiting room line. They think I am having a heart attack. My heart is showing confusing patterns and not operating as they expect. My heart rate is dropping into the 30s; the blood pressure is very low. What is wrong with me?

Maybe there is nothing wrong with me as they ask me questions, considering the possibility that I am an Olympic athlete. I hear a slight chuckle in my head. My patience may have been stretched far beyond that which I thought possible. I have tackled the endurance test of caring for a chronically ill child. My skin has thickened under the insults pummeled my way, but an Olympic athlete, hardly, which leaves us all with no explanations.

As I lay there in the hospital bed, I am able to completely release from all the obligations of life. I expected to feel fear, but there is a sense of peace instead, and I let myself fall into the caring hands of the hospital staff. Life feels like it is slipping away, and I need someone to catch me.

I yearn for someone to hold me, to comfort me, to grasp my hand, to just be there in the moment for me, with me. Tears drip down my face, silent tears of loneliness that release in constant succession splattering down upon my gown. My husband is sitting in the room with me, worlds away, fulfilling his spouse obligation to physically be with me. I feel the sad disconnect as I watch him play games on his cell phone, and I can't believe I am feeling jealousy for a friggin phone, the other woman in the room who is getting all the love.

There are no explanations found in the lines scratched across the EKG. There are no explanations for the pulse that fades into nothingness. There are no medical explanations for any of my symptoms, but maybe the answer is right here, in this very room. They send me home, where I settle in to sleep away the next three days.

⇥⇤

Most marriages don't survive big bombshells that upend their lives with the devastating stresses of a sick child, a true test of a marriage that often results in failure. Maybe it is the additional stress that kills play or the tears that replace smiles. Maybe it is the obligations that tick away days until there is nothing left, nothing left to give or share. Maybe it is living with the frustrations of feeling helpless to change situations out of our control.

Maybe it is just growing apart when two people handle tragedy differently. Maybe he regrets in a different way, a way I don't understand, because he doesn't let me in, into his heart. I'm in there, but it feels like part of me got trapped on the outside, leaving me feeling disconnected and alone. Maybe he grieves silently, in a way he isn't sharing with me.

Some days, I want to throw heavy books at him from across the room. I want him to join me on the same page. I want him to learn alongside me, to read the same books so we can discuss them. I want to talk with him and dig into that mind that I no longer understand. I want to communicate at a depth that reaches the heart.

"What are you still crying for?" my husband asks. Then I cry some more.

He doesn't understand the pain that scars my heart and rips pages throughout my brain. The vaccine reaction didn't upend his whole world the way it did mine. My soul has been turned inside out, and I want him to recognize how much life has changed for me.

He spouts off vaccine facts in analytical manner. I, on the other hand, have changed completely. Sure, I can spout off all the same lists of facts and numbers and data, but I don't want to anymore. I'm sick of facts and figures; so many of them have lied to me. I am immersed in a tangible world, and I feel it; I feel it so deeply in a place where numbers and statistics just aren't invited.

I no longer want to fight or debate or analyze numbers. I have done enough of that on the pediatric battleground. I want to be lost in my emotions, my feelings, and I want to surround myself with things that I love. I am turning inward, being still, listening and open to signs, praying for answers. I am practicing faith. I don't want to fight anymore. I want to find peace.

I am changing. I want my husband to change too, but he is on an entirely different page in an entirely different book.

He tells me, "You changed."

And I yell back, "Of course I changed! How could you go through this experience and not change?" But I can't change him. I can only change myself.

We are married into one family, but we are still two separate people finding our way in the world, and sometimes we don't walk in the same direction. Our journeys may be lovingly intertwined, but they are still our own. There are parts of the trip we walk together and other parts we tackle by ourselves.

I thought we were that couple that would make it through anything. I thought that the realness of true love had a strength all its own to help carry two people together through this difficult world. Where I once felt certainty, I now feel doubt, but I would never consider our time together or our marriage a failure, even if forever doesn't last.

The great divide has gotten to us too, infiltrating my marriage, even though we are united on the same team. I am learning not to need him, while remembering that I still want him. I am learning independence, but I miss my best friend.

The cardiologist tells me that hearts can't be broken, but I disagree. Maybe it is not taught in medical school. Maybe he just doesn't have the science or the tools to explain it, but it happens. History shows the way. Maybe the answers are found in quantum physics or vibrational energy, because it is not something that is seen, it is something that is felt. The heart is much more than a pumping machine to keep blood flowing. It holds an inner wisdom that leads to the magical mystery of the soul.

My heart is aching, ailed with complete sadness, an overwhelming sense of the crooked world crushing me, the lack of love and support from others, and never fully forgiving myself for the damage to my daughter. There is nothing wrong with my heart, but I have internalized pain so deeply that I feel it with every beat.

CHAPTER 45

ON THE BACKS OF BABIES

My new world looks very different than the one I used to live in, yet we haven't moved. My fear has evolved from what is "out there" to fear of what is right here, within ourselves, within our own country. They have tightened their control over us all, and the squeeze feels a lot tighter when you have vulnerable children in your arms. We are becoming one of those "other" countries right under our noses, the kind of country they trained us to fear.

I cry. I cry so much for so many valid reasons. I thought our country was better than this. I have a sickening feeling living in a place where my values don't quite fit. I may be pretty old fashioned for this modern world, but I'm still more progressive than a return to history where barbaric sacrifices were normal or segregated classrooms were considered "separate but equal." I don't want to go back to the days when we were owned by Britain either, the time in our history before we fought for those freedoms we no longer hold so dear. Maybe we are not directly owned by another country anymore. Maybe corporations own us instead.

No, I don't want to go backwards to any of those places in time, even though it seems like my country might be heading that way.

For me, I only want that magical time machine to take me back to the days of bliss with some more magic to have the ignorance snapped right out of me, giving me that impossible opportunity to have said, "No." For me, that one little word would have been the best preventative healthcare of all.

Burdening the little lives with the ills of the world, we insist children be 100% vaccinated with every vaccine that ends up on the pediatric schedule, when our whole neighborhood of adults may never even step foot in a doctor's office. But why do we keep picking on the little kids and their parents, letting them shoulder the burden for the rest of the country?

Adults might be outraged at vaccine mandates for themselves, so instead, we snatch the easy prey. Babies. We annihilate newborn babies directly out of their mommies' bellies in a hospital setting where the most dangerous germs they decided our newborns would encounter is Hepatitis B. Hep B! What kind of *science* supports administering Hep B vaccines to every baby at birth as being beneficial for the newborn? It's not my science. I think it is sinister, right there in plain sight. And they are allowed to do this as the standard of care.

My mind sees the image of the mad scientist rolling his hands over each other, twirling his fingers, and laughing the diabolical laugh, devious in his plans yet disguised under the white cloak of goodness. Characters like fictional Dr. Jekyll and Mr. Hyde are alive and well, but we don't even recognize the true enemies because they mask themselves behind things we trust. I thought this was a battle against germs, but the enemy is much larger.

It's my baby, and it's my guilt, with her pain and her sacrifice. Just like a real soldier, she did her job for her country and then her country abandoned her and left her to suffer. Instead of welcoming our little soldiers, our heroes back from their civic duty, we chastise them, because unfortunately, vaccine injuries fall down on the wrong side of popularity.

The war against germs is being fought on the backs of our babies, drafted into a war under false pretenses, stealing little lives from unsuspecting parents tricked into compliance, unwittingly enlisting their babies with lies.

Our little soldiers are misled to believe they are fighting against germs, "protecting" society, when they are fighting a battle against themselves. With the shot of "protection" their bodies are injected with poisons that ravage their systems from the inside out. They can't simply shoot the invaders and be done with the war. The war battles on inside them, and shooting the invaders would be shooting themselves.

How do you get the invaders to leave when they have become a part of you? Not caught by the usual means, but snuck past the body's usual defenses, taking the route of injection to make their way in. The shots are a Trojan horse, disguised as a benevolent gift, welcomed through an unarmed gate, a soft spot on the chubby thighs. Once inside, they shock the system and work their havoc.

Seizures, convulsions, fevers, diarrhea, blood platelet disorders, encephalitis, inflammation, demyelination, immune dysfunction, diabetes, allergies, rashes… The body goes into overdrive employing every system it knows to rid itself of the enemy.

Some little bodies don't survive this fight. Other bodies suffer serious injuries, some that can be healed, while others remain permanent. But even with healing, there is always a scar, a permanent memory of the trauma held deep inside.

Other bodies don't fight so hard now. They let the intruders stay dormant, but they are always there, sleeper cells ready to turn on at some slight provocation down the road of life. Some bodies seem fine, but deep inside, the foreign matter chews away at the internal integrity of the system, compromising future integrity of the human structure.

I thought we were better than this. When is enough sacrifice enough sacrifice? The enemy is sending in their Trojan Horse, armed with weapons of mass destruction, tiny needles that look harmless but carry a powerful jab, and they are taking down an army of lives.

Where are the vigils, the candle lighting ceremonies, the memorials, the fundraisers? Too controversial to discuss, to talk about, to recognize, so we disregard people, real people who aren't controversial at all, just some accepted casualties of an accepted practice. When we raise awareness to vaccine injury, people get mad, angry at the suggestion, shooting down the message and the messenger. They don't dump buckets of ice on their heads for the cause.

This is a tragedy too, and at best, we have silence. We don't pause for a moment of silence in recognition of the poor souls pulled from the earth too soon. We don't thank the little children for their sacrifice to "protect the herd." We're just silent, at best.

At our worst, we are mean, lashing out at innocent people telling their stories, intimidating injured families into their own silence. Moms and dads crying behind closed doors, in private, without support. At our worst, we portray those crying, grieving parents as the enemy to science and public health, and we torment them some more, bringing them to the breaking point. Because the sacrifice of their child just wasn't enough pain, so we inflict more. At our worst, we are unbelievably awful.

I don't know any other illness that gets vilified in this way, vilified for getting sick, illnesses where the victims get no compassion, only denial or accusations, when "friends" de-friend for mere mentioning of a child's vaccine injury, even though they can't catch anything through a computer screen.

I am not a "poor fool, needing someone to blame," for my daughter's health problems, that are nothing more than a matter of "bad genes." Yes, that is a real insult, I guess from someone who has nothing to worry about the bad gene sort of thing, spoken with an air of cruelty from some bad genes of his own, an oblivious snobbery and complete lack of compassion. Yes, words can say a lot about a person, a person who just doesn't care about the fallen children lining the path, because "bad genes" must make hurting kids like mine okay. Well it is not okay to me, and it is not okay to the thousands of other parents in exactly my position.

How come "bad genes" means no compassion? How come different bad genes get compassion, but bad genes that end in a bad vaccine outcome get hatred and scorn? We are mocked, made fun of, ridiculed for vaccine injury, because we actually have the nerve to blame the vaccines and not just ourselves for some inherited defect that made us susceptible.

All of us are susceptible; some of us just don't know it yet. Answering the question *why us* is so simple now. Why us? Not because we are different, but because we are the same. Why us? Because, as a nation, we allow it.

Those like me will be labeled as "anti-vaxers" and portrayed as the bad guys, fooling us all a little bit more, holding their heads high in genes they feel superior, laughing at our expense, ridiculing our intelligence, while declaring that "anti-vaxers do not understand science." And they fool us all even more with that word they call science, because there is no way we are living by the same definitions.

But this is about people, not science, and it troubles me that sometimes we don't seem to recognize that simple difference. I cry for the people, the poor children we use as guinea pigs for the science we all seem to love. Are we a nation that loves science more than our own children?

Not me, so I cry for this tragedy that has taken hold of my life, wounding my heart and traumatizing my soul. There is no tuning out, no turning the other cheek, no going back to that ignorant place. This is a tragedy too, and so many people don't "get it," while I am getting sick over it. I get it far too well, feeling it deeply, and the thoughts are killing me, from the inside out.

CHAPTER 46

LIFE IS COLLAPSING

I lost my paycheck when my daughter lost her health, but I still have my white picket fence, that little vision of ideal Americana, a symbol of the old fashioned American dream.

Sometimes when foundations start to crumble, little worlds fall apart. The stable earth I once stood firmly upon is now shifting and coming out from beneath me. Life is collapsing for me, right there through the slats of a picket fence, for all to see, and yet no one to notice. Additional stress plus subtracted support = crash and burnout. Behind the white picket fence, I am falling through the cracks.

For my children, I am a boulder, standing strong and steady, with determination and perseverance. But by myself, I am just a bunch of broken pebbles slipping into a hole. I keep hoping someone will grab me, to break my fall and rescue me from my own life. I can't find myself, I can't figure my way out, and many days, I don't have the strength to try.

This is awful, with pain that just will not go away. I thought the pain would get better with time. I thought that having my daughter still alive would be enough to move on from the past. I don't know how to make the pain go away while the crime perpetuates, and I am having a hard time pulling confidence out of myself when all I can hear are echoes of insults in my mind. I don't seem to fit in this world anymore. Our values are different.

I don't understand why I am still crying alone, why everyone is not outraged by these tragedies. I cannot accept these harms to our little babies. Trauma is a big part of that, but so are the day to day casualties of other children, other children taking the fall, new families caught in the net of lies and deceit, parents who think they are doing everything "right," parents just loving their children, just like me.

There are always more tears. With this much crying every day, I thought tears would run out by now. But day in and day out, there is an unending supply of copious amounts of mucus and tears. Tissue boxes are depleted so quickly that rolls of toilet paper have become my constant companion.

Life hurts. The enthusiastic butterflies in my belly went quiet. Maybe I am not such an idealist anymore. Maybe I am a realist, and what I see in real life sucks all around. The world doesn't scare me like it used to; I just hate it instead.

Illness strolls in and sweeps me off my feet on my nineteenth wedding anniversary, ravaging my body with the whirlwind speed of a tornado. Fate found its way into my home through cracks and crevices, slipped in where there was weakness, and took advantage. I had been dying inside, leaving a hollow opening for opportunistic invaders to attack. Maybe the microscopic world behaves a lot like the life sized one.

My brown eyes turn black, one solid color, no depth, no visible pupil, just blackness where light once shone. My fever climbs to 103.5, and it stays there, stuck at a heat I didn't even think possible for adults for any length of time.

My body is difficult to move, anchored to the bed with weight, while my mind floats someplace else, not mentally present in the realm where watching television is too strenuous. My consciousness seems to slip in and out of itself, like I am partway between being in my body and being above my body at the same time, as though I am drifting to someplace out of this world. I am there, but not really there, an observer and a participant in my own life, leaving my own body to protect myself from feeling the pain.

I imagine I am close to death. My heart still aches, my soul is full of sadness, my inner oomph is gone. I lie there, lost in myself for days as my temperature remains high, the pain grows, and the coughing worsens. I expect the fever to break, but as I lie waiting and expecting, it is becoming obvious that I am getting worse and not better. Maybe I am delusional in my own feverish state, but I think quite clearly as the days pass, the very real thought that this illness could take me.

I had fallen deeper than I realized, living where it was dark, and the only light in my eyes were my children. I wore down the shiny armor, burnt out my candles at both ends, and took on years of cumulative stresses. The ravages of guilt, of trauma, of defeat, the toll that wears one down into the depleted adrenals, no more fight left, not even for me. I know that if I can't muster an inner strength, then this might be it. I don't need to ask *why me* this time. I already know.

I had given up on life. I never thought I would be that person, until the day I realize that I am. I didn't realize I had given up until this very moment, this very moment when fate can lead me in either direction. God knows my pain. He gives me a choice, an opportunity to come home or a wakeup call to live.

I know in this ever changing world full of hostility that we made the decision to cut my family short one member, that two kids, one in each arm is all I can hold. The possibility I hadn't considered was that the one less family member could be me.

My husband supports my weight, grasping me under my arms as he drags me to help. Still no broken fever, my diagnosis is pneumonia verified by hospital X-rays. I really don't know how I am going to reignite my own flame in dark hours when my own brown eyes had filled in with blackness. Before, I felt certain that a hospital could save me, and now I am not so sure. They can't give me the will to live. I have to find that on my own.

They send me home with drugs, but my body rejects the whole first dose. Then the power goes out, taking our heat with it. Fully aware, I know this could be the very factor that tips me in one direction or another. Without a fireplace or a generator, I bundle myself up in comforters, keeping my body warm, using the black reclining chair for support to sleep upright.

With a swift current, I remember. I want to live. I conjure up all the love in my heart, all the beautiful memories I had photographed in my mind, all the warmth of an embrace, and the air of my sweet babies' breaths. I remember my strength and all of the fighting I had endured, the battles I had won, and the hardships I survived. I am not ready to give up everything I had fought for to let my children's lives fall into hands not nearly as passionate and loving as my own.

My two beautiful children, the little joys in my day, jump into bed to hug me after returning home from school. They aren't afraid of me. They aren't afraid of germs. They just love. Those few moments of pleasure each day are enough to remind me of who I want to live for, what life is about. They share their spirits and energy with me, and take care of me in the same loving way I had modeled for them. They were paying attention. They noticed. I am not invisible; I am depleted. I used myself up in caring for them, and now these two young children are returning the favor.

My children are my higher purpose, my noble calling, and they need me. They don't care about my past mistakes. They don't care about my imperfections. They even offer forgiveness generously. They just love me, and I still have a lot to learn from them. The tender bonds we had grown reach out to me, arms pulling me back with the grips of love. Maybe it is the country that has its values all wrong, because to my kids, I am pretty special. To my kids, I am worth everything.

I am not living. I am not thriving. I am merely surviving, just barely getting through one day to make it to the next. I treasure sleep, because in my dreams, life is still beautiful. I treasure my kids, because in them, life is still beautiful too. Within them lives the meaning of life.

An unexpected possibility occurs. The crisp cold air feels good in my lungs. The darkness fades away, revealing the true brown of my eyes once more. By almost dying, I remember to live.

CHAPTER 47

THE TOUCH OF GRACE

I learn to take things day by day, with small steps rather than giant leaps, hoping that life will improve, hoping for health to rejuvenate, and hoping mean people will go away. I thought there would be supports to lean on, but instead, I was broken down further with those needling comments, wearing down my armor, chopping away at what was left of my strength.

Life is not easy. But people certainly do have a way of making things worse for each other. I never thought I would escape childhood unscathed, only to meet up with bullies as an adult. I spend days fighting for survival, weakened through all the stress, but sometimes when the holes in the armor start to show, people don't feel for you, they attack your vulnerabilities.

But these are regular people, and their meanness doesn't even compare to the bad guys in high places knowingly ruining people's lives, knowingly harming children and families while preaching it is all good and completely safe. That is a new level of meanness beyond my ordinary comprehension, and I am still having difficulty absorbing this reality. Good people have a hard time understanding how bad real evil can be. It is hard to understand evil at its core when we are not that way ourselves.

But when I have doubts that people can really be that bad, it only takes a small reflection back through history to remind me that they can. Maybe I should have paid more attention in history class, but I did pay attention in religion, and it was people who chose to crucify Jesus. The world that I am living in is not a nice place at all. There must be good left beyond my kids, and I need to find it.

Paying attention to the subtleties surrounding me, I notice the kindness of strangers, with warm smiles that can uplift spirits in seconds. Serendipity grants chance meetings with strangers who just happen to share the same beliefs off the beaten path. Through clouds of meanness, there are still more good guys than bad ones left in this world, I have faith in that. Remembering good people gives me hope.

I agree to have X-rays to make sure the pneumonia has truly passed, because total wellness still eludes me. My lungs look awful, a stark picture in contrasts upon the X-ray. The technician tells me it is scarring, scarring that may never heal, scarring that may be with me for life. I see a small piece of my whole body on the screen, confirming what I have been feeling for years, broken, scarred, and weak. I am well enough to be here alone, but my insides are a mess.

As I pass through the gift shop on the way out of the hospital, a kind woman who works there reaches out to hug me. My disappointment must be obvious. I am at a hospital, and this woman doesn't even seem scared that she might catch something from me. Free from pneumonia, but not fully recovered, and if I believe them, maybe it is not even possible. But, I still believe in possibilities, even if the thought eludes me at the moment. And this woman, a stranger, reaches out to me in a hug of compassion.

With a hug, this woman touches my heart with her kindness, giving me some arms of support. She is the touch of grace, another reminder to look for the blessings in this world, to see goodness even when it is surrounded by a whole lot of bad.

I don't know their names and might not even recollect their appearances, but I remember people like her on a different level, one that touches me far below the surface. I remember hearts reaching out to touch mine, bringing me gratitude for the chance encounters, the small gestures of humanity that offer a boost, even if only for a moment.

Little acts of kindness are sometimes enough to get someone through another day, or another week, or even implant a tiny root into a soul, seeding a life into a whole new direction. Tiny moments and small gestures can have big impacts. Love is the hand up. I came to the hospital for help, but it is this woman in the gift shop who gave me just what I need.

CHAPTER 48

THE GAP

I once thought my reputation was the most valuable thing I could own. I thought it was a piece of me, a reflection of all my hard work and my values. I put all my stock into building my reputation, making sure my past could withstand scrutiny. I was a role model after all, a role model to children, and I wanted my life to be honorable.

I thought a reputation might adequately reflect the truth, but there are forces out there intentionally destroying reputations every day. Intentionally. Every. Day. It might be some small time players at work or some ex-friends choosing sides, but sometimes the schemes and the players have more connections, more power, more intricate ways to tear down lives and destroy the value of a reputation. Rumors move quickly, and so don't those calculated bots and trolls stalking the online world.

A reputation is fragile, broken with mere words and always dependent on the thoughts of others. All that hard work to build it up, only to find some targeted language or some feathery gossip floating freely to infect it. All that building of my reputation, and one reaction to a needle tore it down, demolishing it into nothingness.

Now, I am faced with some emptiness, a lost identity, a worthless reputation, and this great big gap in employment. With true sarcasm, that looks great on a resume.

It is unfortunate that the work we do at home doesn't count towards anything real on a job application. It just counts as a great big gap in work experience, that negative space on paper, an emptiness that gets noticed, making moms easily overlooked. I know this, because I worked in human resources. We were very aware of the gaps too, but we used to give people like me a chance, a chance to pull themselves out of the gap.

Instead of building on a career, I built solid, loving relationships and nurtured developing children. My gap was full to the brim with sleepless nights and busy days, learning, reflecting, reading, and expanding. Holed up in my house, I spent hours upon hours in deep thoughts and study, while occasionally being teased for being "lazy" or not having a "real" job. But it has been this gap in employment where I have accomplished the most growth.

The gap is the place where my brain churns in deep reflection, mashing up memories and making connections. The gap is the place where I explore the terrains that many others are afraid to speak of. The gap is the place where my heart yearns for a better world as I plan my contributions. The gap is the place where my hands have been put to good use holding my children close. The gap is where my eyes cry rivers of love and compassion, and also deep sadness and pain. The gap is where my hands shake, after writing for hours upon hours, recording it all. My life may not look busy to an outsider, but inside the gap, I have been a complete work in progress.

Reclaiming lives is hard work, and I kept busy behind those closed doors. Only I know about all those working nights when I tinkered about alone as everyone slept. Only I know about all those working days that I simply wasn't fortunate enough to earn a paycheck. What others see as a gap, I see as so much more. I have eyes on the inside, just like my husband. That is why he never pressured me to get a "real job." He knew how exhausted and how busy I was with the ones that I had, no less real, just not societally valued.

Boxes and drawers are filled with tangible trinkets, reminders of days passed. I spent hours flipping through teaching scrapbooks with fond memories of students I still love. Long gone and onto their own lives, but forever linked by a single meaningful year together. I miss them. I miss teaching. Yet, I know many public schools may never let me teach again once I publish this book. I don't think many public schools are interested in hiring openly anti-vax teachers. I think they like to fire them instead. Nothing like a wasted education...

Besides, with vaccine mandates moving in on school teachers, I can't comply, the same way I could never teach a pro-vaccine health lesson. But I miss it. Once upon a time, my presence mattered there.

Letters of accolades, thank you notes, none of it mattered after the vaccine reaction. They mattered to me, touching my heart with gratitude for those who took the time to write, to express sincerity through their words. It mattered to me even if none of it helped me keep my job.

In the classroom was where I shined, but now they are just memories. But somewhere, my students live on with some of my love embedded into their foundations. Special kids grow up to be special adults, and the magic of their spirits brighten us all.

I thought I would reclaim my life by going back to work, by getting a teaching job and being in a classroom once again, but being a teacher is dependent on someone else giving me a job, and I am not having a lot of luck with that. All they must see is that great big gap, missing everything that is truly me.

I am too depleted to start any movements, but I find enough strength to push my own little dingy back into the vast sea of possibilities. I gave myself a job, called myself a writer, and made a real book as my goal. For now, there will be no classroom, but my life will be spent with meaning, where I am right at home.

Writing long hand, pouring my heart among the pages, I make connections. Little notebooks on the bedside table, little notebooks in the glove box of my car, little notebooks in my purse, inspiration strikes me everywhere. Within my writing, I find pur-. pose and value, along with passion for something meaningful, passion that brings me back to life. I forgot that I still had it in me, until I put focus on moving forward and light to the darkness.

Soon, I have my little imitator by my side, writing her own short stories in eloquent language above her years. Writing will be good for us all.

CHAPTER 49

THE FARM

We enjoy going back to basics at the farm. I still have no desire to own one or raise my own chickens, but we visit. I haven't forgotten what kids like to do. Their happiness makes me smile, and within that smile, a little bit of me shines on the outside. I've been coming to the farm since the days of just me, when I slung my camera over my neck for photographic adventures, snapping pictures of those animals that l love.

As a mom, I think about things I hadn't considered before, things like rusty barbed fences, animal saliva, and poop covered shoes. I think about tetanus sometimes too, that even though rare, a farm might be just where I could find it.

I watch a young boy playing. He seems to be about two years old, and he is here with his dad. The father sits, watching from a safe distance, close enough to see, but not close enough to hand hold. When my kids were little, I hovered here, closer to my children, closer to the place where I might need to intervene with an animal, or guard that prickly fence from delicate tissue, or wipe animal spit from hands before they make their way to mouths.

The father doesn't seem worried that his baby is touching the metal chicken wire surrounding the goats. I wonder if his child is vaccinated or if he thinks about tetanus. I think about it for him. I worry about that rusty barb wire fence, the same one he doesn't even seem to notice. I yearn to let go a bit more. Today, maybe I just want to be a little bit more like the dad. He is far more relaxed than me, at a place where I worry. He is a dad, and I know that moms and dads generally tend to parent differently, but there are just so many different ways to do this one job right.

My daughter remembers this farm with special memories of days when we used to meet a friend who is no longer my friend. Our friendship had a contingency. She needed me to be pro-vaccine, like her. I think when she looked at my kids she was thinking "harbingers of disease," even though little Bella wasn't harboring any diseases the vaccines themselves hadn't put into her.

To me, I find irony at the farm, one place I still worry a little bit, not about the company I keep, but about that lingering tetanus fear. We can't catch tetanus from each other, but we just might catch it at the farm. My friend didn't seem worried about that at all. She was worried about having us as her companions. If her baby got sick, it couldn't possibly be from the germ filled goat saliva covering her daughter's hands as she passed her an ice cream cone. Naturally, she would look right over that, right onto us.

She seemed willing to hand up my children for sacrifice, if it meant certain protection for her own children, even though no one is offering that kind of guarantee in exchange for our children's lives. She thought that would be fair. But it is not fair — to take our babies, jam them into a one-size-fits-all mold, and hold them down for annihilation. I had a sick child over the procedure, and she didn't. "Life isn't fair" isn't supposed to mean this either.

We are from the same town and attended the same public schools that built up our foundations with a one sided education. We learned through some popular bad teaching methods of our time: to memorize rather than think, to obey rather than to respect, to accept rather than question.

She made it clear to me, in direct words, that she felt she was very smart, much smarter than most people, much smarter than me, before deciding to go her own way. She had great pride in her education, while I felt like mine had let me down. She believes that vaccines save lives. I believe they destroy them. She sees salvation through the tip of the needle. For me, hell lives there.

I don't understand why the people who can't hear me are the same ones who boast about their intelligence. She was fully convinced that she was smart, so it must be me who was stupid. She was convinced that she was right, so it must be me who was wrong. She was too invested in what she already believed to change her mind about anything. Simple words from me could not break through that wall, as words fell to the ground, unheard and wasted. I prefer sponges that absorb and reflect, then squeeze out what doesn't belong. But that is the teacher in me talking, and she was not my student.

I have experiences that I weigh heavier than my training, experiences that carry more weight than an opinion, and real life lessons worth more than any textbook teachings. Some of my experiences are mutually exclusive from what I had learned, so it was easy for me to understand the discrepancies. But without the experience, there was no motivation for her to change. Or see. Or understand. She didn't have to. Her kids are fine.

It is hard to be friends; it is hard to find understanding when there is no meeting of the minds. I didn't need to tell her, but it is hard to leave out the turning point of my whole life in any genuine conversation. It is hard to leave out my daughter. Vaccines don't define us, but their impact has forever changed us, and I still believed that someone might care.

I thought friends might want to know these things I had learned. I thought friends might want to know about my baby. I thought it would be okay to spill some baggage. But it is the part of me that others just have difficulty accepting. She wasn't the first to part ways, or the last, but she may have been the most direct. She didn't leave me second guessing anything.

How does this happen when the only thing we did different is get sick? Losing friends and family is a risk factor not written on any inserts, but the casualties are just as real. If we can't reach a level of understanding with this one issue, this one issue threading itself through all aspects of my life, then friendship fails.

She would not accept me. I cannot accept that vaccine injury even exists. It seemed like she wanted me to accept that vaccine injury is okay, because our fall is for the benefit of some pretend herd. Yet, she would not accept us, for falling ill and feeling ill will towards vaccines. Why couldn't I just fully vaccinate my kids like she did, so I could make this whole issue easy for her — make it go away. But I couldn't. I can't. Life isn't easy. This issue isn't easy, and it will not go away, so she went away instead.

Even though she defended her vaccines, I am not sure she was confident they would actually work. I think she should believe in the product she wanted to push on everybody else. She was not a good salesman at all. But she is a good mom, trying to look out for her own children with eyes and understandings far different than mine. I think she was just scared, but we left with some more memories and another parting of ways over the great divide.

I get it. I understand. I just wish I could get friends to understand me, to understand this issue. I wasn't trying to take her vaccines away; I just wanted her to respect my life, my experiences with those shots that she valued more than our friendship. The world is just not the same for everyone. There is no one-size-fits-all in a nation of diversity, and in a nation of freedom, there shouldn't have to be.

Maybe I am asking too much of people, but aren't some of our most basic universal human needs to be understood, to be heard, to be loved for exactly who we are? This is who I am, forever changed by vaccines, by vaccine injury. To pretend vaccine injury didn't happen to us for the sake of someone else's feelings is not a place I am willing to go. I have gone deep, to the depths of my core, to the darkest nights of my soul, to the places many dare not go. But to pretend this didn't happen, I will not go there, ever.

CHAPTER 50

PUBLIC SCHOOL

With age, my growing girl tackles the huge public school. With passing years of continued improvement, we take steps to go public and brave the local school. No more tiny class sizes, courageous Bella climbs a three-story building with well over a thousand students.

On the first day, I send my girl with lunch money to buy a simple salad, but she is forced to buy one with eggs on it because she touched the container to read the ingredients. She is allergic to eggs to the same degree she is allergic to peanuts.

She tells me she cried, but no one bothered to give her a different lunch, so my little girl went hungry, while the school declared victory at keeping her safe from peanuts. First day of school — total fail — the new kid is forced to sit alone at the peanut free table with a lunch full of another allergen. That might be emotionally scarring, but at least no peanuts.

The school nurses are a blessing, some saving grace to the school, two women who seem to respect our differences and genuinely seem to love my children. Through their guidance, I discover that I can write a note to allow my child the freedom to sit anywhere her classmates sit. Immediately accomplished, problem solved. My little girl gets the luxury to fit in, because her peanut allergies aren't so bad.

When I sit with a stack of papers on the evening after the first day of school, I wonder why I am being asked to sign contracts to attend public school. Some seem harmless, while others are not in a parent's best interests at all, and yet somehow, I am supposed to sign them, as another admittance fee for attendance. Are our signatures required by law?

I face dilemmas like this everywhere, because when I start questioning and thinking outside the box, I notice lots of routine behaviors that don't make sense for the best interests of our families. To the few who will fall outside the range of a typical year of normal expectations, those precise wordings might matter, because they matter to someone, the ones who wrote them, their own little insurance policies that protect themselves.

School is a tough subject for me. School is the place where various perspectives collide and crash into my children. My past within the system creates an inner conflict, some turmoil in my belly, and I don't always know what to think. The teacher in me wants to go back and make a difference in the classroom. The mother in me instinctively wants to pull my own kids back home. But from all my perspectives, I still don't like homework.

I question everything the children bring home from school, and some of the ideas make me uncomfortable. The words of teachers weigh heavy too, and I get upset with some of what they call "facts." I wonder if my kids think I am being difficult. Why do I spend time re-teaching things or getting upset about a flyer that comes home? Sometimes, they say, "Mom, this is no big deal, just throw it away." But I see now, more clearly, how this barrage of information spread by unsuspecting teachers doing their jobs, can lay the foundation for the rest of our lives, impacting future decisions for decades to come.

I notice at my son's school that the large entry sign at the road has the local hospital logo on it. Then I notice that my daughter's school has it too. The sports sign for the high school is sponsored by the local car dealership, like a little billboard of advertising. Educational posters with corporate logos, free book covers with cereal characters — businesses have captured the captive audiences of our children by embedding themselves into our schools, planting seeds of thoughts in the partnerships to learning, a little tiny wedge in their foundation of beliefs. It does matter, the stuff is teaching them too.

I remember the free book covers I once handed out as a teacher. They were corporate advertisements, right there on their textbooks, so kids could learn corporate loyalty, right along with their math. But I suggested they put them on inside out and decorate the empty white space however they would like. I wanted free book covers too. It saved us money. But all those freebies come with a price.

My son gets his report card, a huge one, with lots of confusing grades scattered throughout. There are no simple letters like I was used to, and the content list is far lengthier than the basic core subjects. My son gets assessed each term on six different subsections of health. Well, that just puts up lots of red flags in my head.

It is a lengthy section, with words like "health promotion" and "disease prevention." But, the most troubling part is his grade for his "ability to advocate" to others. The intention might be altruistic, or it might be like a pyramid scheme, but either way, whatever information he learns at school, I think they want him to teach to others, making sure their message gets heard.

What is their message? I don't know, but I have a feeling their teachings on public health might differ from mine. Of course I ask about it, but the teacher tells me she doesn't get to it too often, even though she needs to grade it on the report card. This might be one subject where a bad grade just might make me happier than a good one, because I certainly do not want my little boy singing things like, "No shots, no school," or "Vaccines are good for me." No, I am good with him getting a bad grade. I'm good with him getting six bad grades.

Sending my kids to school, I am learning a lot.

CHAPTER 51
GIRL SCOUTS AND GOODALL

I arrive at the science museum for an overnight adventure with my daughter. This is exactly the kind of activity I relish from my own childhood, like an overnight spent sleeping in military bunks at Battleship Cove in Fall River, Massachusetts with my own Girl Scout troop. All these years later, the recollection is a special thought of childhood. The science museum is not a battleship, but it is still a great night for moms and daughters to make special memories together.

I remind myself that I have nothing else to do this weekend, nothing to accomplish, nowhere to be but here. I can be fully present in this experience with my daughter and have some fun. I am paying attention and appreciating every bit of it. No cell phone in hand or other thoughts flowing through my brain, I have an open mind, ready and willing to take it all in. When I decide to live, to fully show up at the museum, I see many things to write about.

With the museum reserved strictly for the Girl Scout troops, there are no crowds and it is easy for us to make our way through the exhibits. Early in the evening, I stumble upon a gift. In our free exploration time, we enter an exhibit with a game to model scenarios of real life. After we are done playing, we click on the information section to learn how different views of cooperation and competition scenarios affect the world.

To my surprise, there is an information section on health that seems to contradict the marketing campaigns I hear so frequently for vaccines. The museum's computer game has the cooperative "us" view as saving the vaccine for the high risk people, because overuse can cause germs to mutate, just like with the overuse of antibiotics. The game considers the selfish "me" view as taking the vaccine even if you don't need it, simply because everyone else will.

I am at a respected science museum, reading a viewpoint that is almost never mentioned in the discussion of vaccines. It suggests that it is selfish for healthy people to take the flu shot, because the shot should be reserved for only those who most need it. I have heard anti-vax people called selfish before through unfounded bullying, and I feel that a herd that pressures others into taking unwanted vaccines is selfish, but to accept unnecessary vaccines as being selfish — interesting. I have never seen this take before.

I want to know what kind of corporation would promote this idea, so I look for a company sponsorship everywhere and can't find one. There seems to be no name attached to this exhibit, even though there are sponsor names attached to exhibits elsewhere.

The screen flashes off so quickly that I have to play it five times to be able to write it all down, word for word, so that I can quote it correctly. But I am smiling. Seeing this exhibit in the science museum has made my whole night, and there are still hours left to play.

Our sleeping assignment is in a room of stuffed birds, taxidermy, like in a museum of natural history. Dead birds peering at us from behind glass enclosures are creepy, but not one girl is afraid. Indoor camping with dead nature adds to the ambiance, the atmosphere of the night, girls on a camp out inside a science museum, sleeping bags lined up on the hard floor. The backs of children don't yet feel the hardness of the floor, the coldness of the world. Kids are comfortable here.

The next morning, after an uneasy night of noisy campers and flickering flashlights, we are off on an early start to our scheduled showing of a theater presentation. Our film is *Chimpanzees* with Jane Goodall, and I am excited by this selection. I have read her words, I admire her work, and I think she is a great role model for the girls. The film is beautifully displayed across a giant wraparound screen that immerses us in the forest, in Jane's world, a part of the chimps' habitat, for a small glimpse into their lives from the comfort of our seats.

I am moved by some comments I hear, but I can't grasp my notebook fast enough to capture entire quotes in the darkness of the theater. The film provokes thought. By the end, I'm thinking again, asking myself more questions, more questions I wish more of us would ask.

How come it is considered science when we study animals through observation? We call that observation "research." Yet, when scientists are asked to observe our children, parents are told we have no science? They say we have no science, but we have a different kind, the Jane Goodall observation kind. Shouldn't we show our children the same observation efforts we give to the study of animals? Because when I pay attention, I learn all sorts of things, studying humans.

Parents aren't in the laboratory; we're in the field, immersed in the trenches. Our kids are the subjects we have been following intently since birth, as we watch them with focus, using all our senses to connect with this other life. We take notes. We follow schedules. We are there, all the time, and we know far more than an outsider could ever see, could ever know, far more than the doctors or the politicians who try to control us from the outside, not even bothering to look in at the beauty of a family that their negative consequences destroy.

The one thing we might do wrong in the name of science is becoming too attached, but as parents, this is exactly what we do right. Attachments create bonds, unbreakable bonds of unconditional love. And all these people who want to impose their will on us, they don't love us at all. They have no attachments, no strings attached. They walk away from the harm, suffering no consequences of bad decisions they enforce on others, leaving good families to pay the price for the mistakes.

As parents, we must be attached to the outcomes, because we are fully attached to the subjects. That is why we care so much. Just like Jane cares for the future of those chimps, we care for the future of our children and all of humanity. Attachment is good. It means we care more deeply than anyone from the outside could ever know.

Being attached means we are more altruistic in our motivations. Being attached means we make decisions for our children with an honest and pure heart. Being attached means never letting go of our values in order to fit into hypocrisy. Being attached means we will not offer our children up for sacrifice. Being attached goes so much deeper than science. Being attached is good parenting.

I will be there through every hardship we face, every obstacle sent our way. I am not part of a herd, I am part of a family, my family, and I do not run the other way when things go wrong. I don't abandon my children when they make mistakes, and I don't abandon my children when they don't fit in with everyone else. They are a part of me, and I, a part of them, in a mother–child attachment, a completely different kind of immune building science that gets completely ignored.

Our kids don't need another biased study. They need parents fully in the game, paying attention with eyes wide open. Because we do owe our kids protection, protection from all the corruption, and we, as parents, are the only ones watching over our children's best interests, standing guard on the front line. Protection is not a vaccine. Protection is parents, the experts of our children's lives, and we don't need any degrees to qualify. Science sucks when our kids are the experiment.

I love the study of life, it's personal. My daughter's life is personal too. But some feel they have more of a right to be here and will willingly sacrifice the life of another if it brings them feelings of comfort or safety. But to me, living in a world that even thinks like that troubles me a whole lot more than any germ. Those who fit can stay, and those who don't can be tormented; the price of conformity, it's costly, and we are paying with the lives of our children. Because some lives do matter less to some, the ones that are not their own, so to hell with the rest apparently. But in the afterlife, I think roles will be reversed, and different people can go to hell.

CHAPTER 52

SCIENCE, LIKE HOME COOKING

Thoughts of unsettled science swirl through my mind with considerations about all those fallacies they have determined are not up for discussion. I don't want to debate anyway, so I will just stay in my kitchen, conjuring up some stews that ironically remind me of their science, an inexact science, just like home cooking.

The first image that comes to me is those multi-dose vaccine vials that contain several injections inside of one bottle. I never asked the doctor if we were getting our injections from a multi-dose vial or the preservative free single dose vials, because what I had been trained to ask was, "Is there mercury in these shots?"

The doctor didn't ask me if I took chemistry, and he didn't mention anything about Avogadro's number. He didn't even bother to tell me the difference between single dose and multi-dose packaging, because it is different than getting the M separated from the other M and the R. It is about getting each individual's shot packaged separately from everyone else's.

How can a mere human divide the bottle into perfectly even doses? There may be ten doses in one vial, with contents that separate and heavier ingredients that sink to the bottom. Multidose vials are like cocktails, shaken, not stirred, to disperse the ingredients evenly before a syringe is filled in preparation for the injection.

Shaking is not exactly an exact science. I think by probability calculations it must be nearly impossible for two doses to be exactly the same down to mere molecules. Seems to me some kids will get more stuff with their germs, while other kids might be getting more germs with their stuff. It's more like home cooking, with a pinch of this and a pinch of that, when everyone's pinch is not quite the same. What percentage of the shots are the additives, and what percentage is the disease? All possible answers are completely unappetizing.

Molecules may not seem like a big deal, but they are, for the child who gets a shot the day their dose comes from the bottom of the barrel where more heavy metals come to rest. They don't always stay fully suspended in the liquid because they are not homogenized like milk. Those heavy metals sitting on the bottom of the jar need to go somewhere, and no one wants them to end up in their child. Then those little bits of imperfect science, then they matter a whole lot more.

Sometimes, it is more like gambling than home cooking, shaking the jars and tossing the dice, hoping our children don't end up on the losing end of a crap shoot. It is a game, a game of chance, where all the wins go to the businesses and all the losses fall to the families. We can't win this game, unless of course, you are part of the profiting parties, because their idea of the greater good might not include any of us.

Next, let's do some weighing and measuring. The bathroom scale is precise enough. The measuring tape from our sewing kits works just fine too, because the weight and size of the child only matters to parents. Age is all that is considered on the growing vaccine schedule. In cooking, sometimes we halve the ingredients for smaller portions or increase them for larger ones, but infant vaccines are one size, all weights, without exceptions for preemies. Maybe home cooking is even more precise than vaccines.

Home economics has lots of science and math. Moms and dads are good at this stuff. We are not too stupid for science. We are too sweet for the rottenness.

What are some of the ingredients? I think they tossed in some food products just like cooking too — some peanut adjuvant here, some soy adjuvant there, with a pinch of glutamate (MSG), sometimes cultivated on a real egg — creating potential allergies to real cooking and foods, the exact same foods that provoke allergic reactions in my daughter.

Maybe cultivating on eggs creates egg allergies. Maybe peanut adjuvant in shots equals peanut allergies in children. Maybe soy adjuvants create soy allergies. That's definitely some science worth looking into.

I hope someone is checking the expiration dates, because vaccines spoil just like food. Some need to be refrigerated to the proper temperature too. Just like food, sometimes contamination occurs. Sometimes mold grows where we don't want it. Sometimes little pieces of rubber particles from the stoppers flake into the liquid to contaminate the mix. Sometimes glue from the container mixes itself into the ingredients. Sometimes, somehow the HCG pregnancy hormone finds its way in there too.

There is a lot of science involved in vaccines, and that tiny vial holds lots of room for mistakes.

CHAPTER 53

MATH AND RARITY

D o you ever wonder who is conducting the science? The third
graders at my son's school did some great science projects.
Do we trust their work?

I'm not suggesting it would be third graders doing the vaccine
studies; it would be far too dangerous for them to play in that laboratory. It might even be contraindicated with all the hazardous
ingredients. One small spill can require a hazmat team, a hazmat
team to clean up a spilled ingredient that could have otherwise
gone into someone, but onto the floor requires a cleaning crew. At
least with cooking, the food is safe to eat.

Studies have lots of room for errors, even with the most ethical
of researchers. But add some conflicts of interest and financing
contingent upon specific results and we will certainly have lots of
bad science on our hands. But what about the math? I think the
math might be even more telling.

There is the bell curve of statistics where the data that falls
outside the curve can be chopped right off. These are called outliers, those people that don't fit so well into the restrictions of a bell
curve. Imagine wrapping a gift box. The paper has been taped
across the center and now it is time to fold up the edges. But the

edges are too long and will need to be cut to keep the wrapping tidy. All that extra wrapping paper that gets tossed into the trash represents outliers too, people not paper, the people in real life who probably had some sort of reaction. It is really easy to obtain 100% vaccine compliance if all the parents who say, "No," are kicked out, the same way it is easy to show no harm if all the outliers showing injury get chopped out of the data.

Maybe in math those people are statistically insignificant, but in real life, they matter, they matter a lot. Those are the injured, the sacrificed, and they count even if the math ignores them. If researchers are allowed to leave people out of the equation and no one is legally required to report vaccine injuries, then there is a lot of skewed data we put our faith into. That's just playing with numbers. Skew the numbers so our skewed ethics don't look so bad.

But where are these numbers even coming from? Do we ever wonder about the little babies, the people the vaccines were tested on *BEFORE* the determination that they were "safe?" Because I think about those nameless, faceless kids a lot. And I wonder about them, with a heavy heart.

Then there is the math that comes about *AFTER* a vaccine hits the market.

Every time an injured child goes ignored, a seizure gets denied, every time a parent goes unheard, those very real instances when parents beg others to listen, but they don't — all fall to the side of no reaction. Not because it didn't happen, but because no one wants to admit the obvious. "Coincidental," they'll say. And for every "coincidental" we hear, another few kids get hurt by that lie, because the product stays on the market, continuing to harm without consequence. If no one acknowledges vaccine injuries, then injured children get counted as having none.

It is estimated that only 1 out of 10 reactions gets reported, because there is no consequence for not reporting. Without knowing they have a right to file a report without the doctor's permission, many parents will let it go, into the dust. They might not vaccinate anymore, knowing that they have been fully warned, but as for the rest of us, we go on unaware of all those affected families, all those injured children, because they have been silenced, pushing their numbers onto the side that speaks loudly for vaccines. It might not be the truth, but the data records will indicate that xxx amount of doses were given and only xxx (small %) of reactions were reported. But, "reported" is the key word here. With sins of omission, not including data alters reaction percentages by a lot, enough to be quite significant — to parents.

Every injury that goes unreported throws the numbers off balance, straying from accuracy bit by bit, until the truth looks nothing like those numbers, those statistics, those "rarenesses" offered us as assurances, until those numbers look nothing like real life at all. And those are just the numbers after the vaccines hit the market. If we combine the math done during studies and testing, well then, it is just a great big inaccurate mess.

There is some really flimsy data floating around. I don't see how that information is going to inform anyone of anything. Unless, what you want to see is minimal reactions. If you want to believe that vaccine injury is "rare," you will believe the numbers they show you and say, "See — proof — right there in black and white."

And I'd reply, "Sometimes my friend, numbers do lie," because sometimes the people recording them have no interest in accuracy, when warped statistics are better for business.

If vaccine reactions were truly rare, our kids would be examined, like specimens, like aliens. It would be such an oddity that everyone would want to look out of sheer curiosity. Scientists, doctors, and our government would be very interested in what they could find. Rare kids are fascinating.

Maybe reactions aren't rare at all. Maybe they just don't want us to see them, to know about them, putting us in denial, so we deny ourselves and each other, spinning reactions into some other loopy explanations full of holes. Denying the damage with everything in their power, not counting the injuries so the statistics are off, pretending we don't exist so we can't be counted. But they will gladly count us when we refuse more shots, as they tally up the exemptions they keep trying to take away.

If we are only looking for autism, we will miss the rest of the harmful possibilities. If we are only looking past autism, we see nothing at all, except the pure safety they want us to believe. Our kids are real kids, and they are valid proof of vaccine failures. They aren't a threat to public health. Their lives and experiences are important data, valuable to the interests of public health. The public might want to know about them. There is no science or math possible that is ever going to convince us that the lives we live aren't real.

CHAPTER 54
IT'S PSYCHOLOGY

Flipping through old school notebooks, I am reminded of another time in my life when I thought this stuff was important. Hours upon hours spent memorizing, copying sentences, and rewriting information until it traveled by way of osmosis from my hands up through my arms and into my brain. Here in these piles sits what I once valued, old notebooks filled with countless hours of my life, where I found my self-worth. Parts of my old life are slipping away, parts that had no value but to achieve grades, parts I see falling into the trash buckets as I clean through my life.

I traded childhood for book smarts, book smarts that led me wrong. Those achievements cost a lot, sacrificing my playtime for grades, teaching me to look outside myself for validation. I prepared for a lifetime of academics and studies, learning behaviors that taught me discipline, perseverance, hard work, dedication, and lots of subject matter. My training wasn't all bad. I lifted books and exercised my brain, weighing words heavy from an education I valued.

I was taught that the secrets to success could be found throughout the pages of textbooks, that my education would take me places and assure me a financial future of security that leads to a comfortable retirement. I had hopes and dreams for a brighter future, and I was told I would get there with those A's.

The A's made me proud, but they are only letters, and I frittered away my youth to pay for them, completing assignment after assignment of misery in lonely late nights of homework. It felt great to win those academic achievement awards, but in real life, no one is handing out prizes. My book smarts never did feel like tangible skills, which is why, even back then, wearing a dress I had crafted in home economics class was a palpable achievement with self-satisfaction, far more rewarding than earning an A.

As I dusted off my home economics skills, I didn't realize I would need real survival skills. When I dusted off my debating skills, it didn't matter, because the other side kept lying to me. And when I dusted off that diploma, I had no idea that the wisdom would be found somewhere else. Intelligence and fancy degrees don't necessarily confer honesty, ethics, or integrity — some of the most valuable assets of all. The skills and the people we often overlook might be the very ones we need to assure survival in an ever changing world.

I pull out the college textbooks to see what is lurking beneath the covers. Vaccine recommendations right there in the black and white teachings of human development in my psychology textbooks. I studied those textbooks right alongside future social workers and psychologists as I trained for that degree. Yes, I do have a degree in that, but psychology is not the place I would turn when considering the safety and efficacy of vaccines or their impact on human health.

Why is psychology connected to vaccines? Could it be the societal norms, the fear mongering, the study of our herd-like behaviors, social pressures and conformity — all those tactics that seem to hold hands with the vaccination process? Playing with our minds, fulfilling needs of safety and tradition — rituals we had instilled in ourselves as children, rituals we naturally pass along to our own. We pass a lot of things onto our children, much more than genes.

Maybe if I were in college studying psychology today, I would be learning about this new diagnosis of Munchausen syndrome by proxy, and I would be learning that eating healthy has now been declared a mental disorder. Then, there is Oppositional Defiant Disorder, arbitrarily slapped on those people who don't want to obey non-rules from non-authority figures.

Sure, some people like attention; lots of people like attention, but I think we might have better luck finding the extreme personalities on the internet rather than at the doctor's office. Sure, some people will disagree with anything, but seeking a second opinion is not a rebellion. It might be nearly impossible to eat completely healthy in a world that believes industrial waste water is safe for our edible crops, but the people who attempt to succeed are certainly not the crazy ones. And neither are the moms who get unjustly diagnosed with Munchausen's syndrome for going that extra mile to find answers for their legitimately sick children.

There is no medical testing necessary to be labeled with a psychiatric disorder, just subjective opinions and judgments in his-word-against-hers type of life ruining, where titles may carry more weight than sanity or commonsense. Sometimes good parents are labeled with psychology stigmas as easily as being labeled an "anti-vaxer" for simply asking a question.

Who is scrutinizing the sanity and integrity of those who write and apply the manuals to judge others as mentally ill? Being different, not quite fitting into the box of conformity, fighting against unfair rules, perseverance — these are not mental disorders. These are signs of strength, and maybe that is a bit too intimidating for those cooking the books.

CHAPTER 55

IT IS WHAT IT IS... NO!

I suspected her boy had autism long before she told me. As I watched this boy flapping his hands and moving in jerky motions, I recognized these signs. I certainly wasn't an expert, but I studied this boy's movements the same way I had once been studying my own daughter.

One day, the mother strikes up a conversation with me, not the usual small talk or simple pleasantries, but a real dialogue. She has been watching my children too — with admiration — expressing that she notices their good behavior and their kindness. She asks me if her son can play with them. She views my children as strong role models of good behavior, and she wants her son to learn from my kids. She wants her boy to learn some social skills from being in the company of my children.

Did I hear that correctly? She wants my children to role model appropriate behavior for her son with autism? Yes. This might be one of the greatest compliments yet. This mom's simple request was a reminder of our own journey, a reminder to show me just how far we had come, with a request for a favor that was quite the compliment.

This day is a far cry from the days at the library when I was getting reprimanded after story hour classes for my "strong willed" child. The librarian said to me, "You better figure out how to get this strong willed child under control, because if you can't control your two year old, then you'll never be able to control her as a teenager," and then threatened to kick her out of class. But it was the gym program that we had been attending twice a week to improve movements that actually did kick her out.

In our tiniest of efforts to provide a small favor, my children found a new friend. The kids don't talk too much, but no one seems to mind. This boy has a high functioning capability which is not the case for every child diagnosed with autism. This boy has the ability to speak, to connect with others, to make eye contact. He has the capability for play. He can use the bathroom on his own. High functioning autism is not the picture of all autism. Some kids have the same label while living a very different life. We are the lucky ones.

⚒

I cannot redo that fateful day and take back those shots. *What Is* for me is the history I cannot change. But stories are malleable. There are no futures written in stone. When I hear, "It is what it is," I think, don't settle so fast. The only part I must accept is the unchangeable past.

There are countless stories of people who have beaten the odds, who defied all medical logic, who have overcome the unconquerable. We have heard about the persistence and dedication of people who simply did not take, "No," for an answer, the ones who knew that anything is possible. The mother who watches her son play sports, the same son who was told would never walk. Or the mother who was told her daughter would need IV nourishment her whole life, watches her child eating as any other eight year old. Or the parents who were told there simply is nothing to be done to recover from autism, who now have fully functioning children, undistinguishable from their mainstream peers. Where doctors have given no hope, parents are succeeding every day.

There are parents who believe in looking beyond *it is what it is* thinking, into greater possibilities, because they don't believe in the limitation. Possibilities... stones they would have left unturned had they believed that this is all there is, that the future is bleak and hopeless. It is amazing what determined parents can accomplish when they don't take, "No," for an answer. We don't all get the same results when we vaccinate. We don't all get the same results in recovery either, but all our kids are worth every effort to try.

"My doctors told me I would never walk again. My mother told me I would. I believed my mother." This is a quote from Wilma Rudolph, the winner of three Olympic gold medals for running sprints in the 1960 Olympics. What she overcame to get there was polio. She didn't say it was easy, she only proved that it is possible.

When doctors told Wilma she would never walk again, it was her mother that gave her the strength to believe something different, to have faith in possibilities beyond the doctor's words. Wilma beat polio. Then, she succeeded some more, on the track and field stage. But her achievements went even further when she stood for change by bringing integration to a planned segregated event in her honor.

If parents said, "It is what it is," to our vaccine injured children, they would all stay sick. "It is what it is," is not enough to save our children. It cannot be an easy excuse to justify our acceptance of detrimental fates. We need to believe that there is more, that we can do more, until we know in our heart that we have done our very best. We can't give up before we even try.

Sometimes acceptance leads straight into hopelessness, a dark place where some are lost forever. We are not textbooks; our bodies do not necessarily conform to the written science of man. Miracles can happen. Hard work can produce positive results. Instead of accepting "it is what it is," I would rather live with hope and possibilities.

I will not accept that vaccine injury is a necessity of life, or for the greater good, or the kinds of backhanded corruption that leads to these crimes. No, I have no acceptance for that at all. I accept our children unconditionally but never the system that injures them.

When I am told, "It is what it is," that just pisses me off. That is a good thing because anger is an emotion of action. Maybe I am not so comfortable living in this ever changing world that I see, but my American spirit is still alive and well. I know the librarian meant "strong willed" as an insult, but it is clear to me that it is an asset.

I accept my responsibility, I accept my child, I accept my life, but, "getting over it," when it is still occurring, well, that's really hard. "It is what it is," while I sit back and do nothing, well, that is the easy way out. This situation doesn't require acceptance at all. It requires change. In the stillness come the answers, but inaction gets us nowhere.

CHAPTER 56
LOOK HOW FAR WE'VE COME

As the curtain falls on another school year, bitter sweetness fills my heart as fourth grade draws to a close with an award presentation and a talent show. My growing girl has been included in both. The girl who was moving jerky and awkward just received an award for music with accolades for rhythmic movements that resonate sound throughout her whole body. Today is the talent show performances, and Bella is here to dance.

Grace has touched our lives, sometimes unnoticed because my mind visits the past far too often, haunted by memories and visions I wish I had never experienced. But here she is, my big girl, on stage, moving with rhythm. She feels the music through her soul and shakes her hips like a trained dancer. Even her face has cleared up so much. She is well liked, successful in her academics, and now I watch in amazement at my beautiful child, dancing on stage in a talent show that required auditions.

A banner lines the backdrop of the stage. "Look How Far We've Come," it declares. I know it was meant for the kindergarten graduation held earlier in the day, a decoration left behind from their celebration. But I feel those words, inside myself, as though it were a reminder, placed there specifically for me, a thought I often forget when I wallow in the sadness and sickness of the past.

What seems like a normal accomplishment for most parents is a monumental achievement in my eyes. It is not that I thought she wasn't capable of coming this far, but the memories of her gross motor regression have not left my mind. My little girl is finally at a place, a place I always imagined my baby to be before she got knocked down with injury. To see her there on that stage has me smiling and crying simultaneously as my heart's love emanates from my seat and joins her on stage. Maybe I can finally let this all go. Maybe I can finally forgive myself. Maybe I am a good mom after all.

So badly do I want to forget, do I want to move on with life and enjoy what is left of it, enjoy my children's childhood before it all disappears. But the pain is still there. My eyes they have seen too much. I remember. I remember all too well the frightening experiences. I remember the sleepless nights, the continuous studying, the constant checking for breathing. I remember the fear in my heart and the worry that my child would be ripped from my embrace by the grim reaper stalking in the night.

The crowd cheers loudly for Bella's performance. As she walks down the stairs off the stage, her eyes meet mine. I motion to her to come see me before she returns to her own seat. I'm fully crying, the emotions that come over me, watching a simple dance routine. I grab my child and squeeze her in a full body embrace to smother her with my love. She was fantastic! I can't help but cry as my mind scans the past, in some disbelief at the great divide, from where she once was, to where she stands today. I hold my little princess, so proud, so happy. Look how far we've come. And it's good.

Each tear represents a memory, a milestone of accomplishment, a step on this long hard journey. Each tear represents love, love for my baby who is achieving against the odds, not the odds of nature, but the odds of man, taking a beating with each hit of the assault and emerging victorious in her battles. She is beautiful and talented, and I am blessed.

Memories of little achievements, memories of loving moments, a heart full of memories as we journey together. These were tears of joy, flooding me with happy hormones, flooding me with love. Mean people are not going to win this battle. This moment is all mine to relish. This moment is all hers to enjoy, to shine in the spotlight of her accomplishments. Imperceptible setbacks are hidden beneath a glowing spirit of complete joy. This is my baby, not so little anymore. And she is doing just fine.

I can finally see that it was good that I lost my job, because I was absolutely essential to Bella's recovery. It was obvious, and yet I hadn't been giving myself enough credit. Had I sent her off to daycare, I am not convinced we would have achieved the same results.

I researched. I knew what to do in a way that nobody around me could have. Me — what makes me special helped her grow. I didn't pay people for behavioral therapy, I role modeled good behavior. I took her around older children who had already learned to act appropriately. I taught her responses and replies and how to talk to people. I taught her my values and lived them with her. I learned that my shoes can be filled by someone else, but they will never fit quite as perfectly. I learned that I am special, unique, irreplaceable, Mom.

If life hadn't taken an unexpected turn, I would have earned income all these years. Bella would have had the bigger house, but she wouldn't have had me. I didn't realize how valuable I was to her, but it had to be me, and I can see that now. The bigger house — I really wanted that for my kids. But by living in small spaces, we became very close, and I think that is worth a whole lot more.

She is mine! I am so proud to be her mother, feeling pride in my daughter for the remarkable young girl she has become, pride in knowing that I gave every bit I had to see her to this point. This moment, my successful baby, this is worth all the insults, all the negative comments to my self-worth, all the little digs to get a job. No, this is worth so much more. This is worth every sacrifice. I invested me into her, and it has paid off. Look how far we've come.

CHAPTER 57

MY LITTLE BOY

I must admit, I felt the tug of envy seeing lovely images of Princess Kate standing proudly alongside her husband outside the hospital as she held her new baby. It wasn't her royal title, prestige, or her beauty that brought on the twinge, but rather the simple fact that she could stand in platform shoes without falling over so soon after giving birth at a hospital. Maybe she was in lots of pain or hiding secrets behind the smile, but in her light blue polka dot dress, she was the picture of new mom perfection.

I could not have stood holding my baby that close to delivery, and heels would have toppled me over for sure, but seeing Princess Kate hold her little boy reminded me of the birth of my own little boy.

—≈+≈—

By the time my second baby was in my belly, I still wasn't brave enough to attempt delivery without a hospital. I just wasn't as eager to get there.

In the comfort of my home, without hospital protocols to force my laboring behavior, I was surprised when I didn't feel like walking or birthing balls. I felt like sleeping, so I plopped myself into bed for intermittent sleep combined with a Sunday marathon of television episodes. I woke up to involuntary waves of muscles rolling down my belly. The baby was coming through no voluntary physical efforts of my own — and I was still at home!

The quick drive landed me back onto a hospital bed where my body's involuntary efforts stopped. I arrived just in time to avoid all of the birth interventions, including, we thought, the doctor. The hospital staff called in the residents to deliver my baby boy. I was excited to see residents, because I had read that residents had less of a tendency to intervene. After the experience of my first birth, that thought made me happy. No drips of antibiotics, no pain drugs, no obstetrician. Yes!

This was exactly what I wanted until the on-call doctor arrived, relegating the residents to mere observers, deflating my excitement and theirs. I was still glad to see that the weekend doctor wasn't the new female obstetrician I had selected for this second pregnancy. She was another person who promised the natural delivery, until she had me nearly on top of my due date, when she pulled the grass out from under me and replaced it with a medical table for testing and contraptions. As due dates approach, philosophies seem to change.

I didn't even know this man, and one of the first things he did was come at me with the big hook to pop the amniotic sac. My husband was by my side to tell him, "No." No coffee breaks this time. Once again, I didn't even notice, because I was trying to focus inward rather than outward.

My second baby was born, and I am still without the experience of the immediate embrace. My little baby boy emerged with meconium inhaled into his lungs and the cord wrapped around his neck, precipitating a call to the NICU, the neonatal intensive care unit of nurses. My son lay on another table, being held and touched by the hands of nurses rather than my own. This time,

I was grateful to be in a hospital. My son's birth might not have turned out so well at home.

I knew about the Hepatitis B shot this time. With tears in my eyes, I begged the nurses not to give it to him. Unfortunately, the damages from the first delivery resurfaced with the second, opening old wounds, leaving me too badly injured to be with my boy in those early hours. With prayerful trust, I needed to leave him in nurses hands, hoping their behaviors would be the right ones. I'll never really know what happened in the nursery, but I do know that my boy didn't get a fever, and I didn't leave with any little vaccine booklets.

My son was different than my daughter, right from the start, deeper than simply the boy–girl things. He was literally plugged up at birth, with a blocked tear duct that created yellow crusty eyelashes all day, and he lacked a regular pattern of poopy elimination that left him much too easy on diaper changes. He had signs of allergies with food intolerances, cradle cap, and skin sensitivities. He had ear infections that my daughter had been fortunate to avoid.

My little boy was born big, into the 95th percentile, but quickly dropped down and stabilized around 25 percent. He wasn't behaving sickly at all, he just had some inherent traits that might have led somewhere other than healthiness had I vaccinated him to their plan. He had some of those qualities shared by the children whose vaccine injuries manifested as autism. With a sister already injured by vaccines, he was certainly vulnerable. My little boy is exactly the kind of child who is being stolen from this world.

I have a little boy who acts like a typical boy, doing gross things full of germs. He enjoyed sucking on shopping cart handles. Surely, that might kill him, I thought. Then he tried something new. While I was driving, he thought it would be fun to lick the bottom of his sneakers. That is even grosser than the cart handle. Surely, he might die. But he didn't even get sick. Not even a little bit. I waited, and he never got sick. All that grossness straight into his mouth, and everything was fine. He is a boy. This was funny. But I couldn't laugh, or he would do it some more.

I look at my cute wavy haired son, with his mischievous smile, and I thank God I still have him exactly as he was born. My son is lucky. We made mistakes on his sister that he gets to avoid. He is lucky because his sister's cries woke us up. We get lucky, because he is perfect just the way he is, no alterations necessary.

Then, with a heart full of love, I look to my daughter. Tears well up in my eyes, "I'm so glad you are here. I felt like I killed you."

Bella replies, "But you didn't, and I feel like a hero, saving my brother. Stop crying, I'm fine now, just some allergies. I'd like to eat peanut butter cups, but I feel like a hero."

Best buddies, best friends, close to each other, close to my heart, meant to be here, for each other, for me. I gained exactly 35 pounds with both pregnancies, but what I really gained is two wonderful children. I don't see a bad gene anywhere. All I see is the beauty of life. All I see is love.

CHAPTER 58

DAMN TV

Sometimes the TV distracts me from thinking for myself. I like the quiet, the silence of reflection, the silence to concentrate, the silence of peace. But today, I spent the early hours of my day watching a popular morning television show, one of those feel good, happy wake up programs that offers up their version of the news. The tone is upbeat and offers attractive hosts who viewers invite, like friends, into their homes each morning to share little bits of the day.

The day's medical segment included two hosts and one guest doctor having what seemed like a chat rather than a true journalistic interview. The hosts had already chosen sides, working with the doctor to set up her position, like accomplices to aid her speech. They gave the doctor free rein to say whatever she wanted, because she was the only guest there. There were no disparate opinions to argue against, just friendly conversation with a persuasive twist, spouting off the exact same lines that fooled me so many years ago.

I want to believe they are nice and would never do this on purpose. Maybe they are guilty of their own gullibility, or maybe people with good jobs really want to keep them and do what it takes to stay employed. Sometimes, I just don't know, because through those morning lines with smiles was where I learned lots of misinformation too.

Damn TV. The television has been chattering this way for weeks now, conditioning us to fear, just like Pavlov and his dogs, filling our homes with dogma ever since an announcement of a "measles scare" at a famous amusement park. I tell myself that this is just another propaganda piece to train people. I can't help but think of all those misleading words creating mental illusions, swaying parents in only one direction — to vaccinate. In all these years, how many kids have been hurt by these words that encompass complete assurances of vaccine safety, the denial of links to autism, and advocating for all the shots, in combination together, precisely on someone else's schedule?

Why all this hyper focus on the measles? There are far more dangerous, potential pathogens that we seem to ignore. Why elevate a measles concern above the deadly antibiotic resistant hospital infections? I think about those every time I see medical staff wearing their work scrubs about town. There are a whole bunch of scary infections waiting to get us, yet the nation seems to worry the most about the germs of the little ones. Why is that? The public has far scarier things they could worry about, far scarier than measles.

Times have changed, even if the measles haven't. In the early 1990s, there were measles outbreaks that infected thousands, and yet, I don't remember a mass fear at all. Growing up on *Brady Bunch* reruns, I saw a different portrayal of the measles, back when it was an expectation of life and not some deathly fear. Back then, my worries were bigger than the measles too. I was afraid of my husband being sent to the Gulf War, not the measles. And it was mononucleosis that kept me home sick from school for weeks, not the measles.

I guess fear is relative. Measles would have seemed minor in comparison to our experiences, the years of pain and heartache, chronic illnesses that revive themselves over and over again. A week or two is not such a long time in the scheme of a life. I would have welcomed the measles at my door if it could have taken all this pain away and left some lifelong immunity in its place.

I still get upset. This is still so wrong. The media has elevated a few cases of the measles above the thousands upon thousands of cases of vaccine injury, with a sense of urgency that presses for immediate action, encouraging vaccine uptakes and stealing freedoms. Ten years have passed since my daughter was harmed, and nothing about vaccine injury has changed for the better. My baby had so much worse than the measles, and no one cared.

The vaccine didn't let her catch the wild measles. It just bypassed that route and went straight to the side effects. My baby girl was ignored and denied, all while suffering pains and ailments matching the bad side effects of the measles, the ones they use to frighten us all about the real measles. On paper, it looks like a success — no wild measles. But in real life, it looks tragic, like a total failure, and still, no one cared.

Now, we have real measles spreading wildly, not like wildfire, but here and there, blaming the cases on the unvaccinated at an amusement park. We don't really know if the illnesses are from the vaccine strain shedding or the wild strain, but in many minds, it doesn't matter. People care, even if their kids aren't sick. Even if their family never runs into contagion, they care. Because the media is training people to be scared of parents like me who don't want to hurt their children with the vaccines that already caused so much hurting.

Some parents have vulnerable children, like I do, but they fight on the other side of the argument, in opposition to families like mine, not realizing that mine and theirs might be more similar than they realize. But they want others to vaccinate to protect their kids with herd immunity, angry that we don't want to hurt our children to "protect" theirs, calling parents like me selfish, even though I would never expect or ask someone to risk harming their own child to protect mine. I just don't believe life works that way, and I don't believe vaccines work that way either.

Media outlets everywhere put sharp focus on those they call "anti-vaxers," looking through biased lenses and slanted perspectives, injecting living people into their rants, putting real lives like mine up for debate. Parents are verbally attacked, like punching bags, portraying those who dare to question like villains blowing breaths of fire to scare everyone. I might expose some illusions, but I'm not on the news frightening anyone. It's not me creating mass hysteria over a few cases of the measles. Broadcast after broadcast creates fear, instigates hostility, and sends people away panicking — but they blame the "anti-vaxers" for that too.

These media pieces work. They work to scare us and divide us, even if they are based on hearsay without real facts, even if they are paid for by corporate sponsors who control what gets said on their dime, like commercials or infomercials rather than real news. They have us confused about good and bad, right and wrong, steering the focus to distract us from the real issues. They own the spotlights, so they get to choose what we see, what they shine light upon, what goes dark. Pitting parents against parents, by dividing us, we are weakened, wasting our energies fighting the wrong battles with the wrong people.

They spread conflict. They spread the culture of bullying. They spread verbal disease and hatred into society, spreading far more illness than any "anti-vaxer" out there, creating a society where my personal terrorists might be my own neighbors, people who want us outted with targets on the door, people who feel they have a right to know who we are so they can avoid us, on purpose, missing out on connection, connection with people who have a lot to offer.

But many won't see our value through the wall of shame, through the dividers set up to tear us apart; they won't see value through the bars of imprisonment in the land of diminishing freedoms. Before the land caves in on us all, I hope we can find some common ground in the land of the free, a country that has sacrificed so much bloodshed for liberty.

CHAPTER 59

THE WORDS OF THE PRESIDENT

It is the start of February in 2015. "You should get your kids vaccinated. It's good for them," President Obama announces on television, stamping his opinion on the vaccine debate.

I have been working on this book for so many years, I thought it could be irrelevant by now, but sadly, the words of the president have just matched that second grade teacher so many years ago. It has been ten years since that day in the lunchroom, nearly ten years exact, but this is a sadder day for America and all our vulnerable children, because his words reach beyond the scope of a tiny lunchroom. They reach through screens across America, infecting minds everywhere.

Forgive them Father, for they know not what they do, all those innocent, obedient parents who will line up just like I did for appointments full of shots. Because, "there aren't reasons to not," in the words of the president. Well, I have lots of good reasons, scattered throughout my written words, but I'm not the president or a doctor. But I am a mom, who is paying attention, and I do have that psychology degree. I know they are playing us, like a tag team in wrestling, politics and the media taking turns in the ring, working in collusion to teach us one thing and reinforcing it with the other, as if they were many different faces of the same information.

I met Barack Obama and his family at a political event in New Hampshire, that little state that seems to wield big power in presidential elections. Everyone who wants to come is welcome to this type of gathering, and this one took place in the front yard at the home of a local supporter. Strangers lined the streets with their cars, walked into this residential neighborhood, and stood for two hours waiting and watching, long before titles were bestowed and Mr. Obama was still campaigning to be the democratic nominee for the 2008 election. With an open field, candidates from both sides of the aisle flocked the state. He wasn't the only candidate I watched at that time, but the Obama family had an energy about them that excited the crowd and made people feel hopeful for change. I guess I was still hoping change would have taken a different direction.

Back then, politicians didn't want to touch the vaccine debate. The controversy just might lose elections if candidates expressed safety concerns, so mostly they stayed mum. Now, the president states that "the science is pretty indisputable." I wonder to whose science he is referring. How could the science be indisputable, if it is the science we are fighting over? An oxymoron, those two words should not go together, because science is always changing. That is how we advance.

Science is meant to be up for debate, but I guess we didn't pay enough to get our side invited because suffering doesn't seem to count. It takes money to get heard. Hearing us would require change, and I think they have more interest in keeping things exactly the same. They would rather declare "science settled" and move on, stomping with disregard for every human life that has ever been harmed by a vaccine, ensuring a future where injuries continue to happen.

I hear what he says, but I wonder what the president truly believes. Many politicians are jumping into a pro-vaccine stance, but I'm not sure they touch the stuff themselves. I just don't understand how the president of the United States, who has access to everything, would ever come to this same conclusion in his personal life.

My mind imagines someone behind the scenes telling him to say one thing, but do another, like pinching him and offering little whispers, making sure he skips the shots for his own girls. That is what friends would do for each other, warn them, not push them into harm, and with friends in high places watching his back, he might be getting different advice than the rest of us.

Somehow, from the highest job in the land, his words trickle down to the people. Some of us hear in disbelief, but many will believe. His words weight heavy, sinking my heart straight into my belly. This is awful, the president's speech creating another great divide among his united people.

I was hoping the president would stand up as a leader and tell his people to stop bullying each other, but instead, he chose sides, alienating a whole class from his united people. It is a sad day for me, a sad day for this country. With statements that once sounded innocent, I think the president has just declared war on our children.

Behind the president come his armies, his armies of followers taking his words steps further to jump on a bullying bandwagon to rip good parents like me to shreds, picking the side of an easy win with an opinion backed by the leader of the land. More people follow along, because this bullying stuff looks fun while everyone is getting away with it. But that train is driving a slippery slope, crossing into criminal territories with bias intimidation, harassment, and acceptance of hate crimes as long as the targets are slapped with labels they call "anti-vax." With the "do as I say, not as I do," hypocrisy, our "anti-bullying" society is having a field day at our expense, and it is not only accepted, but encouraged.

Word travels to more people, people who buy into the hatred and the divisionism. The fights get mean, flashing judgments behind the pretty smiles, giggling with the jokes at our expense, letting only their friends speak on their microphones, a bunch of kids who don't play fair. A whole bunch of doctors, brave enough for bleeps, swear at us on late night television. Laugh at the expense of others, laugh at my daughter's expense, my expense, my family's expense, but hey, that part of life is not fun for us, so we don't laugh at all.

I don't understand why bullying some groups of people is good fun, while statements that offend another group just might have serious consequences. People with really good jobs get fired for misspeaks or politically incorrect statements, but make fun of someone not clearly pro-vaccine or someone with a vaccine wounded soldier and it's all cool.

Insensitivity runs amuck. Classes of people are dehumanized so others will forget to feel. Assaults flow rampant, assaults on our humanness, assaults on our characters, assaults on our freedoms, tearing us down so they can build up the support to assault our bodies. As article after article emerges and late night comics make us the butt of their jokes and talk shows have no shame emulating the pro-vaccine bullies, we watch from our homes in more disbelief at the cruelty in this world, the cruelty right here in America that is beginning to look a bit more barbaric each day. The bullying has gotten worse, elevated exponentially with the words of the president, because now we face another unwanted side effect, the president's words just made bullying "anti-vaxers" popular.

The infection is spreading; prejudices disperse beyond the television sets, beyond the living rooms, beyond the doctors' offices and into the world of politics where the removal of our freedoms is encouraged by the scared. Maybe just an unintended consequence of the president's vocal opinion or the very purpose of his words, but within a week, many states are working faster than ever to remove parental choice rights and vaccine exemptions for school. Some states want to go so far as to force homeschoolers, some extend the boundaries onto teachers, but many are working feverishly behind the scenes to "get 'er done."

Word spreads into the classrooms infecting teaching materials and district personnel. Word trickles down to our children and to the parents demanding to know who these unvaccinated children are. They don't want to know the stories, just their names, so they can label them and out them just like level three sex offenders, fighting to get postings on the school walls, outing the unvaccinated publicly, right alongside the posters of freebies, and corporate sponsored signs. I wonder if instead of exposing the unvaccinated, it might visually expose some conflicts of interest instead. But who knows, we might walk past in a hurry, texting on our cell phones, and we won't notice any of it.

The pro-vaccination agenda says the vaccine science is conclusive and has no interest in bringing both sides to the debate table. They don't want to come if the opposing team is invited, arguing that the science is settled. But what if sometimes *it is what it is* just isn't?

In my attic, I keep some posters I used to hang in my classroom, my fifth grade classroom, before I ever considered the thought of vaccines. The quote that strikes me is one by Orville Wright, "If we all worked on the assumption that what is accepted as true is really true, there would be little hope of advance."

Are we to say that this is as far as we can come? That we already know everything there is to know about science? That we know so much more than our ancestors and yet there is nothing left for our children to discover? That our science ends here, at the tip of their words? If Orville Wright believed that kind of limitation, it would have hindered his ability to fly.

Science is never finalized; it evolves. Where we find controversy, we find more than one side, more than one argument, more than one truth, and more than one science. The words science, fact, and truth are not synonyms, and there are no scientific laws that apply to vaccines. Beyond our current data, beyond our imaginations lie more frontiers left to discover.

Science has been wrong in the past, disproven time and time again. The passing of time always seems to reveal the truth, as the unfolding of history reveals our mistakes. In hindsight, everything looks obvious, but at one time, we didn't see any of it. Science is not perfect or infallible, and sometimes scientists have regrets too.

I have been living in the past hoping to learn from it, while my country is moving forward so quickly it is leaping backwards in progress. The history we are creating today looks eerily similar to catastrophic world histories that we only seem to discover is wrong when it is already too late. Unfortunately, I am not on the safe side. No, there is no vaccine to protect us from mass hysteria. I am not one of the masses anymore; I lost my herd a long time ago.

I am under no illusions here. Families like mine are under attack, civil rights abuses, harassment, and bullying, encouraged by those holding the microphones. I am under no illusions of protection from my country. When people like me become the enemy, well then, I know we've been screwed, because now they have changed the very definitions of good and bad on us too, confusing so many people, on purpose. Because the day that good mothers who did everything right become the bad guys, society is messed up. Maybe for the first time in my life, I appreciate not fitting in.

CHAPTER 60

THE FALL OF CALIFORNIA

"No shots, no school. No shots, no school." I heard this slogan for the first time when I enrolled my daughter in public school as the admissions coordinator parroted the line to me several times. Many states use this mantra even though exemptions are available. When I asked the woman for the proper form number, she acted like she genuinely didn't know what I was talking about. "No shots, no school. No shots, no school," she repeated some more. It was as though the woman didn't know what else to say.

Maybe she didn't know. Maybe there aren't that many children "opting out" for the nation to make such a big deal about it. But the parents of the vaccine injured make a big deal about it, because it IS a big deal to us. It means the very lives of our children. We are just trying to save them in a different way, a way people just don't imagine until the child that reacts badly is yours.

I'm lucky. I live in a state that still has the right to choose, but good thing I know my rights, because no one at the school would have told me.

June 2015. Just days before Independence Day, California has fallen, into the darkness, following the lead of the governments in those trail blazing states that came before it, Mississippi and West Virginia. With the stroke of a pen and the mark of a signature, the governor of California signed vaccine bill SB-277 into law, stamping his approval to remove all religious and philosophical exemptions to vaccination on the pathways to schools, enforcing pharmaceutical vaccines, the gateway drugs to the doors of an education.

Why did he choose to follow in the footsteps of those two states trailing the nation in health rankings? Why did he choose to overrule the parents who packed the halls pleading for the rulers not to do this to our children? Why did he just appoint doctors as the gatekeepers to school, bestowing a lot of power on a profession that makes so many mistakes? The conflicts of interests are written all over the walls, but that was overlooked, in favor of a manhunt, to round up the few children some parents tried to slip away for protection.

Of course, parents have the option to move, like fugitives running state to state in search of freedoms, leaving jobs, leaving communities, leaving behind everything they worked hard for. Forced to start over, not knowing if they can truly settle down because they might have to up and move again to protect their children from unfair laws that will hurt them. No job security, no personal security, good people driven away because of misinformation, prejudices and now a law.

This is not what the American dream is supposed to look like. American citizens, American families, good people who are not fugitives, not criminals, but running away, running in search of someplace that hasn't gone vaccine insane. Or they can stay and homeschool, the option money can buy. Hardworking Americans grow up with the promise of an American dream and sacrifice it all for the love of their children, their vaccine vulnerable children they would do anything to protect.

Laws like this just mean less, less, less, reducing student populations and money allocations. Those kids come from caring families, and they won't be there anymore. The parents will pull the kids out of school first and figure out life second, because priorities do change when you have children, and they come first.

But what everyone else will be missing will be the kids themselves, great, wonderful kids who deserve to be in school right alongside their peers, their friends, their neighbors — kids the same age, learning side by side. These kids are treated like the discards of society, but they are the overlooked blessings, the undervalued potential, undervalued life, life others feel have less of a right to be here.

No exemptions forces good people into bad dilemmas, pushing them into moves they just can't win. When there are no good options, deciding between the lesser of two evils is not a real choice. Being forced into actions they wouldn't otherwise make for themselves, well then, that is not real freedom.

Vaccinations have been linked to schools for years, but why? The answer came to me in a Huffington post article written by Mrs. Rosalind Carter, the wife of the former president.

I have fond memories of President Carter from long before I knew what politics were all about, when parties just meant cupcakes and friends. He was the sitting president the year I entered first grade, one of those formative school years when children believe every word a teacher says, when children look up to the people adults point out as role models, those days when little kids deeply respect the highest job in the land.

There was even a girl in my first grade class who seemed to know him. She brought pictures to school from her family's trip to Washington, D.C. She posed right alongside the president of United States, right there at the White House. To a six-year-old child, that makes quite the impression.

To a first grader, the president of the United States is pretty special. Looking up to him with pig tails in my hair and eyes of admiration, I was no exception. I was much too young to know the inner workings of his presidency, I only know that feeling of pride that a child of innocence feels when she believes in the promise of her country and believes the man in charge is one of the good guys.

To a fortysomething, all that was a mere memory as I read the article with incredible disappointment. In her own words, Mrs. Carter shares pride in her accomplishments about getting vaccine requirements connected to school admissions in all fifty states.

Is this just another one of those instances when good intentions seem to turn out all wrong? People like me are now on the opposing side trying to explain how good intentions sometimes ruin lives, how ideal thoughts on paper reflect in the real world. Oh, Mrs. Carter, I wish you never pushed for vaccine requirements for school admissions. It has created a mess for people like me. I know you have a charity that works in opposition to my beliefs, but vaccine injury is very real; I wish you could see that. I wish for another impossible do-over to make those laws disappear, to return the states to the state they were once in, when vaccine requirements weren't legally connected to school admittance at all.

California is one of our own, one of our united states, and what happens there matters to us all. Immersion of my life into this issue, we cannot be separated. These laws matter because they threaten our very survival along with all of our American ideals. They steal our religion and our freedoms, the exact values our country was founded on. But they can't take our faith, and this is a test.

My husband reminds me that not everyone is obsessed with this topic the way I am, that most people don't think about it every day and night like I do, that others don't care enough to let it overcome their lives. So how come I spend every day immersed in vaccines, making thoughtful observations and reflections, picking up the pieces of vaccine injuries and broken lives, how come people like me will lose our very rights to say, "No," the people who think about this issue day in and day out?

Ten years of my life immersing myself in vaccines, the science of vaccines, the politics of vaccines, the psychology of vaccines, and recovery from vaccine injury. Ten years, every day, on my mind, in my thoughts, in my news feed, in the science, that vaccines have touched my life, touched my family's life. Maybe it qualifies as an obsession or maybe even my life's work, but *EVERY DAY* is not an exaggeration.

Ten years of study, and I earned no degree, no medical honors, garnishing only criticism, negative names, and questions about my intelligence. Ten years is a long time, fully immersed in a life of vaccines. It is even longer than the length of study most doctors complete, because that is ten years on top of my master's degree.

Ten years have passed since I started paying attention, ten years since my little baby faced a battle that she thankfully won. Ten years have passed, and life looks nothing like I imagined. In ten years, it seems like everything has changed, for me. In ten years, it seems like nothing has changed at all, except to get worse.

I've put in the time. I've earned my right to make this decision for my family. Our debt to society has already been paid. So how come the people who aren't obsessing over this issue get to be the ones to make the decisions for the rest of us?

This is a tough day. A deep feeling of uneasiness has just over-taken my body. I cried while my kids and the neighbors played outside. I cried while friends packed for vacations. I cried for something that affects me deeply, fully aware that for some this issue is barely a blip on the TV screen. I cried because the world I live in has just gotten a whole lot sadder, a whole lot less free, and I don't even live in California.

While I spent the day in sadness, life went about as normal for everyone around me. Life goes on. Others are preparing for the holiday, ready to celebrate freedom, the same freedom I keep watching slip away.

CHAPTER 61

KILLING KIDS WITH MANDATES

Having less free time to myself, lack of sleep, disappearing privacy, shared spaces — these were the kinds of freedoms I expected to lose by becoming a mom. I voluntarily gave up those personal freedoms with the decision to have a child, knowing that I would one day gain them all back.

Trained in obedience, I never thought I would have problems with laws. My life felt free enough, living among my comfortable confines, before I had small children in my arms, before I had anything that mattered quite so much. With vulnerable children, I feel the walls closing in on us, reining in our freedoms, threatening our very survival and suffocating our breathing room.

Owning ourselves, seems so commonsense, so innately a gift, and yet that is the very basic right they seem intent to steal. Night time raids on our freedoms, in the darkness of secrecy, they slip in their riders with sneaky intent, a surprise attack on our liberties. We thought we had more rights, but they took them away from us and gave them to corporations instead. Who owns us? With so much of our DNA already owned and patented by someone else, I guess the obvious answer is now questionable.

I never want to see the day where the America I love will no longer have freedom, freedom they take away inside government offices using weapons of pens. No, pens don't seem scary at all, until we find out they have signed our lives away. If it becomes a law to harm children with forced vaccinations, and we refuse, well then, suddenly good parents become criminals, and there is nothing right about that at all.

Harming already injured children by continuing to vaccinate is no longer a mistake, no longer an unknown casualty, it's a premeditated crime. It is not an accident when they keep doing it, on purpose.

It won't be long before the ripples wave beyond the families of those injured by vaccines, the days when vaccines are mandated for work, the days when children are force vaccinated while their crying parents are on the sidelines, held back at gunpoint, the days when we live in fear, hiding behind closed doors, afraid of our neighbors, not because of their germs, but because of what they might do to us. This is what the nation is coming to, and it is not just in the future, it has already happened, right here in the U.S.A.

It would be wrong to force something on someone that was bad for him, like a sucker punch with something "unavoidably unsafe." So, let's just keep calling vaccines "good for us," so that we can all justify harming each other with forced assaults into anarchy, the frenzy of the fanatics who do bad things to others in the name of good. Isn't that what terrorism is about? I never wanted to go to war, but now I find my family under attack, attack of the needles, those deadly weapons of mass destruction. Because those needles won't just destroy my family, they'll destroy some of yours too.

But it will be too late. And it won't be fair, because fair and equal are not the same. Some of us have more risk than others, but we'll have no freedom to say no, so we'll suffer more damages and have no recourse, as they steal the decision, but leave the repercussions up to the parents. Mistakes will be played out on a large scale, someone else's mistakes enforced on innocent people who are forced to pay the consequences and their broken hearts reach a tipping point of no return.

We vaccinate everybody, because injuries do not ensure medical exemptions or a settlement for damages. Nope, we just pull those kids up by their bootstraps and shove their broken bodies back on that horse, to take some more jabs for the team of deserters. They will say they need to protect "those who can't be vaccinated," but these are our kids, who they refuse to recognize, so they'll stab them to death.

Without the nearly impossible medical exemption that must be written by doctors who mostly deny vaccine injury, those *who can't be vaccinated* will be lined up first. They'll be the ones who are not up to date, the ones who stopped midway through the program, the ones whose parents said, "Enough is enough." Yes, they are first, because they are the ones who have some catching up to do.

Then, they will say it is for the best, protecting the herd and those who can't be vaccinated. And what the ignorant people simply following orders won't know — is that they are the very same people. They are vaccinating those who can't be vaccinated against their will. And it isn't for their protection, even though they want you to believe that it is.

Even if one day down the road, the people snap to their senses to stop the madness, it might be too late. Freedom will be gone and the casualties will have escalated. Forced procedures will kill somebody, and murder is still a crime in both God's laws and man's laws. Decimation of all those people *who can't be vaccinated*, BUT ARE, will put blood on their hands, wiping out a whole group of potential human resources.

By wiping away our freedoms, and stealing our exemptions, they'll kill our children and call themselves "good" for doing it. MURDER. They will commit murder, but the crimes will be deflected with more politically acceptable labels, labels like SIDS and an even newer term for SIDS smacked on the older kids, leaving parents with the grief of a loss they may never quite understand.

But they won't see it this way, not at first, until maybe some of their own fall ill. Until maybe some of them start questioning the mass hysteria. Until maybe someone reaches out with care, not to warp our words, but to hear them, with the genuine intent of an open mind. Until maybe one day we miss the freedom and realize we liked living in a free country rather than a dictatorship for profits. Until maybe we realize that it is discrimination, plain and simple, hate crimes committed against our fellow man, and maybe the people can start to question who really belongs in jail here.

They declare a war on germs and use needles as weapons, and they harm those very kids that we love. And as we watch them fall, we'll be reminded that it is "for the best," or "the greater good," all those slogans that will help justify this for us. Somewhere down the way, we might forget where the battle started or exactly when, but we might one day pause to notice the casualties and wonder why.

The cloaks of silence will try to smother our voices and the clouds of darkness will try to hide us from view. But we'll still be here, crying from inside our homes, dying inside, wondering what happened to our free country that forces this kind of misery upon people, wondering why so many still do not care. I cry out in pain, wondering why these great children of mine are considered acceptable losses.

I dream about change while I worry about survival, imagining a world where we don't annihilate each other on purpose. I live in a world where the ability to say, "No," is the key to survival. I don't want to see any more lives cut short dealing with the pains of injections that shoot far deeper than an injection site.

I had hoped the worst days of my life were over, but my world is being shaken all over again. I was hoping to never have to worry about another vaccine reaction again in my lifetime. I fought hard to save my little baby from her medical injury, and unfair laws threaten to undo all that hard work, threaten the lives that I care about so deeply. When the sacrifice is not yours, you don't worry about it so much. But when it is, it is something you never stop thinking about.

Even if I had let this all go, it comes back to haunt me. Because they want to force, against instincts, against common sense, against God, against my wishes, putting us directly on the front lines, all over again, to rekindle the heartaches and the tragedies. I feel like I don't really live in the civilized world I thought I did, but some sort of jungle where we have to fight for the right to our lives each and every day. So, I'm always on edge, with no illusions of safety, ready to step up and fight for my children's lives. I can cry all I want, but as a mother, I am not allowed to be a wimp.

CHAPTER 62
CRIMES, PUNISHMENTS, AND REASONABLE DOUBTS

W̲e choose sides without really knowing what each side represents, not completely certain what each side stands for, just a bunch of judgments built upon assumptions of what we believe are truths. Then we pick a team, believing that the side we stand on is the right side, and we stand firm in our denial or degradation of the other sides. We want to know without making connection, want to judge without looking deeper, want to find faults in others while overlooking them in ourselves.

Entangled in the web of misleading distortions of reality, others make assumptions that are wrong, judging on caricatures that hardly resemble the truth, taking the tiniest glimpse of an outside that has been painted over with graffiti, surface perusals that overlook the inner layers hiding beneath the defamations of character, misreading us through the eyes of prejudices instilled through our trainings.

I have immersed myself in vaccine reflection for ten years now, but some parents will leave their pediatrician's office after one well visit and watch a couple of TV programs called news, and they will think they know more about vaccines than me. I've gotten used to that.

What bothers me are the people who take the extra steps beyond the thoughts of superiority and the ridicule, standing on their righteous soap boxes from imaginary places of perfection proclaiming judgments that those who don't vaccinate are bad parents. Some stand even taller as they equate not vaccinating with child abuse, suggesting we go to jail or face death penalties, making ignorant judgments of parents they know nothing about. I would also suggest they don't know much about vaccines, but they condemn regardless and would like to see the innocent punished.

Maybe people wouldn't be so quick to make false accusations of child abuse if they knew it is a felony.

Good fortune at dodging a vaccine reaction has left some with the reassurance that they are right, determined to inflict their personal beliefs onto the rest of us, pushing their luck on our genes, with the smugness of certainty spoken by those who have never been there, never walked the steps in the shoes of another.

To me, the child abuse would have occurred if I had let the doctors continue to harm my daughter. If we continued to poke her with needles that made her so sick. If I purposefully sacrificed my son, knowing he was at risk. If we remained obedient to the wishes of others, letting them make detrimental decisions for us. Why is society trying to accuse good parents of crimes when it is the hands of others bringing our kids harm?

Society keeps punishing its fall guys, poking fun, alienating, making ignorant judgments that threaten us. I don't know if they mean to throw us under the bus some more so that our hearts can be rolled over a few more times. I don't know if some people have just lost their souls. I don't understand why they fear the very children they will say they are trying to protect, those in the herd who can't be vaccinated. I don't understand having such faith in a product without any real confidence that it will work. And I don't understand how we can bypass all these poor sick vaccine injured children and still tell them that vaccination is "for the best."

Sometimes I feel like I don't understand at all, living among rationalizations in a world that just doesn't make sense. My heart is pure. My arms cling to my babies in a shield of protection. My love encompasses their beings. Somehow, protecting my babies, my family from further harms, inflicts me with labels like "selfish," and "anti-vaxer," and every term imaginable that means the same as stupid. But I think that earns me the title of "Mom."

Vaccine status is all some people want to know about us. What a shame. That is not information that makes someone human, that is what makes someone a number, a statistic, a compliant number as close to 100% as they can get. There is no tolerance for differences, mathematically or humanely. People don't make connections when they follow the dots to somewhere else, never slowing down long enough to ponder, to walk the path of stepping stones, crossing the bridge to understanding.

We fight with each other, parent versus parent, because it is easier, the little guy versus the little guy. It is too difficult to take on the large corporations, the entire educational system, the laws, the lobbyists, the politicians. Parent versus parent is the easy fight. Changing our country and its indoctrinated beliefs, that is the real challenge.

⟫⟪

Mandatory vaccination is like a possible death sentence for people who have done nothing wrong, a possible death sentences without any trials. It is estimated that 1 in 25 people on death row have done nothing wrong either. And just like twelve jurors can be wrong, so can the majority of a population. That's scary, not minor childhood illnesses.

There is a reason why we judge "beyond a reasonable doubt." It is because it is better to have a guilty man go free than an innocent man go to jail. If we are going to steal a man's liberty, then we better be sure, really sure.

And if we are not sure "beyond a reasonable doubt" the safety and efficacy of vaccines, we cannot remove liberty and enforce them. The fact that there is so much controversy is the reasonable doubt, right there, reasonable doubt that one side is not the only side, reasonable doubt to both safety and efficacy.

Very reasonable people have very reasonable doubts, very real concerns that have plenty of science, because science extends far beyond the boundaries of the United States. Science is not perfect, and people are not perfect, leaving more reasonable doubts. Ethics are questionable, leaving more reasonable doubts. Conflicts of interest leave more reasonable doubts, along with all those warped statistics.

To steal a man's freedom when there is reasonable doubt is not even legal for a person who might actually be a criminal. Why would we legalize the criminalization of innocent families doing right by their children? The benefit of the doubt has to fall to the parents. We deserve it.

The same doctors who deny injury spout off rarity, bought politicians write legislation for their financiers rather than their constituents, the court system declares vaccines "unavoidably unsafe," while still enforcing their use. Now, they are dragging in the police department and social services to enforce non-rules on law abiding citizens. So, before parents start suing each other over vaccine status, make sure you caught the right guy, because with all those innocent people in jails, it is possible to have it all wrong.

Why isn't anybody going to jail? Sometimes the parents do when vaccine injury medically looks like child abuse or shaken baby syndrome, but those who actually committed the crimes walk away free of charges, because legally they can't be held liable. Their protection is written right into our laws. The absence of liability can create an absence of ethics.

Doctors use all sorts of behaviors, I argue might be criminal. I know that no one is held liable for vaccine injuries or defective shots, but I often wonder if the techniques they use to achieve compliance are criminal, things like fraud, coercion, intimidation, creating duress, lying in the expert opinion, withholding facts, false pretenses — all those techniques that get other people to act in their favor.

They convince us, that this is freedom. Yes, for the doctor it seems to be complete freedom to say and do whatever he pleases to achieve his goals. But for parents, it is entirely something else. But instead of doctors getting charged with crimes for the methods they use to coerce parents to "decide" in their favor, they would rather turn the tables and charge parents with crimes instead, crimes like negligence, for actions like thinking.

Which decision can I live with? The one I can make myself. When one side makes the decisions that the other side is forced to live by, that is not like freedom at all.

But it would be so much easier for them if they could just change the laws, because this all takes work on their part, spending too much time on someone like me, trying to convince me to behave in a way that I know is bad for us. So if they can just rewrite the laws to steal freedom, then doctors won't have to waste so much of their time trying to convince the inconvincible. Because we are not stupid, we are strong. And it is not science they are selling us; they just use that word a lot.

Thoughtful consideration is what good parents do, not obedient apathy. But independent thinking somehow labels good parents as bad guys? I am being a good mom by thinking. I am being a good mom when I stand up for my children's best interests. I am being a good mom when I resist the peer pressure that is bad for us. I am being a good mom because I care, and I think, and I love.

I am being a good mom when I have the strength to make the difficult decisions that are unpopular. The goal of good parenting is not to win a popularity contest, but to raise wonderful children full of our values, not full of someone else's values or all that crap they want to put in them. Those who question get labeled with bad names, even though what they do is good parenting.

We are good parents, doing right by our children, and none of our decisions are easy. Some of us are wound deeply, tightly woven in an intricate fabric embedded into our beings, and we cannot be known in the length of time it takes to make surface assessments. We think deeply about our decisions, and we feel deeply in ways that pain our hearts and bruise our muscles, aching for life, love, and people, in a world we once thought we knew. Our lives are not easy, thanks to everyone else making it just that much more difficult for us.

Most parents like me are probably reformed vaxers rather than non-vaxers, but people on the outside will take liberty to call us whatever they feel like anyway, even when mistaken identities are never the truth. Reformed alcoholics are not called "anti-alcohol." Reformed criminals are not called "anti-crime." Reformed drug addicts are not called "anti-drug." We call people reformed, we call them better, we call them recovered, we call them healed. Me too. I am in recovery from vaccination, after taking many steps to reclaim a life.

If we drop the labels, I'm simply a mom, doing the best I know how in an imperfect world. I don't make my decisions lightly; I wrestle with them and roll them around in my brain, putting a lifetime of reflection and thought into decisions that matter. A mile in my shoes will not lead you back to the arms of vaccines, and days in my shoes might just make you an "anti-vaxer" too. But that is just a label, it isn't the heart of what matters. I might be called an "anti-vaxer" in this battle, but I am not one of the bad guys.

CHAPTER 63
LETTING GO

B eautiful long baby lashes look up into the face of a mom. It is one of my favorite visions of motherhood, and yet I can barely look without tears. I wonder what is going on in that infant brain. I imagine the piercing of the skin in those little bodies with fat, squishy thighs. I see joy and feel pain at the very same time. I love children so much. I still can't believe I live in a world that hurts them on purpose.

I hadn't realized when my son was born that he would be the last of my children. My love overflowed instantly for this tiny person, and our deep bond was instantaneous. He was a happy baby filled with incredible joy at simply being alive, and he brought laughter into our home.

I didn't fully realize that each day with him would be my last opportunity to experience the thrill of babies. He was born into the unknown, when my daughter was still sick. Even though his insatiable hunger woke me up twice every night for the whole first year, I hadn't fully awakened yet. I knew it was the vaccines, but I wasn't sure what else was at play or how to right the wrongs.

The attic holds memories of a past that came and went too quickly, remnants of baby products, tubs full of clothing, bins of keepsakes, childhood in a box, packed away for another day. The feelings are bittersweet. It is hard to let go. As I invested in these items, I was hoping three children might have the opportunity to use them, but it turns out, there are just two. Saying goodbye to these things symbolizes the finality of our family, the truth that we are done having children. But it is hard to let go, because I wanted one more.

I hung onto the baby stuff for some future that never came. I wanted one more baby, one more little person to love, but with the passing of time, the world appears to be heading downhill quickly. My mind wonders if it isn't for the best that we remain a family of four. Maybe I just wanted the chance to do it right, do it better, do it perfectly. Letting the stuff go, reminds me that I will have neither, no more babies, no do-overs.

As I sit among piles of clothing ready to donate, I reflect upon the memories associated with each tiny outfit. It is easy to part with the newer outfits. It is the tattered shreds that hold all the love, worn right into the fibers of the cloth. Those hold a special place in a special box for safekeeping. But I am keeping the sick outfits too, to remind me to never forget. I think forgetting is impossible, but one look instantly transports me back in time to the place where this story began.

The day of the seizure, Bella was wearing light colored blue jeans in 1970s style, with frayed edges at the bell bottoms. Her hot pink top had long sleeves and an adornment of a popular story book character. I imprinted the outfit on purpose, committed it to memory — the day our lives would change forever. Then, there are those soft cotton red and white striped pajamas that comforted my baby through illnesses. I saved those too.

Sitting on the floor, surrounded by piles of clothes and baby supplies, I contemplate life, the last child, the births, the people, the threats, the television... How did I get here? I'm just one mom, surrounded by all this stuff that I thought symbolized motherhood, but the only thing our babies truly need — is us.

Something had been stolen from our lives, but what was lost could not be found in things. My beautiful baby girl had been harmed, and none of these things could make up for that. There is no THING in the world that can make up for that.

Crimes were committed against my little angel, and there is no justice, no penalties for the perpetrators. They are still criminals, nonetheless, stealing lives from our lives, stealing futures from our past, rewriting stories into oblivion. Nothing can make up for that.

There is nothing I can buy to remove the pain. I can only buy distractions from it. Holes cannot be filled with purchases, and a house full of stuff will never fill the void in my heart. With all the crazy weather, I am learning that stuff doesn't matter so much. In an instant, it can all blow away, and I will still be grateful for what is left, the people that bring meaning to a life. The very things I never thought I would have are sometimes the only things that keep me going. Of course, it is because they are not things, and that's what makes them so special.

I toss away the very last diaper box that I was storing books in. They are not little kids anymore. They are growing up, and letting go is a part of life. Letting go of stuff, letting the kids go out into the big world, no more holding onto the badness, making room for forgiveness. Parting with all this stuff doesn't represent finalities at all; it clears space for new beginnings. At some point, I realized I wanted freedom more than stuff. With letting go, I am working on that.

CHAPTER 64
MOVING ON

There goes my heart, driving slowly away in a little grey car. Bella rolls down the window of the backseat to tell me she loves me one more time. Bella is excited for her first big adventure, two hours from home. We'll miss each other, but we are not sad. We are happy to be at this place where she can go off with a friend and have a unique experience that is different than the daily routines of our own lives.

In every sense, she is a normal, healthy kid who happens to bring along a little extra baggage: an injector of epinephrine, homeopathic arnica, our own sunblock, some hydrogen peroxide, and special face soap. She is on this journey with a family who may not do things our way but respects and honors our wishes. I am grateful they see Bella as the beautiful person she is, a kind friend to their own daughter, and welcome her into their world. They are happy that we have trusted enough to let Bella go with them. This is a big step for us, a leap of faith into letting go.

A cord once tied us together, but now we are attached through invisible bonds that can be felt rather than seen. But with careful observation, the eyes are the window to the soul, displaying the truth in the endearing looks of love. We have connection without touch. I'm letting go, because she is fully attached.

She needs to go live. She needs to have a life, live a life, even if we are not safe. As crooked as I know this world to be, I still encourage my kids to join it. They need to go live to make life worth living. Survival is not the only goal. A quality life fulfills us with so much more.

Being alive comes with risk. Death can find us at our bed; the earth can swallow us up and claim the life we live in true uncertainty. We are not really safe, not really immune. Our days are numbered whether we are faced with a sharp reminder or casually forget that we are not immortal. Life is short, the world is dangerous, things are out of our control, but instead of fearing life itself, we might as well go live it. Accepting the risks of life is the gamble we all take with the decision to bring children into this world.

Life doesn't come with guarantees. Safety is an illusion. We all have our own false sense of security, behind the walls of our houses (that can crumble in a storm), with people we believe will always be there for us (and sometimes they are not), behind a reputation not yet marred by scandal (when scandal can simply mean having an opinion on a controversial topic), insurance we depend on in case of tragedy (that decides not to pay for the loss). We teeter a fine line in our comfort zone, feeling safe but unbalanced enough that a quick shove from the universe can knock us down.

We can plan, we can prepare, we can be resilient, but we really can't hide because sometimes fate finds us anyway. One day, all our comforts can be stripped away, our identity, our security, our home, our health, our money. But when we lose everything, we have nothing to lose. Life is still waiting for us.

When my daughter got sick, I was living safe, with a false sense of security. When I got sick, I lost my sense of security, but I was still living safe. Now, I can just feel secure in who I am while living in an unsafe and unpredictable world. I would rather have wasted learnings than a wasted life.

Life gives us choices and risks and personal paths full of unexpected turns. Life is a great big contradiction, full of uncertainty. No one taught me all the missing pieces while I was still in school. Life brings the rest of the education, because when I pay attention, life is a good teacher.

I am moving now, with some momentum into the future, practicing the art of letting go. Letting go... Certainly if I can loosen the grip on the person, the living thing most valuable to me in this world, I can let go of some other things I've been hanging onto as well, like anger, fear, and stuff.

Let it all go — because that's the stuff I won't even miss. They don't lighten my being the way my daughter's smile can brighten my day. They don't comfort me like my girl's petite arms wrapped around me in a loving hug. They don't lighten the burden I carry through life. Instead, they are heavy.

I tried to forgive some medical practitioners for their ignorance, my friends for their betrayals, but I still hadn't forgiven myself for my own ignorance, being much too hard on the one person who truly loved, who truly tried to make this right, the one person who suffered alongside Bella. Because hurting your own child is not something one gets over lightly. But certainly if I can forgive the others, I can learn to forgive myself. I can offer more kindness and love to myself. I can let myself off the hook and be set free.

I remember one certain woman I reached out to for advice, a woman in my exact same position, a woman who made a mistake just like I did. It was a long time ago, but I remember her saying to me, "It is not your fault. It is not your fault." She repeated herself many times to me, and somehow I managed to ignore her, until now, when I hear her words ringing in my ears, over and over again, reminding me to forgive myself, reminding me that it is not my fault. She offered words that care, words I saved, words I treasure in their help with letting go. "It's not your fault," my mind repeats, spurring the release of tears from my eyes. I can't even say these words aloud without letting go.

CHAPTER 65

MAKING SACRIFICES

I hug my son with tears in my eyes. "I don't think you understand the sacrifices that have been made for you," I whisper under my breath, not meaning for him to hear me.

He is too young to understand. Maybe I don't fully understand the sacrifices that have been made for me either. Maybe most of us don't. Maybe if we don't have soldiers in our families we don't truly understand the extent of the sacrifices.

Sacrifice upon sacrifice, soldiers fighting for freedoms, sacrificing their lives for freedoms that get stolen from us by our own government in the country that they risked everything to fight for. Little children sacrificed for the slogan of "the greater good," the herd mentality of a bullying herd that expects others to sacrifice for their benefit.

More soldiers, more lives sacrificed. The parents of our American soldiers, sacrificing their children for their country, and what thanks do they get? The country tries to rip away the very same freedoms that all the bloodshed was meant to preserve.

Sacrifice after sacrifice wasted, lives lost to preserve the very foundation of our country, lives lost that cannot be reclaimed.

When we voluntarily hand over our freedoms, we throw away some more lives, while disregarding the ones who have already been sacrificed fighting for liberty. Are we truly thankful for the unending sacrifices for our freedoms? Because we are losing them so readily, without much protest from those of us not on the front lines.

There has been so much sacrifice on our behalf, that now some of us seem to expect it, like an entitlement to being American, while having a completely un-American attitude to get their way. Fighting for forced medical procedures, expecting others to take risks on their behalf, stomping on freedoms, inalienable rights, and our independence, why do some feel entitled to the sacrifices of others?

Well, to sit back and take that sort of treatment, that sort of insult to our humanity, and attack on our freedoms, that is un-American too. We are Americans. We stand for freedom. We can't just sit back and watch them take it all away, handing over freedoms that our military soldiers died for, to kill some more kids for a corrupt cause. That is double indemnity, paying twice, once for the freedom and again when they take it away, disrespecting all the lives throughout history that have fought for us. Those freedoms cost so much. Have we forgotten to value them?

We sacrifice for our children, just as others who came before us sacrificed for us. Soldiers may not live in our families, but they sacrifice their lives for us too. My grandfather, a World War II veteran — I think of him a lot, wishing he were still alive so that I could appreciate him and his services some more.

I can't speak of the trauma that impacts a man in the face of war, but we might have one thing in common, a country that denies us our injuries and doesn't always welcome us back with the full respect deserved. Because soldiers do service for their country and we let them down too. We let them fall through the cracks, in a nation of riches, where the words *homeless* and *veteran* should never be used together, because it should never be a soldier's reality.

Honorable service deserves honor, respect, and support. Our vaccine wounded children deserve that too.

Why aren't families recognized for their sacrifices and left alone to live what left they have of their lives in peace? Why aren't they recognized for their sacrifice, for their contributions to the herd? Why aren't they thanked and appreciated for their service to the country and given honorable discharges, releasing them from further service, further commitments, and honorable exemptions from further vaccinations?

Why do we have to hurt our kids in the first place in order to exempt them from further harm? Siblings should be exempt by blood, because no parent deserves to have more than one child suffer the same horrific fate that will already haunt them for a lifetime. My daughter should get an honorable discharge, and my son should qualify for something similar to the military's Sole Survivor Policy, exempting siblings from service.

There is no honor. We are brushed under carpets, trampled on woe, clouded in veils of secrecy. Children get shafted, denied, or written off as unexplained deaths that were more than clear. This is a tragedy too, a tragedy I wish more of us could see, a tragedy that is not going anywhere as long as we ignore it.

I'm one of the lucky ones. I get to hold hands with my little girl and take her with me into the future.

CHAPTER 66

PATRIOTS RISING

"Choose happiness." It sounds so simple. I see that sentiment more and more each day, but I don't think life is that easy. If we keep choosing happiness and fun and distractions, while they work to steal away freedoms, one day, life as we know it will come to an end. Then, it won't be so easy to choose happiness anymore, because the freedom that once brought happiness might be gone. It is much easier to choose happiness from a comfy home full of luxuries than a prison cell enclosed by bars.

I don't know if any of the great world changers chose happiness, because some seemed to choose right, at all cost and huge personal sacrifice, sacrificing pieces of themselves to make life better for others. They chose difficult, because doing the right thing is not always popular, not always in the majority, and definitely not the easy way out. So they risked, they made sacrifices, they suffered, because they couldn't settle for *it is what it is* either. They demanded change. They fought for change. They cared and made a difference as they battled on the side of right rather than taking the easy win in a popularity contest.

I have always admired these personal heroes of mine: the protestors, the familiar names standing side by side with unsung heroes, people who stand up for causes they believe in, causes I believe in, not getting paid like lobbyists, but doing it anyway. Yes, I admire those people from afar, from a perspective in time that could only exist because of their efforts. I look back and forward with gratitude for shifting the times, shifting the culture, a new outlook built up a little more correct because of their determina-. tion to make things right, by making sacrifices.

Today, history continues, with celebrities brave enough to speak out, politicians who dare cross the line, doctors and nurses cutting ties to convention against threats to their careers, the whistleblowers sounding alarms, and all those other heroes working for justice. They are working for us, not against us. Right now, we might not see that, we might not value these warriors, because in the midst of a controversy, their names might get slammed. Tarnished reputations come with the territory. But, while others sling mud, I send gratitude. I look to them with admiration, just like other great heroes that make sacrifices for right.

I cry alone, but deep down, I know that I am not alone, even though it feels so isolating. I know there are so many other parents out there, just like me, crying over tragedies to precious little lives. I am one of many, a harsh reality that is both a source of sadness and my strength. If they believe we have some magical powers to resurrect dead diseases they have declared extinct, then certainly we have strength in numbers.

Sometimes I am not so sure we aren't a silent majority, hiding out where we think it is safe. Because vaccine injury has only multiplied since the day of my daughter's downhill plunge. There are many more like me, many more asking questions, telling stories, and making connections. Maybe we are so common that people hardly notice the devastation anymore. We just don't know if we are in this alone, like it feels, or if there are a whole bunch of others with identical feelings, living in obscurity.

Maybe sharing our stories is not safe in a world full of hate, but it is not safe to sit back and keep quiet either, because they have started an attack on our freedoms. If we just let them, they win easily, without a fight as we surrender in our living rooms. They are coming to steal our rights, and there will be no safety anywhere. It doesn't really matter if we are herds or sheep or lone warriors, the wolves are out to get us all.

We must speak up, we must share our stories, we must not remain quiet, divided or separate. We must honor the lives of the sacrifices shed by our grown soldiers in uniform and our tiny soldiers in birthday suits. We need minds brave enough to break the molds, hearts full enough to share, a will that is more powerful than fear, and stamina to stand strong.

We need more hearts united for change, more words of truth hitting the eyes of readers, more bodies standing strong in the halls of medicine and the chambers of government. Let our speech be the outlets of our hearts, pouring our feelings through the ink that hits the paper, the clicks that hit the keyboard, the words that touch a note. Strength in numbers, strength in humanity, power within.

⇌╫⇋

There is a real life story of a grocery store chain called Market Basket. It is a New England local, but the people made national news when both employees and customers just stopped showing up, uniting together to boycott the stores. The employees wanted their beloved CEO back, a CEO that had been pushed out of his position in closed door details to which I am not privy. The customers stood with the employees, shopping elsewhere, paying more, driving farther.

As the people united together in a band of protest, their absence spoke loudly. Together, the people had the power to cripple a large business, taking the chain down from packed aisles to bar-on nothingness in weeks. It is an amazing story of people united for a cause, sacrificing money and livelihoods, standing in unity for one single man who was welcomed back in victory to the grocery store chain that flourishes once more.

I cheered for the people of Market Basket, not because I once worked there myself, but because I was so proud of my fellow Americans. The spirit of Rocky was the little bit of Philadelphia I took home with me, much more valuable than souvenirs, so much more than a movie, and here it was, on display in my own backyard, in the hearts and minds of so many others, the underdog, the little guy, overcoming all odds to have a fighting chance, and maybe even win.

Our kids don't have time to wait for others to figure out the whys. They don't have time to wait for the funding of science that doesn't go deep enough to discover the truth. We don't have time to wait for someone else. Sometimes the buck stops with us, bringing with it that powerful reminder of the faith that gives me strength, IN GOD WE TRUST.

Our time is now, drafted to make a stand, called to question, protect, and defend. Protection is me. Change is me. Action is me. But I'm not alone. I'm just doing my part, as an American, as a parent, standing my ground. This is my country, of the people, by the people, and for the people.

We shouldn't have to win boxing matches to exercise our human rights, but the more the pro-vaccine agenda attacks, more and more parents show up, exposing themselves to reveal another side. Caring parents show up in droves, packing the aisles of state houses, driving for hours, waiting for hours. California is a big state, and trips to the capital are not convenient for a vast majority of the population. In other states, the massive outpouring of parents has already defeated the vaccine push, preserving freedoms for children and parents. In the unity, in the bravery, in the efforts, I find faith, hope, and love. I see the Rocky spirit lives within our people and our nation, and we are not threats at all. We're Patriots!

There are lots of heroes left in this world, but we might not notice them. They don't wear capes, and they can only fly with the help of an airplane. We don't always know who the heroes are in this world, because they might look exactly like us. We may have footsteps that get washed away in the tides of denial, but our tears join together in an ocean of strength. The waves of change are within us.

CHAPTER 67
CHILDREN LEAD THE WAY

All the young children warmly greeted their classmate with hugs and smiles. The little girl had been out of school for a week with chicken pox, and not one of the children was afraid to touch her. The little girl even lifted the leg of her pant to show the remaining spots along her calves. My curious daughter looked on, ready to touch them. I flinched for a moment, knowing that my daughter would fulfill her curiosity by touching those spots sometime during the day when I was no longer around to guard her behaviors.

As I cringed, the children offered no hesitation, only love and kindness, and welcome hugs for the friend they missed. I am reflecting on a day from kindergarten when my daughter and her classmates shared sweet warmth and tender, genuine affection with each other.

I think back to those loving classmates, the little children who knew better than to fear each other, spreading their love and kindness, and yes, germs with each other, without fear, without concern, just an innate knowing that it is much better to live life as friends. Sometimes, I might still wince at a yuck factor, but it is good to see caring kids loving each other, leaving me with hope and a smile.

The beauty of life involves sharing love and friendship that naturally bring with it some germs, but it is still so much more beautiful when shared together. That's why we have friends, and family, and children, because life is better with good company. It is this loving connection that actually improves immune function so we don't have to worry so much about the germs.

Life in a bubble of isolation, alone, will deteriorate the spirit so detrimentally, that even without germs, one could be much closer to the death and illness we all seem to fear. Studies show that it is the support systems in our lives, the people themselves who add to our longevity. Relationships with others bring happiness too. I heard "70% of it" according to another study. Life is just better with good people in it, and friends will add to happiness and longevity better than any vaccine.

I imagine a world where people are valued without fear. There are a lot of scary things we can catch from each other, far scarier than those childhood illnesses. There are far scarier and more prevalent germs that are far more dangerous, and there are far scarier mental mindsets too. Yes, there is a lot going around, far more dangerous than germs. I hope my kids don't catch any of these: mass hysteria, vaccine insanity, bullying arrogance, or prejudicial ignorance. There are plenty of things to be afraid of in this world. Little children are not one of them.

How can we be friends if we fear each other? How can we understand if we build walls? Everyone carries germs, but life is so much better with friends. The children are trying to teach us a lot. Showing love between two friends is really what life is all about. Teaching led me to children. Now, children lead the way.

CHAPTER 68
SHARING OUR STORIES

Years ago, I had one focus, get my daughter well. That's it. My only focus was her. I spent time examining every single eyelash, combing my fingers through the strands of her soft fine hair, and tracking the roadmaps of her veins with a fingertip gently caressing the top of her skin. I couldn't finish this book any sooner, because I was too close, too close to make meaning from the whole picture. With the distance of time, I found the space for understanding.

That is the beauty of taking a long time, sticking with it through the ups and downs, growing perspective beyond the bull's-eye, radiating out to encompass current events and an ever changing universe that affects us on a deeply personal level, right there in the center, in the heart of our personal world.

The only way to fully express is to go there, to the places I never wanted to revisit. As I write about it, as I speak about it, I find myself dabbling in all those controversial topics they tell us not to discuss. When digging starts, roots are entwined everywhere, entangling themselves in places that seem to have no connection, and yet they do, underground. I can apply my vaccine logic everywhere, because even when I try, I can't get away from them.

Our real lives are getting denied, but on paper, I am recording history, our history, and the pages accept it all, no judgments, no denials. Complete acceptance in a world where outcasts have trouble finding acceptance, always needing to stand up and justify our equal rights to be here.

I used to enjoy a television segment where a dart was thrown onto the United States map, landing by chance in a specific county. A flip through that location's phone book and a point of the finger selected a random resident, a stranger with a story. *Everybody Has a Story* declared the title. Yes, everyone has a story, including me.

I used to believe that I had to know all the answers first, or that I had to have my own life in perfect order before I could offer something to share. I still have more questions than answers, more uncertainties than certainties. I have made lots of observations and insights into a life I once thought I knew. I thought the story was going to be all about Bella, but as I wrote, I realized it is even more about me. Maybe I need to find more acceptance for myself, from myself, with deeper understanding and generous forgiveness. I don't claim to be perfect, but I am worthy.

I have been working at this book for years, without pay or a publishing date. I had to believe, because I knew I was working on something really important to my heart. This is my life, my daughter's life, and I have let you in on the most personal aspects of who we are. To me, that is worth a lot, because I am private, and I don't like to share. But I cannot ignore this calling, this call to action to speak up. I cannot remain silent and pretend our lives don't matter.

They want us to go away and stay hidden, while they steal some more lives in the cloaks of darkness. No! "Let there be light," and the light shines in, exposing both good and bad. Then you can choose sides, but at least you'll be able to see who and what you are getting.

The concept of role model has changed. What once meant inaction in the form of abstinence from those off limits activities now becomes action for cause. This role requires courage and bravery, and I don't know if I possess enough of those qualities to fill the shoes. I am forced to find strength, because business as usual just might kill one of us. Are you sure God that I am strong enough for this? But, I do not question God too much anymore. With faith, I trust.

It's my turn to speak up and take my turn at the plate, begging for others to hear. I am a mom, without a microphone, going against my very nature, taking a risk, standing in my truth. It is my turn to speak up, a very private person miles out of her comfort zone. I have taken years to find the strength, the strength within me, to tell our story.

I'm coming to the end, and I find myself pausing a lot. This is a big step, and sometimes I am still not sure I want to take it. I get tempted to resort to distractions; I'm scared. It takes guts, guts that are tied in nervous knots. But the cause is so important, so much bigger than me. I hear my calling, and I answer. Because as reluctant as I am, the bigger regret would be to do nothing, to say nothing, to surrender without a fight. Because our kids are worth it, they are worth our sacrifices, because love is the greatest motivation of all — and sometimes it brings happiness worth a life.

I write as chronological as possible, but our story is not a time line. It is a journey, a journey of exploration into the dark nights of the soul through the lightness in the good. This book is a lifetime of knowledge applied, a test of all that I have learned, and a trial of endurance to completion. Maybe I hadn't wasted any learning, because finally, I can see value in it all.

Sometimes minds meet, sometimes hearts touch, and we realize that the other side wasn't as expected, wasn't as we thought, wasn't what we judged, because the world isn't as it seems. There is no black and white, and scratching at the surface will never produce the treasure of depth. Looking from the inside grants an entirely new perspective and the wisdom of empathy. In the mirror of reflection, I see so many others who look just like me. This issue isn't about science degrees or advanced educations; it is about being human.

Sometimes life is the best teacher. When people share their stories, others get the privilege of the lesson without the hardship of the ordeal. Gifts we give to each other. Gifts full of value and meaning. Gifts shared from one human to another, soul to soul, heart to heart. It is how the world should be done. Letting it go, for the greater good. Nothing is wasted; it is shared, from my heart to yours.

CHAPTER 69
FOREVER CHANGED

My coworkers are lovely, and we get to know each other as mutual lovers of nature who care for the environment. I took this job as a getaway, a short weekly retreat from being immersed in vaccine writing, a chance at starting over, working with people, and being back in the interactive world of human connection.

I had no motivations for my writing; this job was to be the escape from this book, my small attempt at finding balance and bringing my light back. I signed up as a tour guide to rekindle the teacher in me, but a fortuitous change lands me into the butterfly house of a children's garden. I make the connection. My experience here is an important part of my story.

Butterflies have gaps too. For a couple of weeks, they look like busy caterpillars, voraciously eating away, always hungry for more, fattening, thickening, lengthening, growing. Then one day, they just stop. We don't know exactly when it will happen. We just see a big caterpillar and know it is near ready.

They wind themselves up, attaching to a safe place nearby, using tethers they create from within, binding themselves to the plants that once nourished them. Then they are just there, hiding out in plain sight, camouflaged by their surroundings so well that we might not see them.

A chrysalis waits, dangling where only the most curious might venture to search, blending in with leaves, branches, and flowers. Right there among all the life is another life, a life that looks still, a life in the gap, a life hanging in the balance. Delicate yet strong, simple yet amazing, blowing in the wind, yet firmly attached.

To the outside, it might look dead. Brown ones look like crumpled up leaves that have fallen from an autumn tree. Green ones blend with living leaves. But to the outside, they all look still. When we watch them and wait, they look like they are doing nothing at all. People walk by, people get bored, people continue on their way, because it just looks like nothing is happening.

Then, in a surprise instant, the butterfly scratches its way out, shedding that remaining skin, a translucent sheath so much thinner than paper, sliding right out of its encasing to emerge in this world. Broken free from its shell, broken free from confinement, the life is reborn in new form. All the original stuff is still there, and yet it emerges completely different and forever changed.

Some people are lucky enough to see, while others never quite meet up with that fortuitous timing. It happens so fast that only a moment of distraction misses a moment that is quickly gone.

Butterflies are not ready to fly right away. They have an adjustment period where they transform themselves from a soggy wet rag to pressed stiff perfection. They have to unfurl their wings, wings that emerge crumpled from confinement in tight quarters. They send power through their veins, filling up their wings, building strength and firmness, straightening, lengthening, and tightening the muscles.

Then, there is a pause, a bit more quiet time to allow the wings to fully dry. It only takes a couple hours, sitting in stillness, before we watch for the first flutter. Butterflies practice flapping their wings before the eventual take off, getting ready to move, testing their strength, preparing to fly.

People are fascinated by this process. I am fascinated by this process. What went silent as a caterpillar emerges as a butterfly. But in between, it looks like nothing is happening. But in that gap, in that space in time, transformation has been occurring, like biological magic right in front of our eyes, and yet we can't see it. The inner workings are masked by a skin, a shell, a chrysalis we call it.

When the butterfly emerges, there is no doubt that it was busy, that it had undergone an amazing transformation, right in the gap, that space and time that looked still from the outside. No one would even dare say it had been lazy.

We don't always appreciate the work that is being done when we see nothing at all, the behind the scenes kind of busyness that keeps illusions alive. Transformations are like magical new beginnings, but there is always that gap, the gap that looks still to the world. We shouldn't overlook it so easily. The gap is the space where magic can happen.

Beautiful butterflies are important pollinators, getting their feet dirty spreading the gifts of life that make fruit and flowers grow. They also represent amazing transformations. I used to be told that people can't change, but with time and effort, I know they can. My metamorphosis might not look so pretty, and my outside is not more beautiful than it once was, but growth takes time. I don't emanate as elegant as the butterfly as I push out of my shell, shedding hypocrisy and fears.

Thank you, God, for rescuing me from my mistakes. We walk hand and hand, my growing girl and I, now of similar heights and similar shoe sizes. We smile at each other, just knowing... We are the lucky ones. The spirit of Rocky lives within us, and the monumental staircase represents the journey, each small step a personal victory in the uphill climb, a personal victory on the bumps of life's roads. Those steps lead straight to the entryway of the Philadelphia Museum of Art, reminding me that living life is an art, not a science.

This isn't the end. It is a new beginning. I'm moving forward, forever changed. The touch of grace gives me a little boost, and I am just as ready as an emerging butterfly, ready to take flight.

ABOUT THE AUTHOR

Bridget Long holds a bachelor's degree in psychology and a master's degree in education. Though her passion is teaching, her greatest joys come from being a mother.

32720236R00212

Made in the USA
Middletown, DE
16 June 2016